THE STAGES OF
ECONOMIC GROWTH

THE STAGES OF ECONOMIC GROWTH

A NON-COMMUNIST MANIFESTO

SECOND EDITION

W. W. ROSTOW

Professor of Economics and History
The University of Texas at Austin

CAMBRIDGE
AT THE UNIVERSITY PRESS

PUBLISHED BY
THE SYNDICS OF THE CAMBRIDGE UNIVERSITY PRESS

Bentley House, 200 Euston Road, London N.W.1
American Branch: 32 East 57th Street, New York, N.Y.10022

© CAMBRIDGE UNIVERSITY PRESS 1960

This edition © CAMBRIDGE UNIVERSITY PRESS 1971

ISBN: 0 521 08100 9
PAPERBACK: 0 521 09650 2

First published 1960
Reprinted   1960, 1961, 1962, 1963, 1964, 1965,
                 1966, 1967, 1968, 1969
Second Edition 1971, 1973

Library of Congress Catalogue Card Number: 70-152634

First printed in Great Britain
at the University Printing House, Cambridge
Reprinted in the United States of America

TO

ALISON, TATIANA AND

WILLIAM ROSE

CONTENTS

Contents

PREFACE TO THE SECOND EDITION

I

In considering a second edition of *The Stages of Economic Growth*, a decade after its publication, I weighed the question of revising the text itself. For two reasons I decided to confine changes to this Preface and to Appendix B, 'The critics and the evidence'.

First, the analytic bone-structure of the argument.

For reasons set out in Appendix B, I am not inclined to alter the basic approach to the stages of growth; and I regard the evidence accumulated over the past decade on the past and on the contemporary world as, on the whole, reinforcing, not weakening, the concept of stages of growth. This has been an extraordinarily fruitful decade of research in economic history and in the study of growth in the contemporary world. I would not for a moment argue that the text would be identical if it were written afresh. There are important bodies of data and analyses which I would certainly take into account. But I concluded this was best done through an Appendix rather than by rewriting the text.

The Stages of Economic Growth is an effort to map a large problem. It is not an encyclopedia of economic history. An effort to introduce, within its text, the new data available on the various nations and regions of the world would alter its character and purpose.

Despite the heat generated in certain portions of the debate about the stages of growth, the heart of the controversy lies in a quite straightforward technical difference of view: should growth be analysed in terms of broad aggregates (like GNP, the proportion of income invested, the proportion of GNP generated in primary, manufacturing, and service sectors, etc.)? Or, must these aggregates be linked to movements in the sectors and sub-sectors within which new technologies are actually absorbed efficiently into an economy? If one takes the former view, then the dating of take-off and subsequent stages appears fuzzy and impressionistic. If one takes the latter view—and is prepared to dig out the data—the stages emerge with reasonable clarity, out of the past and in the world around us. (In the March, 1970, issue of the *Journal of Economic History* I apply the stages approach to the evolution of regions and nations since 1945, 'The Past Quarter-Century as Economic History and the Tasks of International Economic Organization'.)

Professor Simon Kuznets has led the attack on the stages of growth on this question of the appropriate degree of disaggregation; and, quite properly, his extraordinary scholarship as a statistical analyst of growth has influenced others. But, in this part of my work I am a child of his earlier marriage. It was his *Secular Movements in Production and Prices* (1930) which, more than any other single work, set me off on the approach I have long taken to the analysis of growth, linking, as it easily does, to the essentially sectoral and sub-sectoral approach an historian instinctively takes to how things actually happened at particular times and places in the past.

This passage from Kuznets' *Secular Movements* (pp. 3–4, 5, and 10) suggests its connection to stages of growth analysis:

This picture of economic development suffers a curious change as we examine it first in a rather wide sphere, then in a narrow one. If we take the world from the end of the eighteenth century, there unrolls before us a process of uninterrupted and seemingly unslackened growth. We observe a ceaseless expansion of production and trade, a constant growth in the volume of power used, in the extraction of raw materials, in the quality and quantity of finished products.

But if we single out the various nations or the separate branches of industry, the picture becomes less uniform. Some nations seem to have led the world at one time, others at another. Some industries were developing most rapidly at the beginning of the century, others at the end. Within single countries or within single branches of industries (on a world scale) there has not been uniform, unretarded growth. Great Britain has relinquished the lead in the economic world because its own growth, so vigorous through the period 1780–1850, has slackened. She has been overtaken by rapidly developing Germany and the United States. The texile industries which had so spectacular a rise toward the close of the eighteenth and the beginning of the nineteenth century ceded first place to pig iron, then to steel, while in turn the electrical industries assumed the leadership in the '80s and '90s.

The view becomes further variegated if we distinguish the different industries in their national units. The rapid development of the English textiles came much earlier than that of the American. The Belgian coal output had reached nearly stable levels in the beginning of the twentieth century when American and German coal production were still showing substantial growth. Industries within the limits of one country frequently show a retardation of development as compared either with the national industry as a whole or with the same industry on a world-wide scale...

As we observe the various industries within a given national system, we see that the lead in development shifts from one branch to another. The main reason for this shift seems to be that a rapidly developing industry does not continue its vigorous growth indefinitely, but slackens its pace after a time, and is overtaken by industries whose period of rapid development comes later. Within any country we observe a succession of different branches of activity leading the process of development, and in each mature industry we notice a conspicuous slackening in the rate of increase. For example, the vigorous development of copper mining during the years 1880–1900 in the United States did not continue unabated, nor did that of steel after 1870–1900, nor railroad construction after 1830–1880...

In many industries there comes a time when the basic technical conditions are revolutionized. When such a fundamental change takes place, a new era begins. In the manufacturing industries it is frequently the period when the machine process first supplants hand labour to a substantial extent. In the extractive industries, it is either the moment when the sources and use of a commodity are discovered (petroleum) or when a new and wide application is found for a commodity hitherto but little used. As concrete examples of such periods, one may mention the decade 1780–90 for the cotton industry and pig iron production in Great Britain, the decade of 1860–70 for steel, the decade of the '80s for the copper industry, the decade of the '30s for anthracite, and of the '40s for bituminous coal in the United States, the first and second decades of the nineteenth century for zinc smelting (Belgium-Saxony), the '60s for petroleum (United States), and the decade of the '70s for lead (United States). In all these cases we observe a revolutionary invention or discovery applied to the industrial process which becomes the chief method of production. Our generation has been the eye-witness of such changes in the automobile and radio industries.

But these powerful insights—linking the introduction of new technologies and the national paths of output—have not been pursued by Kuznets and those who have followed his lead. Because of the Keynesian revolution, the generation on an international basis of national income and investment data, and the way the international community has chosen to organize data on output (influenced, perhaps, by Colin Clark's pioneering efforts), the statistician has faced a temptation and a dilemma. The temptation has been to plunge in and exploit the data that are easily accessible and capable of organization for purposes of international comparison. The dilemma is that these data do not easily permit statistical analysts, on an international basis, to get hold of the sectors and sub-sectors where the new technologies actually come in and from which their spreading effects are generated; for we all agree that modern growth is rooted in the progressive diffusion of new technologies on an efficient basis. The analytic task is generally quite possible on a national basis, especially if the analyst is prepared to use incomplete time series and non-statistical data. But one cannot easily generate at this level of disaggregation a statistical base that permits elegant international cross-comparisons, especially for the historical past.

I would not question another man's decision about his research priorities and strategy; and we are all ardent consumers of the aggregative data on growth mobilized by Kuznets. But I do regret that the early Kuznets insights were lost sight of for a time. (They were, incidentally, shared in the early 1930's by Walther Hoffmann and Arthur F. Burns.) And, as Appendix B tries to make clear, I believe they are in the process of re-emerging from both historical and contemporary studies, statistical and non-statistical; for example, something like the sequence of key sectoral complexes arises from Hollis B. Chenery and Lance Taylor's 'Development Patterns: Among Countries and Over Time', *The Review of Economics and Statistics*, November 1968, pp. 405–12. Because this process of linking the aggregates and sectoral analysis is well under way—in statistical as well as national analyses of growth—we are, I believe, moving closer together on this central issue. Therefore, Appendix B is not a polemical document but an effort to find common ground and to narrow, rather than widen, differences of view.

I would, however, reaffirm what I have said before: Without appropriate disaggregation the study of growth is *Hamlet* without the Prince, or playing the piano while wearing mittens. We certainly need the large aggregates; and we are all greatly in the debt of Clark, Kuznets, Chenery, and others who have analysed patterns in these aggregates. But, as an historian and student of growth in the contemporary nations, rich and poor, I am confident that we have much unfinished business ahead in relating them in an orderly way to the sectors where the critical linkage of technology and production occurs so that the analysis of modern growth can become, in Warren Weaver's phrase, a field of 'organized complexity'.

In retrospect, I believe this point should have been put more strongly in the first edition of *The Stages of Economic Growth*. Because it was proportioned as a small book, I confined the statement of the problem to some four pages at the close of chapter 2 entitled 'A Dynamic Theory of Production'. I made footnote reference to my earlier work on the role of sectoral analysis in the study of growth, on which this passage was based: *The Process of Economic Growth* (Oxford, 1953 and 1960); and 'Trends in the Allocation of Resources in Secular Growth', chapter 15 of *Economic Progress*, ed. Leon H. Dupriez, with the assistance of Douglas C. Hague (Louvain, 1955). Evidently, this did not suffice to force the issue with clarity; but I am not sure that anything short of grinding, protracted debate would have forced clarification, given the intellectual interests and resistances at stake.

One reason for the resistance to the stages approach is that it denies the statistical analyst the easy use, in good conscience, of GNP per capita as a measure of growth. If the degree of efficient absorption of technologies is taken as a basic measure of growth (as it should be), one can have relatively rich and relatively poor countries at the same stage of growth, depending on population/resource balances, export capabilities, tourism, foreign aid, etc. Argentina, for example, was a much richer country in take-off than India; Canada than Russia. Moreover, because high mass-consumption depends on income per capita (and the income elasticity of demand), one can have nations moving into that stage before they have absorbed fully and efficiently the technologies that go with their versions of technological maturity; e.g. Australia, Canada, and, at the extreme margin, Kuwait.

It would have been considerably easier for all of us if GNP per capita (or some equivalent measure of income) could have been used to define the stages of growth. And there are, as Appendix B indicates, rough average patterns in societies that go with such measures.

But without piercing the veil of these averages and getting at the extent to which technologies are absorbed efficiently in particular cases, we are using a blunt tool and emerging with sometimes misleading results.

In any case, everything I have learned about growth over the past decade convinces me that the underlying sectoral, disaggregated approach to growth incorporated in *The Stages* is sound. And a high proportion of the debate about *The Stages* centres about this matter, which is pursued, along with other aspects of the debate, in Appendix B.

II

A second factor has led me to confine the revision of *The Stages* to this Preface and Appendix B. This book is both a scientific effort and a tract for the times. Writing in the late 1950's, I brought the tools it incorporates to bear on a number of quite specific questions which concerned a good many of us at that time:

What were the problems and possibilities for America (and other foreseeably rich nations) beyond high mass-consumption?

What were the prospects for growth in the Soviet Union and the meaning of relative U.S.–U.S.S.R. growth rates?

What were the prospects for U.S.–U.S.S.R. relations, as the march of the stages of growth forced a partial diffusion of power away from Washington and Moscow?

What were the prospects for moving from Cold War to stable peace in this world of diffusing power?

What were the prospects in the southern developing regions of the world; how did they relate to the prospects for peace; and what ought we, in the developed north, do to help them?

In assessing whether the portions of the text dealing with these matters should now be revised, I put two questions: In retrospect, were the analyses of these questions faulty? How have these issues changed, in their shape and content, over the past decade?

I did not go far in speculating about life beyond high mass-consumption, except to raise a number of questions that men, societies, and governments would have to answer as they turned to explore new frontiers (pp. 11–12, 90–2, 156). Aside from posing the questions, the fundamental contribution of the argument on this point was to assert that the automobile–durable consumers' goods–suburbia sectoral complex had lost in the 1950's the capacity to drive forward American growth. A decade later, this point is now, I believe, quite clear. (Incidentally, the emphasis given in those passages to the postwar rise in the American birth rate was belied, to a degree, by its decline in the 1960's.)

As for the Soviet growth rate, sectoral analysis (pp. 102–3) proved helpful; and the warning—'beware of linear projections'—germane. As predicted—and the prediction was controversial at the time—the Soviet growth rate decelerated in the 1960's. The issue of whether, how, and at what pace the U.S.S.R. should move forward into the automobile–durable consumers' goods complex did become a central question of policy in Moscow, symbolized by the decision to install the Fiat plant in the Soviet Union

The predicted diffusion of power away from Washington and Moscow did occur in the 1960's—with the Cuba missile crisis and its outcome (and the related exacerbation of the Sino–Soviet split) an historical watershed. The United States and the Soviet Union moved to limit the scope of this diffusion through the non-proliferation treaty which, in turn, enforced certain constraints on the two major nuclear powers, which will have to be honoured if nuclear proliferation is to be confined to its present amply dangerous limits.

At certain points the diffusion of power moved Moscow and Washington into parallelism (e.g., the India–Pakistan war of 1965) and encouraged limited movement towards normalization of U.S.-Soviet relations. But dangerous cross-purposes remained in Southeast Asia and the Middle East. The 1960's did not see an end to the Cold War, although it clearly saw a transitional process away from its rather simple pattern in, say, the time of Stalin.

Finally, the world political community did respond to a significant degree in the 1960's to the challenge of development in the southern regions of the world, yielding the India–Pakistan consortia, the Alliance for Progress, and the broad concept of The Decade of Development. By no means all developing nations achieved self-sustained growth in the 1960's or, even, moved into take-off. But progress was sufficient, in each of the developing regions, to demonstrate that the job could be done if birth rates could be brought down and adequate support sustained from the more advanced nations. In every region there are now examples of rapid and quite regular economic and social progress conducted in loyalty to national cultures, in an environment of political independence, geared to nationally defined ambitions. But as the Pearson Report (*Partners in Development*, 1969) and other studies suggest, the task is incomplete; and the development agenda for the 1970's remains formidable.

Without in any way claiming omniscience, I believe the insights into the contemporary world flowing from the stages of growth in the late 1950's did not prove misleading; but, evidently, a decade and more later we know more than we did then, and there is a great deal more to be said about these issues.

My contribution to their further analysis, as of 1970, is incorporated in another book, *Politics and the Stages of Growth*.

Immediately upon completing *The Stages of Economic Growth*, early in 1959, I decided to elaborate its political dimensions. I had long been interested in the interweaving of politics and economics, but had consciously limited the treatment of politics in this book. As I stated in the Preface to the first edition, I regarded this book as 'both a theory about economic growth and a more general, if still highly partial, theory about modern history as a whole'. With the publication of *Politics and the Stages of Growth*, I have tried to widen the perspective I can contribute to modern history as a whole.

For these reasons, then, chapters 6–10 are left to stand as written; and the reader, if interested, will have to turn elsewhere for the observations I would now make on the subject-matter of those chapters.

AUSTIN, TEXAS   W. W. ROSTOW
June 1970

PREFACE TO THE FIRST EDITION

This book is the product of both a highly spontaneous and a highly protracted effort.

Proximately, it derives from a set of lectures prepared and delivered at Cambridge University in the autumn of 1958. While there on sabbatical leave from M.I.T., I was invited by the Faculty of Economics and Politics to present views on 'The Process of Industrialization' to an undergraduate audience. This book emerged directly from the effort to respond to that invitation, bearing still the marks of the occasion in its informality and non-technical character.

On the other hand the book fulfils, at least *ad interim*, a decision made when I was an undergraduate at Yale, in the mid-1930's. At that time I decided to work professionally on two problems: the relatively narrow problem of bringing modern economic theory to bear on economic history; and the broader problem of relating economic to social and political forces, in the workings of whole societies. As a student and teacher these two questions have engaged me ever since.

Specifically, I found Marx's solution to the problem of linking economic and non-economic behaviour—and the solutions of others who had grappled with it—unsatisfactory, without then feeling prepared to offer an alternative. Over the intervening years I explored facets of the relationship: in work on Britain of the nineteenth century; in teaching American history at Oxford and Cambridge; in studies of modern Russia, China, and the United States; and in elaborating general views on the process of economic growth. In addition, the experience of working from time to time on problems of military and foreign policy added some illumination. This book unifies what I have thus far learned about the central problem from all these directions.

The views presented here might have been elaborated, in a more conventional treatise, at greater length, in greater detail, and with greater professional refinement. But there may be some virtue in articulating new ideas briefly and simply to an intelligent non-professional audience. There are devices of obscurity and diversionary temptations that are denied the teacher of undergraduates. In any case, I owe a real debt to the lively and challenging students at Cambridge who came to hear the lectures, and whose response gave the enterprise an authentic air of intellectual adventure.

Chapter 4 is substantially reprinted, with excisions, from 'The Take-off into Self-Sustained Growth', published in the *Economic Journal*, March 1956, and here included with the kind permission of the editors.

I am in the debt of others as well, in Cambridge and beyond, who commented on this set of ideas. I should wish to thank, in particular, Lawrence Barss, Kenneth Berrill, Denis Brogan, Richard Goodwin, Richard Hofstadter, Richard Kahn, Albert Kervyn, W. J. Macpherson, Gunnar Myrdal, M. M. Postan, E. A. Radice, C. Raphael, Sir Dennis Robertson, Joan Robinson, George Rosen, P. N. Rosenstein-Rodan, Arthur Schlesinger, Sr, Charles Wilson, and the staff of *The Economist* for observations which, whether wholly accepted or not, proved extremely helpful.

I owe a quite specific and substantial debt to my wife, Elspeth Davies Rostow. While I was working in the summer of 1957 on a study of recent American military and foreign policy, she insisted that it was necessary to bring to bear the insights that economic history might afford. It was directly from that injunction, and from the protracted dialogue that followed, that the full sequence of stages-of-growth first fell into place, as well as certain of the contemporary applications here developed in chapters 7–9.

A longer-term and more diffuse debt is owed to my colleagues at M.I.T., who generously commented on various segments of this argument as they were formulated and, notably, to the students in my graduate seminar in economic history since 1950, who actively shared in the creation of this structure of thought.

The preparation of this book was rendered both pleasant and easy by the facilities made available to me by the Faculty of Economics and Politics at Cambridge and those who run the Marshall Library. Their willingness to assist a transient teacher, in the midst of their urgent responsibilities, was memorable.

Preface to the First Edition

The charts in chapter 6, illustrating the diffusion of the private automobile, and the supporting data presented in the Appendix, are the work of John Longden, who most generously turned from his own work to help dramatize that portion of the argument.

Finally, I would wish to thank those at M.I.T. who granted me a sabbatical year, and the Carnegie Corporation, which offered the freedom and resources of a Reflective Year Grant. It is not easy, in contemporary academic life, to find a setting where one can concentrate one's attention wholly on the elaboration of a single line of thought.

W. W. ROSTOW

MARSHALL LIBRARY
CAMBRIDGE
March 1959

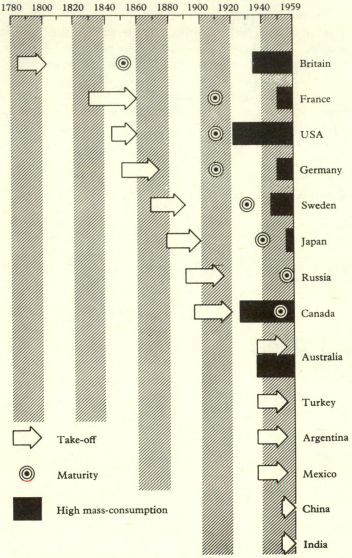

1780 1800 1820 1840 1860 1880 1900 1920 1940 1959

Britain
France
USA
Germany
Sweden
Japan
Russia
Canada
Australia
Turkey
Argentina
Mexico
China
India

⇨ Take-off

◉ Maturity

■ High mass-consumption

Chart of the stages of economic growth in selected countries. Note that Canada and Australia have entered the stage of high mass-consumption before reaching maturity. [By courtesy of the *Economist*.]

CHAPTER I

INTRODUCTION

This book presents an economic historian's way of generalizing the sweep of modern history. The form of this generalization is a set of stages-of-growth.

I have gradually come to the view that it is possible and, for certain limited purposes, it is useful to break down the story of each national economy—and sometimes the story of regions—according to this set of stages. They constitute, in the end, both a theory about economic growth and a more general, if still highly partial, theory about modern history as a whole.

But any way of looking at things that pretends to bring within its orbit, let us say, significant aspects of late eighteenth-century Britain and Khrushchev's Russia; Meiji Japan and Canada of the pre-1914 railway boom; Alexander Hamilton's United States and Mao's China; Bismarck's Germany and Nasser's Egypt—any such scheme is bound, to put it mildly, to have certain limitations.

I cannot emphasize too strongly at the outset, that the stages-of-growth are an arbitrary and limited way of looking at the sequence of modern history: and they are, in no absolute sense, a correct way. They are designed, in fact, to dramatize not merely the uniformities in the sequence of modernization but also—and equally—the uniqueness of each nation's experience.

As Croce said in discussing the limits of historical materialism: '...whilst it is possible to reduce to general concepts the particular factors of reality which appear in history...it is not possible to work up into general concepts the single complex whole formed by these factors'.* We shall be concerned here, then, with certain 'particular factors of reality' which appear to run through the story of the modern world since about 1700.

Having accepted and emphasized the limited nature of the enterprise, it should be noted that the stages-of-growth are designed

* B. Croce, *Historical Materialism and the Economics of Karl Marx*, tr. C. M. Meredith (London), pp. 3–4.

to grapple with a quite substantial range of issues. Under what impulses did traditional, agricultural societies begin the process of their modernization? When and how did regular growth come to be a built-in feature of each society? What forces drove the process of sustained growth along and determined its contours? What common social and political features of the growth process may be discerned at each stage? And in which directions did the uniqueness of each society express itself at each stage? What forces have determined the relations between the more developed and less developed areas; and what relation, if any, did the relative sequence of growth bear to the outbreak of war? And, finally, where is compound interest* taking us? Is it taking us to Communism; or to the affluent suburbs, nicely rounded out with social overhead capital; to destruction; to the moon; or where?

The stages-of-growth are designed to get at these matters; and, since they constitute an alternative to Karl Marx's theory of modern history, I have given over the final chapter to a comparison between his way of looking at things and mine.

But this should be clear: although the stages-of-growth are an economic way of looking at whole societies, they in no sense imply that the worlds of politics, social organization, and of culture are a mere superstructure built upon and derived uniquely from the economy. On the contrary, we accept from the beginning the perception on which Marx, in the end, turned his back and which Engels was only willing to acknowledge whole-heartedly as a very old man; namely, that societies are interacting organisms. While it is true that economic change has political and social consequence, economic change is, itself, viewed here as the consequence of political and social as well as narrowly economic forces. And in terms of human motivation, many of the most profound economic changes are viewed as the consequence of non-economic human motives and aspirations. The student of economic growth concerned with its foundation in human motivation should never forget Keynes's dictum: 'If human nature felt no temptation to take a chance no satisfaction (profit apart) in constructing a factory, a rail-

---

* This phrase is used as a shorthand way of suggesting that growth normally proceeds by geometric progression, much as a savings account if interest is left to compound with principal.

way, a mine or a farm, there might not be much investment merely as a result of cold calculation.'*

The exposition begins with an impressionistic definition of the five major stages-of-growth and a brief statement of the dynamic theory of production which is their bone-structure. The four chapters that follow consider more analytically, and illustrate from history and from contemporary experience, the stages beyond the traditional society: the preconditions period, the take-off, maturity, and the period of diffusion on a mass basis of durable consumers' goods and services.

Chapter 7 examines the comparative patterns of growth of Russia and the United States over the past century, a matter of both historical and contemporary interest.

Chapter 8 applies the stages-of-growth to the question of aggression and war, down to the early 1950's, the question conventionally raised under the rubric of imperialism.

Chapter 9 carries forward this analysis of the relation between growth and war into the future, considering the nature of the problem of peace, when examined from the perspective of the stages-of-growth.

And, finally, in chapter 10 we examine explicitly the relationship between the stages-of-growth and the Marxist system.

Now, then, what are these stages-of-growth?

* *General Theory*, p. 150.

CHAPTER 2

THE FIVE STAGES-OF-GROWTH—
A SUMMARY

It is possible to identify all societies, in their economic dimensions, as lying within one of five categories: the traditional society, the preconditions for take-off, the take-off, the drive to maturity, and the age of high mass-consumption.

THE TRADITIONAL SOCIETY

First, the traditional society. A traditional society is one whose structure is developed within limited production functions, based on pre-Newtonian science and technology, and on pre-Newtonian attitudes towards the physical world. Newton is here used as a symbol for that watershed in history when men came widely to believe that the external world was subject to a few knowable laws, and was systematically capable of productive manipulation.

The conception of the traditional society is, however, in no sense static; and it would not exclude increases in output. Acreage could be expanded; some *ad hoc* technical innovations, often highly productive innovations, could be introduced in trade, industry and agriculture; productivity could rise with, for example, the improvement of irrigation works or the discovery and diffusion of a new crop. But the central fact about the traditional society was that a ceiling existed on the level of attainable output per head. This ceiling resulted from the fact that the potentialities which flow from modern science and technology were either not available or not regularly and systematically applied.

Both in the longer past and in recent times the story of traditional societies was thus a story of endless change. The area and volume of trade within them and between them fluctuated, for example, with the degree of political and social turbulence, the efficiency of central rule, the upkeep of the roads. Population—and, within limits, the level of life—rose and fell not only with the sequence

4

of the harvests, but with the incidence of war and of plague. Varying degrees of manufacture developed; but, as in agriculture, the level of productivity was limited by the inaccessibility of modern science, its applications, and its frame of mind.

Generally speaking, these societies, because of the limitation on productivity, had to devote a very high proportion of their resources to agriculture; and flowing from the agricultural system there was an hierarchical social structure, with relatively narrow scope—but some scope—for vertical mobility. Family and clan connexions played a large role in social organization. The value system of these societies was generally geared to what might be called a long-run fatalism; that is, the assumption that the range of possibilities open to one's grandchildren would be just about what it had been for one's grandparents. But this long-run fatalism by no means excluded the short-run option that, within a considerable range, it was possible and legitimate for the individual to strive to improve his lot, within his lifetime. In Chinese villages, for example, there was an endless struggle to acquire or to avoid losing land, yielding a situation where land rarely remained within the same family for a century.

Although central political rule—in one form or another—often existed in traditional societies, transcending the relatively self-sufficient regions, the centre of gravity of political power generally lay in the regions, in the hands of those who owned or controlled the land. The landowner maintained fluctuating but usually profound influence over such central political power as existed, backed by its entourage of civil servants and soldiers, imbued with attitudes and controlled by interests transcending the regions.

In terms of history then, with the phrase 'traditional society' we are grouping the whole pre-Newtonian world: the dynasties in China; the civilization of the Middle East and the Mediterranean; the world of medieval Europe. And to them we add the post-Newtonian societies which, for a time, remained untouched or unmoved by man's new capability for regularly manipulating his environment to his economic advantage.

To place these infinitely various, changing societies in a single category, on the ground that they all shared a ceiling on the productivity of their economic techniques, is to say very little indeed. But we are, after all, merely clearing the way in order to get at the subject of this book; that is, the post-traditional societies, in which each of the major characteristics of the traditional society was altered in such ways as to permit regular growth: its politics, social structure, and (to a degree) its values, as well as its economy.

THE PRECONDITIONS FOR TAKE-OFF

The second stage of growth embraces societies in the process of transition; that is, the period when the preconditions for take-off are developed; for it takes time to transform a traditional society in the ways necessary for it to exploit the fruits of modern science, to fend off diminishing returns, and thus to enjoy the blessings and choices opened up by the march of compound interest.

The preconditions for take-off were initially developed, in a clearly marked way, in Western Europe of the late seventeenth and early eighteenth centuries as the insights of modern science began to be translated into new production functions in both agriculture and industry, in a setting given dynamism by the lateral expansion of world markets and the international competition for them. But all that lies behind the break-up of the Middle Ages is relevant to the creation of the preconditions for take-off in Western Europe. Among the Western European states, Britain, favoured by geography, natural resources, trading possibilities, social and political structure, was the first to develop fully the preconditions for take-off.

The more general case in modern history, however, saw the stage of preconditions arise not endogenously but from some external intrusion by more advanced societies. These invasions—literal or figurative—shocked the traditional society and began or hastened its undoing; but they also set in motion ideas and sentiments which initiated the process by which a modern alternative to the traditional society was constructed out of the old culture.

The idea spreads not merely that economic progress is possible, but that economic progress is a necessary condition for some other purpose, judged to be good: be it national dignity, private profit, the general welfare, or a better life for the children. Education, for some at least, broadens and changes to suit the needs of modern economic activity. New types of enterprising men come forward—

6

in the private economy, in government, or both—willing to mobilize savings and to take risks in pursuit of profit or modernization. Banks and other institutions for mobilizing capital appear. Investment increases, notably in transport, communications, and in raw materials in which other nations may have an economic interest. The scope of commerce, internal and external, widens. And, here and there, modern manufacturing enterprise appears, using the new methods. But all this activity proceeds at a limited pace within an economy and a society still mainly characterized by traditional low-productivity methods, by the old social structure and values, and by the regionally based political institutions that developed in conjunction with them.

In many recent cases, for example, the traditional society persisted side by side with modern economic activities, conducted for limited economic purposes by a colonial or quasi-colonial power.

Although the period of transition—between the traditional society and the take-off—saw major changes in both the economy itself and in the balance of social values, a decisive feature was often political. Politically, the building of an effective centralized national state—on the basis of coalitions touched with a new nationalism, in opposition to the traditional landed regional interests, the colonial power, or both, was a decisive aspect of the preconditions period; and it was, almost universally, a necessary condition for take-off.

There is a great deal more that needs to be said about the preconditions period, but we shall leave it for chapter 3, where the anatomy of the transition from a traditional to a modern society is examined.

THE TAKE-OFF

We come now to the great watershed in the life of modern societies: the third stage in this sequence, the take-off. The take-off is the interval when the old blocks and resistances to steady growth are finally overcome. The forces making for economic progress, which yielded limited bursts and enclaves of modern activity, expand and come to dominate the society. Growth becomes its normal condition. Compound interest becomes built, as it were, into its habits and institutional structure.

In Britain and the well-endowed parts of the world populated substantially from Britain (the United States, Canada etc.) the proximate stimulus for take-off was mainly (but not wholly) technological. In the more general case, the take-off awaited not only the build-up of social overhead capital and a surge of technological development in industry and agriculture, but also the emergence to political power of a group prepared to regard the modernization of the economy as serious, high-order political business.

During the take-off, the rate of effective investment and savings may rise from, say, 5% of the national income to 10% or more; although where heavy social overhead capital investment was required to create the technical preconditions for take-off the investment rate in the preconditions period could be higher than 5%, as, for example, in Canada before the 1890's and Argentina before 1914. In such cases capital imports usually formed a high proportion of total investment in the preconditions period and sometimes even during the take-off itself, as in Russia and Canada during their pre-1914 railway booms.

During the take-off new industries expand rapidly, yielding profits a large proportion of which are reinvested in new plant; and these new industries, in turn, stimulate, through their rapidly expanding requirement for factory workers, the services to support them, and for other manufactured goods, a further expansion in urban areas and in other modern industrial plants. The whole process of expansion in the modern sector yields an increase of income in the hands of those who not only save at high rates but place their savings at the disposal of those engaged in modern sector activities. The new class of entrepreneurs expands; and it directs the enlarging flows of investment in the private sector. The economy exploits hitherto unused natural resources and methods of production.

New techniques spread in agriculture as well as industry, as agriculture is commercialized, and increasing numbers of farmers are prepared to accept the new methods and the deep changes they bring to ways of life. The revolutionary changes in agricultural productivity are an essential condition for successful take-off; for modernization of a society increases radically its bill for agricultural products. In a decade or two both the basic structure of the economy and the social and political structure of the society are transformed in such a way that a steady rate of growth can be, thereafter, regularly sustained.

As indicated in chapter 4, one can approximately allocate the take-off of Britain to the two decades after 1783; France and the United States to the several decades preceding 1860; Germany, the third quarter of the nineteenth century; Japan, the fourth quarter of the nineteenth century; Russia and Canada the quarter-century or so preceding 1914; while during the 1950's India and China have, in quite different ways, launched their respective take-offs.

THE DRIVE TO MATURITY

After take-off there follows a long interval of sustained if fluctuating progress, as the now regularly growing economy drives to extend modern technology over the whole front of its economic activity. Some 10–20 % of the national income is steadily invested, permitting output regularly to outstrip the increase in population. The make-up of the economy changes unceasingly as technique improves, new industries accelerate, older industries level off. The economy finds its place in the international economy: goods formerly imported are produced at home; new import requirements develop, and new export commodities to match them. The society makes such terms as it will with the requirements of modern efficient production, balancing off the new against the older values and institutions, or revising the latter in such ways as to support rather than to retard the growth process.

Some sixty years after take-off begins (say, forty years after the end of take-off) what may be called maturity is generally attained. The economy, focused during the take-off around a relatively narrow complex of industry and technology, has extended its range into more refined and technologically often more complex processes; for example, there may be a shift in focus from the coal, iron, and heavy engineering industries of the railway phase to machine-tools, chemicals, and electrical equipment. This, for example, was the transition through which Germany, Britain, France, and the United States had passed by the end of the nineteenth century or shortly thereafter. But there are other sectoral patterns which have been followed in the sequence from take-off to maturity, which are considered in chapter 5.

Formally, we can define maturity as the stage in which an economy demonstrates the capacity to move beyond the original industries which powered its take-off and to absorb and to apply efficiently over a very wide range of its resources—if not the whole range— the most advanced fruits of (then) modern technology. This is the stage in which an economy demonstrates that it has the technological and entrepreneurial skills to produce not everything, but anything that it chooses to produce. It may lack (like contemporary Sweden and Switzerland, for example) the raw materials or other supply conditions required to produce a given type of output economically; but its dependence is a matter of economic choice or political priority rather than a technological or institutional necessity.

Historically, it would appear that something like sixty years was required to move a society from the beginning of take-off to maturity. Analytically the explanation for some such interval may lie in the powerful arithmetic of compound interest applied to the capital stock, combined with the broader consequences for a society's ability to absorb modern technology of three successive generations living under a regime where growth is the normal condition. But, clearly, no dogmatism is justified about the exact length of the interval from take-off to maturity.

THE AGE OF HIGH MASS-CONSUMPTION

We come now to the age of high mass-consumption, where, in time, the leading sectors shift towards durable consumers' goods and services: a phase from which Americans are beginning to emerge; whose not unequivocal joys Western Europe and Japan are beginning energetically to probe; and with which Soviet society is engaged in an uneasy flirtation.

As societies achieved maturity in the twentieth century two things happened: real income per head rose to a point where a large number of persons gained a command over consumption which transcended basic food, shelter, and clothing; and the structure of the working force changed in ways which increased not only the proportion of urban to total population, but also the proportion of the population working in offices or in skilled factory jobs—aware of and anxious to acquire the consumption fruits of a mature economy.

In addition to these economic changes, the society ceased to accept the further extension of modern technology as an overriding objective. It is in this post-maturity stage, for example, that, through the political process, Western societies have chosen to allocate increased resources to social welfare and security. The emergence of the welfare state is one manifestation of a society's moving beyond technical maturity; but it is also at this stage that resources tend increasingly to be directed to the production of consumers' durables and to the diffusion of services on a mass basis, if consumers' sovereignty reigns. The sewing-machine, the bicycle, and then the various electric-powered household gadgets were gradually diffused. Historically, however, the decisive element has been the cheap mass automobile with its quite revolutionary effects— social as well as economic—on the life and expectations of society.

For the United States, the turning point was, perhaps, Henry Ford's moving assembly line of 1913–14; but it was in the 1920's, and again in the post-war decade, 1946–56, that this stage of growth was pressed to, virtually, its logical conclusion. In the 1950's Western Europe and Japan appear to have fully entered this phase, accounting substantially for a momentum in their economies quite unexpected in the immediate post-war years. The Soviet Union is technically ready for this stage, and, by every sign, its citizens hunger for it; but Communist leaders face difficult political and social problems of adjustment if this stage is launched.

BEYOND CONSUMPTION

Beyond, it is impossible to predict, except perhaps to observe that Americans, at least, have behaved in the past decade as if diminishing relative marginal utility sets in, after a point, for durable consumers' goods; and they have chosen, at the margin, larger families— behaviour in the pattern of Buddenbrooks dynamics.* Americans have behaved as if, having been born into a system that provided economic security and high mass-consumption, they placed a lower

* In Thomas Mann's novel of three generations, the first sought money; the second, born to money, sought social and civic position; the third, born to comfort and family prestige, looked to the life of music. The phrase is designed to suggest, then, the changing aspirations of generations, as they place a low value on what they take for granted and seek new forms of satisfaction.

valuation on acquiring additional increments of real income in the conventional form as opposed to the advantages and values of an enlarged family. But even in this adventure in generalization it is a shade too soon to create—on the basis of one case—a new stage-of-growth, based on babies, in succession to the age of consumers' durables: as economists might say, the income-elasticity of demand for babies may well vary from society to society. But it is true that the implications of the baby boom along with the not wholly unrelated deficit in social overhead capital are likely to dominate the American economy over the next decade rather than the further diffusion of consumers' durables.

Here then, in an impressionistic rather than an analytic way, are the stages-of-growth which can be distinguished once a traditional society begins its modernization: the transitional period when the preconditions for take-off are created generally in response to the intrusion of a foreign power, converging with certain domestic forces making for modernization; the take-off itself; the sweep into maturity generally taking up the life of about two further generations; and then, finally, if the rise of income has matched the spread of technological virtuosity (which, as we shall see, it need not immediately do) the diversion of the fully mature economy to the provision of durable consumers' goods and services (as well as the welfare state) for its increasingly urban—and then suburban—population. Beyond lies the question of whether or not secular spiritual stagnation will arise, and, if it does, how man might fend it off: a matter considered in chapter 6.

In the four chapters that follow we shall take a harder, and more rigorous look at the preconditions, the take-off, the drive to maturity, and the processes which have led to the age of high mass-consumption. But even in this introductory chapter one characteristic of this system should be made clear.

A DYNAMIC THEORY OF PRODUCTION

These stages are not merely descriptive. They are not merely a way of generalizing certain factual observations about the sequence of development of modern societies. They have an inner logic and continuity. They have an analytic bone-structure, rooted in a dynamic theory of production.

The classical theory of production is formulated under essentially static assumptions which freeze—or permit only once-over change—in the variables most relevant to the process of economic growth. As modern economists have sought to merge classical production theory with Keynesian income analysis they have introduced the dynamic variables: population, technology, entrepreneurship etc. But they have tended to do so in forms so rigid and general that their models cannot grip the essential phenomena of growth, as they appear to an economic historian. We require a dynamic theory of production which isolates not only the distribution of income between consumption, saving, and investment (and the balance of production between consumers and capital goods) but which focuses directly and in some detail on the composition of investment and on developments within particular sectors of the economy. The argument that follows is based on such a flexible, disaggregated theory of production.

When the conventional limits on the theory of production are widened, it is possible to define theoretical equilibrium positions not only for output, investment, and consumption as a whole, but for each sector of the economy.*

Within the framework set by forces determining the total level of output, sectoral optimum positions are determined on the side of demand, by the levels of income and of population, and by the character of tastes; on the side of supply, by the state of technology and the quality of entrepreneurship, as the latter determines the proportion of technically available and potentially profitable innovations actually incorporated in the capital stock.†

In addition, one must introduce an extremely significant empirical hypothesis: namely, that deceleration is the normal optimum path of a sector, due to a variety of factors operating on it, from the side of both supply and demand.‡

---

* W.W. Rostow, *The Process of Economic Growth* (Oxford, 1953), especially chapter IV. Also 'Trends in the Allocation of Resources in Secular Growth', chapter 15 of *Economic Progress*, ed. Leon H. Dupriez, with the assistance of Douglas C. Hague (Louvain, 1955).

† In a closed model, a dynamic theory of production must account for changing stocks of basic and applied science, as sectoral aspects of investment, which is done in *The Process of Economic Growth*, especially pp. 22–5.

‡ *Process of Economic Growth*, pp. 96–103.

The equilibria which emerge from the application of these criteria are a set of sectoral paths, from which flows, as first derivatives, a sequence of optimum patterns of investment.

Historical patterns of investment did not, of course, exactly follow these optimum patterns. They were distorted by imperfections in the private investment process, by the policies of governments, and by the impact of wars. Wars temporarily altered the profitable directions of investment by setting up arbitrary demands and by changing the conditions of supply; they destroyed capital; and, occasionally, they accelerated the development of new technology relevant to the peacetime economy and shifted the political and social framework in ways conducive to peacetime growth.* The historical sequence of business-cycles and trend-periods results from these deviations of actual from optimal patterns; and such fluctuations, along with the impact of wars, yield historical paths of growth which differ from those which the optima, calculated before the event, would have yielded.

Nevertheless, the economic history of growing societies takes a part of its rude shape from the effort of societies to approximate the optimum sectoral paths.

At any period of time, the rate of growth in the sectors will vary greatly; and it is possible to isolate empirically certain leading sectors, at early stages of their evolution, whose rapid rate of expansion plays an essential direct and indirect role in maintaining the overall momentum of the economy.† For some purposes it is useful to characterize an economy in terms of its leading sectors; and a part of the technical basis for the stages of growth lies in the changing sequence of leading sectors. In essence it is the fact that sectors tend to have a rapid growth-phase, early in their life, that makes it possible and useful to regard economic history as a sequence of stages rather than merely as a continuum, within which nature never makes a jump.

The stages-of-growth also require, however, that elasticities of demand be taken into account, and that this familiar concept be

---

* *Process of Economic Growth*, chapter VII, especially pp. 164-7.

† For a discussion of the leading sectors, their direct and indirect consequences, and the diverse routes of their impact, see 'Trends in the Allocation of Resources in Secular Growth', *loc. cit.*

widened; for these rapid growth phases in the sectors derive not merely from the discontinuity of production functions but also from high price- or income-elasticities of demand. Leading sectors are determined not merely by the changing flow of technology and the changing willingness of entrepreneurs to accept available innovations: they are also partially determined by those types of demand which have exhibited high elasticity with respect to price, income, or both.

The demand for resources has resulted, however, not merely from demands set up by private taste and choice, but also from social decisions and from the policies of governments—whether democratically responsive or not. It is necessary, therefore, to look at the choices made by societies in the disposition of their resources in terms which transcend conventional market processes. It is necessary to look at their welfare functions, in the widest sense, including the non-economic processes which determined them.

The course of birth-rates, for example, represents one form of welfare choice made by societies, as income has changed; and population curves reflect (in addition to changing death-rates) how the calculus about family size was made in the various stages; from the usual (but not universal) decline in birth-rates, during or soon after the take-off, as urbanization took hold and progress became a palpable possibility, to the recent rise, as Americans (and others in societies marked by high mass-consumption) have appeared to seek in larger families values beyond those afforded by economic security and by an ample supply of durable consumers' goods and services.

And there are other decisions as well that societies have made as the choices open to them have been altered by the unfolding process of economic growth; and these broad collective decisions, determined by many factors—deep in history, culture, and the active political process—outside the market-place, have interplayed with the dynamics of market demand, risk-taking, technology and entrepreneurship, to determine the specific content of the stages of growth for each society.

How, for example, should the traditional society react to the intrusion of a more advanced power: with cohesion, promptness, and vigour, like the Japanese; by making a virtue of fecklessness, like the oppressed Irish of the eighteenth century; by slowly and reluctantly altering the traditional society, like the Chinese?

When independent modern nationhood is achieved, how should the national energies be disposed: in external aggression, to right old wrongs or to exploit newly created or perceived possibilities for enlarged national power; in completing and refining the political victory of the new national government over old regional interests; or in modernizing the economy?

Once growth is under way, with the take-off, to what extent should the requirements of diffusing modern technology and maximizing the rate of growth be moderated by the desire to increase consumption *per capita* and to increase welfare?

When technological maturity is reached, and the nation has at its command a modernized and differentiated industrial machine, to what ends should it be put, and in what proportions: to increase social security, through the welfare state; to expand mass-consumption into the range of durable consumers' goods and services; to increase the nation's stature and power on the world scene; or to increase leisure?

And then the question beyond, where history offers us only fragments: what to do when the increase in real income itself loses its charm? Babies, boredom, three-day week-ends, the moon, or the creation of new inner, human frontiers in substitution for the imperatives of scarcity?

In surveying now the broad contours of each stage-of-growth, we are examining, then, not merely the sectoral structure of economies, as they transformed themselves for growth, and grew; we are also examining a succession of strategic choices made by various societies concerning the disposition of their resources, which include but transcend the income- and price-elasticities of demand.

CHAPTER 3

THE PRECONDITIONS FOR TAKE-OFF

THE TWO CASES

We consider in this chapter the preconditions for take-off: the transitional era when a society prepares itself—or is prepared by external forces—for sustained growth.

It is necessary to begin by distinguishing two kinds of cases history has to offer.

There is first what might be called the general case. This case fits not merely the evolution of most of Europe but also the greater part of Asia, the Middle East, and Africa. In this general case the creation of the preconditions for take-off required fundamental changes in a well-established traditional society: changes which touched and substantially altered the social structure and political system as well as techniques of production.

Then there is the second case. This case covers the small group of nations that were, in a sense, 'born free':* the United States, Australia, New Zealand, Canada, and, perhaps, a few others. These nations were created mainly out of a Britain already far along in the transitional process. Moreover, they were founded by social groups —usually one type of non-conformist or another—who were at the margin of the dynamic transitional process slowly going forward within Britain. Finally their physical settings—of wild but abundant land and other natural resources—discouraged the maintenance of such elements in the traditional structure as were transplanted, and they accelerated the transitional process by offering extremely attractive incentives to get on with economic growth. Thus the nations within the second case never became so deeply caught up in the structures, politics and values of the traditional society; and, therefore, the process of their transition to modern growth was mainly economic and technical. The creation of the preconditions for take-off was largely a matter of building social overhead capital—railways,

* A phrase used by Louis Hartz in *The Liberal Tradition in America* (New York, 1955).

ports and roads—and of finding an economic setting in which a shift from agriculture and trade to manufacture was profitable; for, in the first instance, comparative advantage lay in agriculture and the production of food-stuffs and raw materials for export.

The distinction between the two cases is real enough; but looked at closely the lines of demarcation turn out to be not all that sharp. The United States, for example, created for itself a kind of traditional society in the South, as an appendage to Lancashire, and then New England's cotton mills; and the long, slow disengagement of the South from its peculiar version of a traditional society belongs clearly in the general rather than the special case. Canada, moreover, has had its regional problem of a sort of traditional society in Quebec. The take-off of the American South is a phenomenon of the last two decades; while the take-off in Quebec may only now be getting whole-heartedly under way.

There are other types of fuzziness as well. Are the Latin American states to be regarded as in the general case, or among the lucky offspring of already transitional Europe? On the whole, we would judge, they belong in the general case; that is, they began with a version of a traditional society—often a merging of traditional Latin Europe and native traditional cultures--which required fundamental change before the mixed blessings of compound interest could be attained; but the Latin American cases vary among themselves. Similarly, Scandinavia, somewhat like Britain itself, faced less searching problems than many other parts of Europe in shaking off the limiting parameters of the traditional society. Sweden is almost in the second rather than the first category.

Nevertheless, the distinction between the two cases, properly and modestly used, is helpful.

This chapter is concentrated on the general case; that is, on the process, within a traditional society, by which the preconditions for take-off are created.

THE NATURE OF THE TRANSITION

The transition we are examining has, evidently, many dimensions. A society predominantly agricultural—with, in fact, usually 75% or more of its working force in agriculture—must shift to a predominance for industry, communications, trade and services.

A society whose economic, social and political arrangements are built around the life of relatively small—mainly self-sufficient—regions must orient its commerce and its thought to the nation and to a still larger international setting.

The view towards the having of children—initially the residual blessing and affirmation of immortality in a hard life, of relatively fixed horizons—must change in ways which ultimately yield a decline in the birth-rate, as the possibility of progress and the decline in the need for unskilled farm labour create a new calculus.

The income above minimum levels of consumption, largely concentrated in the hands of those who own land, must be shifted into the hands of those who will spend it on roads and railroads, schools and factories rather than on country houses and servants, personal ornaments and temples.

Men must come to be valued in the society not for their connexion with clan or class, or, even, their guild; but for their individual ability to perform certain specific, increasingly specialized functions.

And, above all, the concept must be spread that man need not regard his physical environment as virtually a factor given by nature and providence, but as an ordered world which, if rationally understood, can be manipulated in ways which yield productive change and, in one dimension at least, progress.

All of this—and more—is involved in the passage of a traditional to a modern growing society. Now, how shall we go about analysing this transition? How shall we try to give to it a certain intellectual order?

We shall turn first to its economic aspects—in a reasonably narrow sense—and then to its non-economic dimensions.

THE ANALYSIS OF THE TRANSITION

The modern economist—or perhaps one should say, given the recent shift of interest to growth, the modern economist of a decade ago—might have been inclined to say to the historian something of this sort: 'This complexity about whole societies is all very well; and it is no doubt of some interest to you and your kind; but don't make such heavy weather of it. What you are talking about is a rise in the rate of investment and in the *per capita* stock of capital. Get the investment-rate up to the point where the increase in output outstrips the rate of population increase—to, say, a rate of investment over 10% of national income—and the job is done. The difference between a traditional and a modern society is merely a question of whether its investment-rate is low relative to population increase —let us say under 5% of national income; or whether it has risen up to 10% or over. With a capital/output ratio of about 3, a 10% investment-rate will outstrip any likely population growth; and there you are, with a regular increase in output per head.'

And what the old-fashioned modern economist might have said was, of course, quite true.

But to get the rate of investment up some men in the society must be able to manipulate and apply—and in a closed system they must be able to create—modern science and useful cost-reducing inventions.

Some other men in the society must be prepared to undergo the strain and risks of leadership in bringing the flow of available inventions productively into the capital stock.

Some other men in the society must be prepared to lend their money on long term, at high risk, to back the innovating entrepreneurs—not in money-lending, playing the exchanges, foreign trade or real estate—but in modern industry.

And the population at large must be prepared to accept training for—and then to operate—an economic system whose methods are subject to regular change, and one which also increasingly confines the individual in large, disciplined organizations allocating to him specialized narrow, recurrent tasks.

In short, the rise in the rate of investment—which the economist conjures up to summarize the transition—requires a radical shift in the society's effective attitude toward fundamental and applied science; toward the initiation of change in productive technique; toward the taking of risk; and toward the conditions and methods of work.

One must say a change in effective attitude—rather than merely a change in attitude—because what is involved here is not some vague change in psychological or sociological orientation, but a change translated into working institutions and procedures. Such change is not to be established by retrospective Gallup polls, but by the comparative examination of political, social and economic performance in response to similar objective profit possibilities.

Having peered briefly inside the process of investment in a world of changing production functions, we can conclude by agreeing that, in the end, the essence of the transition can be described legitimately as a rise in the rate of investment to a level which regularly, substantially and perceptibly outstrips population growth; although, when this is said, it carries no implication that the rise in the investment-rate is an ultimate cause.

TWO SECTORAL PROBLEMS

The rise of the investment-rate, as well as reflecting these more profound societal changes, is also the consequence of developments in particular sectors of the economy, where the transformation of the economy actually takes place. The analysis of economic growth can, then, proceed only a short and highly abstracted way without disaggregation.

To illustrate the need to pierce the veil of aggregative analysis in the transitional period we shall look briefly now at two particular problems shared, in one way or another, by all societies which have learned how to grow: the problem of increased productivity in agriculture and the extractive industries; and the problem of social overhead capital.

AGRICULTURE AND THE EXTRACTIVE INDUSTRIES

Although a good deal of the early growth process hinges on the food-supply, the first of these two sectoral problems is properly to be defined as that of agriculture and the extractive industries. The general requirement of the transition is to apply quick-yielding changes in productivity to the most accessible and naturally productive resources. Generally, this means higher productivity in food-production. But it may also mean wool, cotton, or silk—as in nineteenth-century New Zealand, the American South, and Japan. And in Sweden it meant timber; in Malaya, rubber; in the Middle

East, oil; and in certain American regions, Australia, and Alaska, gold helped to do the trick.

The point is that it takes more than industry to industrialize. Industry itself takes time to develop momentum and competitive competence; in the meanwhile there is certain to be a big social overhead capital bill to meet; and there is almost certain to be a radically increased population to feed. In a generalized sense modernization takes a lot of working capital; and a good part of this working capital must come from rapid increases in output achieved by higher productivity in agriculture and the extractive industries.

More specifically the attempt simultaneously to expand fixed capital—of long gestation period—and to feed an expanding population requires both increased food output at home and/or increased imports from abroad. Capital imports can help, of course, but in the end loans must be serviced; and the servicing of loans requires enlarged exports.

It is, therefore, an essential condition for a successful transition that investment be increased and—even more important—that the hitherto unexploited back-log of innovations be brought to bear on a society's land and other natural resources, where quick increases in output are possible.

Having made the general case in terms of requirements for working capital, look for a moment more closely at the question of agriculture and the food-supply. There are, in fact, three distinct major roles agriculture must play in the transitional process between a traditional society and a successful take-off.

First, agriculture must supply more food. Food is needed to meet the likely rise in population, without yielding either starvation or a depletion of foreign exchange available for purposes essential to growth. But increased supplies and increased transfers of food out of rural areas are needed for another reason: to feed the urban populations which are certain to grow at a disproportionately high rate during the transition. And, in most cases, increased agricultural supplies are needed as well to help meet the foreign exchange bill for capital development: either positively by earning foreign exchange, as in the United States, Russia, Canada, and several other nations which generated and maintained agricultural surpluses while

22

their populations were growing (and their urban populations growing faster than the population as a whole); or negatively, to minimize the foreign exchange bill for food—like a whole series of nations from Britain in the 1790's to Israel in the 1950's.

The central fact is that, in the transitional period, industry is not likely to have established a sufficiently large and productive base to earn enough foreign exchange to meet the increments in the nation's food bill via increased imports. Population increases, urbanization, and increased foreign exchange requirements for fixed and working capital are all thus likely to conspire to exert a peculiar pressure on the agricultural sector in the transitional process. Put another way, the rate of increase in output in agriculture may set the limit within which the transition to modernization proceeds.

But this is not all. Agriculture may enter the picture in a related but quite distinctive way, from the side of demand as well as supply. Let us assume that the governmental sector in this transitional economy is not so large that its expanded demand can support the rapid growth of industry. Let us assume that some of the potential leading sectors are in consumers' goods—as, indeed, has often been the case: not only cotton textiles—as in England and New England—but a wide range of import substitutes, as in a number of Latin American cases. In addition, the modern sector can—and often should—be built in part on items of capital for agriculture: farm machinery, chemical fertilizers, diesel pumps etc. In short, an environment of rising real incomes in agriculture, rooted in increased productivity, may be an important stimulus to new modern industrial sectors essential to the take-off.

The income side of the productivity revolution in agriculture may be important even in those cases where the transition to industrialization is not based on consumers' goods industries; for it is from rising rural incomes that increased taxes of one sort or another can be drawn—necessary to finance the government's functions in the transition—without imposing either starvation on the peasants or inflation on the urban population.

And there is a third distinctive role for agriculture in the transitional period which goes beyond its functions in supplying resources, effective demand or tax revenues: agriculture must yield up a substantial part of its surplus income to the modern sector. At the core of the *Wealth of Nations*—lost among propositions about pins and free trade—is Adam Smith's perception that surplus income derived from ownership of land must, somehow, be transferred out of the hands of those who would sterilize it in prodigal living into the hands of the productive men who will invest it in the modern sector and then regularly plough back their profits as output and productivity rise.

In their nineteenth-century land-reform schemes this is precisely what Japan, Russia, and many other nations have done during the transition in an effort to increase the supply of capital available for social overhead and other essential modernizing processes.

It is thus the multiple, distinctive, but converging consequences of the revolution in agriculture which give to it a peculiar importance in the period of preconditions. Agriculture must supply expanded food, expanded markets, and an expanded supply of loanable funds to the modern sector.

Generalized observations about capital formation in the aggregate do not significantly illuminate these essential multiple connexions between agricultural and industrial growth.

SOCIAL OVERHEAD CAPITAL

Similarly, the conventional mode for dealing with capital formation in terms of national income aggregates does not usefully illuminate the crucial role, in the preconditions period, of the build-up of social overhead capital. Where data exist on the level and pattern of capital formation in pre-take-off societies—and for the take-off as well—it is clear that a very high proportion of total investment must go into transport and other social overhead outlays.*

Aside from their quantitative importance, social overhead outlays have three characteristics which distinguish them from investment in general, as usually presented in aggregative models. First, their

* See, for example, A. K. Cairncross, *Home and Foreign Investment, 1870–1913* (Cambridge, 1953), chapter III. pp. 44–8, on the composition of Canadian investment during the take-off period (say, 1895–1915). See also, for the pattern of investment in Sweden and the role within it of railway and housing investment in the period 1870–90, E. Lindahl and others, *National Income of Sweden, 1861–1930* (Stockholm, 1937), especially pp. 257–66.

periods of gestation and of pay-off are usually long. Unlike double-cropping or the application of chemical fertilizers, a railway system is unlikely to yield its results in a year or two from the time its construction is undertaken, although it will yield large benefits over a very long time. Second, social overhead capital is generally lumpy. You either build the line from, say, Chicago to San Francisco or you do not: an incomplete railway line is of limited use, although many other forms of investment—in industry and agriculture—can proceed usefully by small increments. Third, of its nature, the profits from social overhead capital often return to the community as a whole—through indirect chains of causation—rather than directly to the initiating entrepreneurs.

Taken together, these three characteristics of social overhead capital—the long periods of gestation and pay-off, the lumpiness, and the indirect routes of pay-off—decree that governments must generally play an extremely important role in the process of building social overhead capital; which means governments must generally play an extremely important role in the preconditions period. Put another way, social overhead capital cannot be formed—in some of its most essential forms—by an enlarging flow of ploughed-back profits from an initially small base. You cannot get well started unless you can mobilize quite large initial capital sums.

Thus, even in so highly capitalist a transitional society as the United States between 1815 and 1840, state and local governments played a major role in initiating the build-up of social overhead capital. The Erie Canal was built by the New York State legislature; and the great American continental railway networks were built with enormous federal subsidies in the form of land grants.

The argument about agriculture and social overhead capital in transitional societies underlines a point of method and a point of substance. The point of method is that orderly disaggregation is necessary for an analysis of economic growth that comes to grips with the key strategic factors. Aggregates which may be useful for purposes of short-run income analysis conceal more than they illuminate when carried over into the analysis of growth. The point of substance is that the preparation of a viable base for a modern

25

industrial structure requires that quite revolutionary changes be brought about in two non-industrial sectors: agriculture and social overhead capital, most notably in transport.

NON-ECONOMIC CHANGE

We turn, now, to the non-economic side of the preconditions for take-off.

The broad lines of societal change necessary to prepare a traditional society for regular growth are becoming familiar enough. It would be widely agreed that a new élite—a new leadership—must emerge and be given scope to begin the building of a modern industrial society; and, while the Protestant ethic by no means represents a set of values uniquely suitable for modernization, it is essential that the members of this new élite regard modernization as a possible task, serving some end they judge to be ethically good or otherwise advantageous.

Sociologically this new élite must—to a degree—supersede in social and political authority the old land-based élite, whose grasp on income above minimum levels of consumption must be broken where it proves impossible simply to divert that income smoothly into the modern sector.

And more generally—in rural as in urban areas—the horizon of expectations must lift; and men must become prepared for a life of change and specialized function.

Something like this group of sociological and psychological changes would now be agreed to be at the heart of the creation of the preconditions for take-off. But this is an insufficient view. While in no way denying the significance of some such changes in attitude, value, social structure and expectations, we would emphasize, in addition, the role of the political process and of political motive in the transition.

As a matter of historical fact a reactive nationalism—reacting against intrusion from more advanced nations—has been a most important and powerful motive force in the transition from traditional to modern societies, at least as important as the profit motive. Men holding effective authority or influence have been willing to uproot traditional societies not, primarily, to make more money but

26

because the traditional society failed—or threatened to fail—to protect them from humiliation by foreigners. Leave Britain aside for a moment and consider the circumstances and motives that set traditional societies in other regions on the road to modernization.

In Germany it was certainly a nationalism based on past humilia- *examples of nationalism* tion and future hope that did the job: the memory of Napoleon, and the Prussian perception of the potentialities for power of German unity and German nationalism. It was German nationalism which stole the revolution of 1848 at Frankfurt and made the framework within which the German take-off occurred—the Junkers and the men of the East, more than the men of trade and the liberals of the West. In Russia it was a series of military intrusions and defeats, stretching out over a century, which was the great engine of change: Napoleon's invasion, the Crimean War, the Russo-Japanese War, and then, finally, the First World War. In Japan it was the demonstration effect not of high profits or manufactured consumers' *disputed* goods, but of the Opium War in China in the early 1840's and Commodore Perry's seven black ships a decade later that cast the die for modernization. And in China, the deeply entrenched traditional society yielded only slowly and painfully; but it did, in the end, yield to a century of humiliations from abroad that it could not prevent.

And so also, of course, with the colonial areas of the southern half of the world. But there, in the colonies, a dual demonstration effect operated.

Although imperial powers pursued policies which did not always optimize the development of the preconditions for take-off, they could not avoid bringing about transformation in thought, knowledge, institutions and the supply of social overhead capital which moved the colonial society along the transitional path; and they often included modernization of a sort as one explicit object of colonial policy.

In any case, the reality of the effective power that went with an ability to wield modern technology was demonstrated and the more thoughtful local people drew appropriate conclusions. Ports, docks, roads, and later, railways were built; a centralized tax system was imposed; some colonials were drawn into those minimum modern economic activities necessary to conduct trade to produce what the colonial power wished to export and what could profitably be produced locally for the expanding urban and commercialized agricultural markets; some modern goods and services were diffused sufficiently to alter the conception of an attainable level of consumption; the opportunity for a Western education was opened to a few, at least; and a concept of nationalism, transcending the old ties to clan or region, inevitably crystallized around an accumulating resentment of colonial rule.

In the end, out of these semi-modernized settings, local coalitions emerged which generated political and, in some cases, military pressure capable of forcing withdrawal; coalitions created by both the positive and negative types of demonstration.

Xenophobic nationalism or that peculiar form of it which developed in colonial areas has not, of course, been a unique motive in bringing about the modernization of traditional societies. The merchant has been always present, seeing in modernization not only the removal of obstacles to enlarged markets and profits but also the high status denied him—despite his wealth—in the traditional society. And there have almost always been intellectuals who saw in modernization ways of increasing the dignity or value of human life, for individuals and for the nation as a whole. And the soldier—an absolutely crucial figure of the transition—often brought much more to the job than resentment of foreign domination and dreams of future national glory on foreign fields of battle.

THE TRANSITIONAL COALITIONS

There is no doubt that without the affront to human and national dignity caused by the intrusion of more advanced powers, the rate of modernization of traditional societies over the past century-and-a-half would have been much slower than, in fact, it has been. Out of mixed interests and motives, coalitions were formed in these traditional or early transitional societies which aimed to make a strong modern national government and which were prepared to deal with the enemies of this objective: that is, they were prepared to struggle against the political and social groups rooted in regionally based agriculture, joined in some cases by the colonial or quasi-colonial power.

These transitional coalitions often shared only one solid common conviction; namely, that they had a stake in the creation of an independent modern state. Historically, these coalitions often had a political (or military) wing and an economic wing, each wing representing somewhat different motives and objectives in the formation of the new or modernized nation; thus, in Germany, the coalition of Junkers and the Western men of commerce and industry; in Japan, the samurai and the grain merchants; in post-1861 Russia, the commercial middle class and the more enterprising civil servants and soldiers.

These nineteenth-century coalitions obviously bear a family resemblance to the post-medieval coalitions of king and urban middle class that helped create the states of Western Europe, as well as to such twentieth-century coalitions of soldiers, merchants and intellectuals as that which was developed with success in Turkey, which failed in Nationalist China, and whose destinies are still in question in most of the southern half of the world.

THE ALTERNATIVE DIRECTIONS OF NATIONALISM

Now we come to the crux of the matter. Nationalism can be turned in any one of several directions. It can be turned outward to right real or believed past humiliations suffered on the world scene or to exploit real or believed opportunities for national aggrandizement which appear for the first time as realistic possibilities, once the new modern state is established and the economy develops some momentum; nationalism can be held inward and focused on the political consolidation of the victory won by the national over the regionally based power; or nationalism can be turned to the tasks of economic, social, and political modernization which have been obstructed by the old regionally based, usually aristocratic societal structure, by the former colonial power, or by both in coalition.

Once modern nationhood is established, different elements in the coalition press to mobilize the newly triumphant nationalist political sentiment in different directions: the soldiers, say, abroad; the professional politicians, to drive home the triumph of the centre over the region; the merchants, to economic development; the intellectuals, to social, political and legal reform.

The cast of policy at home and abroad of newly created or newly modernized states hinges greatly, then, on the balance of power within the coalition which emerges and the balance in which the various alternative objectives of nationalism are pursued.

A scholar at M.I.T., Mr Lawrence Barss, believes in fact that the road to modernization was generally traversed in two distinct phases: in the first phase the effective political coalition wanted the fruits of modernization, but it was in fact weighted too heavily with interests and attitudes from the traditional past to do the things that needed doing to make a modern society. Then, finally, there came into power, in a second transitional phase (which he calls the 'transformation') a generation of men who were not merely anxious to assert national independence but were prepared to create an urban-based modern society. Then, at last, the preconditions for take-off were completed.

Whether or not the Barss two-phase transition proves to be a consistent part of the common experience of the preconditions period it is clear that the length of time and the vicissitudes of transition from traditional to modern status depend substantially on the degree to which local talent, energy, and resources are channelled on to the domestic tasks of modernization as opposed to alternative possible objectives of nationalism; and this channelling must, in the general case, be in substantial part a function of political leadership.

This is so because the central government has essential, major technical tasks to perform in the period of preconditions. There is no need for the government to own the means of production; on the contrary. But the government must be capable of organizing the nation so that unified commercial markets develop; it must create and maintain a tax and fiscal system which diverts resources into modern uses, if necessary at the expense of the old rent-collectors; and it must lead the way through the whole spectrum of national policy—from tariffs to education and public health— toward the modernization of the economy and the society of which it is a part. For, as emphasized earlier, it is the inescapable responsibility of the state to make sure the stock of social overhead capital required for take-off is built; and it is likely as well that only vigorous

30

leadership from the central government can bring about those radical changes in the productivity of agriculture and the use of other natural resources whose quick achievement may also constitute a precondition for take-off.

THE FIRST TAKE-OFF

This way of looking at things poses an interesting historical problem. If the break-up of traditional societies is judged to have been induced by the transmission of demonstration effects from other societies, how shall we account for the first take-off, that of Great Britain?

The classic answer to that question is also the most obvious and sensible; and it may be the one nearest historical truth. It is, essentially, that in the late eighteenth century, while many parts of Western Europe were caught up in a version of the preconditions process, only in Britain were the necessary and sufficient conditions fulfilled for a take-off. This combination of necessary and sufficient conditions for take-off in Britain was the result of the convergence of a number of quite independent circumstances, a kind of statistical accident of history which, once having occurred, was irreversible, like the loss of innocence.

How does the classic answer unfold?

It unfolds, essentially, from two features of post-medieval Europe: the discovery and rediscovery of regions beyond Western Europe, and the initially slow but then accelerating development of modern scientific knowledge and attitudes.

From the discovery of new territories a whole chain of developments resulted, in which most of Western Europe shared, in varying degree. First there was the expansion of trade, including trade in new commodities, both foods and textiles—and even such raw materials as the new dyes. With the rise of commerce came a rise in shipping and, perhaps more important, a rise in the institutions of credit and commerce; and above all a rise of men devoted to commerce: men concerned with fine calculations of profit and loss, men of wide horizons, whose attitudes communicated themselves in various ways throughout their societies.

The new territories and the trade that developed with them were a profound lateral innovation in Western European society; lateral as distinct from the kind of vertical innovation incorporated in, say, the steam-engine or the spinning machines.

The meaning and impact of this lateral innovation was heightened and given a peculiar turn because it occurred in a system of inherently competitive nation states. The dynastic struggles, over who would control the fixed quantity of European real estate, became mixed up with the question of who would control the flows of trade and who would derive from them the maximum favourable balance of bullion, naval stores, and the like. But, as Charles Wilson points out, the concern of governments with trade transcended primitive concerns with military or even political power on the international scene. The pursuit and protection of a favourable trade balance was, says Wilson,

in many countries an obsession with statesmen and the achievement of a favourable balance of trade a prime object of policy. The explanation of the seeming paradox must lie in the close relationship between governments and strong groups with vested interests in foreign trade...as well as in the fiscal interests of governments themselves. More than that, a trade stoppage might produce unemployment and danger to public order in particular areas, or even a threat to national security. In England Jamaican cotton was increasingly used in the Lancashire cotton industry. West Indian dyes were essential for the treatment of dark cloths in Yorkshire and the West Country. Raw silk from Smyrna and Leghorn was necessary for the silk spinners of the English midlands and the weavers of Spitalfields.*

And Wilson's catalogue of vital interconnexions, reaching deep into each national society, rolls on.

Thus, quite aside from questions of power, the great lateral innovation had, in the Smithian sense, widened the market, producing new types of specialization and interdependence, including international interdependence in manufacturing.

The second general force operating in Western Europe was the spirit of science and productive gadgeteering, of Galileo and Leonardo down to Newton, Bacon, and the flood of eighteenth-century men caught up in what Ashton aptly calls 'the impulse to contrive':† the men who wrestled purposefully to break the bottle-

---

* *The New Cambridge Modern History*, vol. VII (Cambridge, 1957), p. 45.

† T. S. Ashton, *An Economic History of England: the Eighteenth Century* (London, 1955), p. 104.

necks in fuel-supply for iron-making, in spinning, in the efficiency of steam-engines, and so on.

Something like this background of competitive trading and purposeful contriving—with all its ramified consequences—accompanied by a strengthening of national governments, partly in response to the problems of international competition—is the setting of the preconditions period for Western Europe, taken as a whole.

Now, why Britain? Why not France? Why not the most advanced of the preconditions countries of the seventeenth century—the Netherlands—that taught the others so much?

Here, again, there is a familiar catalogue. The Dutch became too committed to finance and trade, without an adequate manufacturing base—partly because they lacked raw materials at home, partly because the financial and trading groups predominated rather than the manufacturers. And then, when Britain and France threw their full weight into the competition for trade, in the eighteenth century, the Netherlands lacked either the economic resources or the naval and military resources to stay in the commercial lead or to create an industrial take-off.

What about the French? They were too rough with their Protestants. They were politically and socially too inflexible, caught up not merely in a class society but a caste society. The best minds and spirits of eighteenth-century France, so the classical story goes, had to think about political, social and religious revolution rather than economic revolution. Moreover the French were committed heavily to ground warfare in Europe; and they cheated on shipping and naval strength at an historical moment when ships mattered greatly.

And so Britain, with more basic industrial resources than the Netherlands; more nonconformists, and more ships than France; with its political, social, and religious revolution fought out by 1688 —Britain alone was in a position to weave together cotton manufacture, coal and iron technology, the steam-engine, and ample foreign trade to pull it off.

It is fair to ask also, why not the United States? The United States, after all, had an ample domestic market, was even kinder than

Britain to its Nonconformists, and wasted even less of its resources than Britain in war. Here we are properly told that the attractions of ample fertile land and trade based on the possession of rich natural resources were too great to draw sufficient energy, talent, and resources into industry in the eighteenth century. Also, to some degree, the mercantilist policy imposed by Britain in the American colonies might have slowed down the preconditions a bit. And, one can add, in the American colonies—as in many other colonial societies—the best minds and most energetic spirits tended to be drawn into problems of politics until independence was achieved and consolidated; that is, from about the middle of the eighteenth century forward. It is only after 1815—with the passage of the generation of men who created independence and a working constitution—that American society began to concentrate the energies of its ablest men on the adventure of developing a modern continental economy.

Something like this we can take to be the classical tale.

But it is possible to pose a further question: why was eighteenth-century Britain more tolerant of its Nonconformists than France; why had it emerged from the seventeenth century with, relatively, so flexible a social structure, with a sense of nationalism that softened those political and social rigidities that gave France such difficulty and permitted the innovators of the industrial revolution to do their job?

An answer to these deeper questions places Britain back in the general case, to some significant degree. The general case is of a society modernizing itself in a nationalist reaction to intrusion or the threat of intrusion from more advanced powers abroad. The British experience of freeing itself from the Church in Rome, and from the Spanish power that backed it in the sixteenth century; the phase of relatively spacious Elizabethan nationalism; the painfully achieved national consensus of the seventeenth century, brought about by 1688, accompanied by an obsessive effort to break Britain free of what was regarded as the quasi-colonial relationship to the Dutch; the eighteenth-century struggles with the larger and apparently more powerful French...all of this is a not wholly unfamiliar story of reactive nationalism, creating a setting in which

34

modernization—in its post-1688 context—was a widely sanctioned, and even encouraged, goal.

It is possible, then, that British nationalism, transcending caste loyalties, created by a series of intrusions and challenges to a lesser island off a dominant mainland, may have been a major force in creating a relatively flexible social matrix within which the process of building the preconditions for take-off was hastened in Britain; and in that limited sense the first take-off takes its place, despite many unique features, with the others.

CHAPTER 4

THE TAKE-OFF

THE ACHIEVEMENT OF REGULAR GROWTH

We turn now to analyse narrowly that decisive interval in the history of a society when growth becomes its normal condition. We consider how it comes about that the slow-moving changes of the preconditions period, when forces of modernization contend against the habits and institutions, the values and vested interests of the traditional society, make a decisive break-through; and compound interest gets built into the society's structure.

As suggested in chapter 3, take-offs have occurred in two quite different types of societies; and, therefore, the process of establishing preconditions for take-off has varied. In the first and most general case the achievement of preconditions for take-off required major changes in political and social structure and even in effective social values. In the second case take-off was delayed not by political, social and cultural obstacles but by the high (and even expanding) levels of welfare that could be achieved by exploiting land and natural resources. In this second case take-off was initiated by a more narrowly economic process as, for example, in the northern United States, Australia and, perhaps, Sweden. And, you will recall, as one would expect in the essentially biological field of economic growth, history offers mixed as well as pure cases.

The beginning of take-off can usually be traced to a particular sharp stimulus. The stimulus may take the form of a political revolution which affects directly the balance of social power and effective values, the character of economic institutions, the distribution of income, the pattern of investment outlays and the proportion of potential innovations actually applied. Such was the case, for example, with the German revolution of 1848, the Meiji restoration in Japan of 1868, and the more recent achievement of Indian independence and the Communist victory in China. It may come about through a technological (including transport) innovation, which sets in motion a chain of secondary expansion in modern sectors and has powerful potential external economy effects which the society exploits. It may take the form of a newly favourable international environment, such as the opening of British and French markets to Swedish timber in the 1860's or a sharp relative rise in export prices and/or large new capital imports, as in the case of the United States from the late 1840's, Canada and Russia from the mid-1890's; but it may also come as a challenge posed by an unfavourable shift in the international environment, such as a sharp fall in the terms of trade (or a war-time blockage of foreign trade) requiring the rapid development of manufactured import substitutes, as with the Argentine and Australia from 1930 to 1945.

What is essential here is not the form of stimulus but the fact that the prior development of the society and its economy result in a positive, sustained, and self-reinforcing response to it: the result is not a once-over change in production functions or in the volume of investment, but a higher proportion of potential innovations accepted in a more or less regular flow, and a higher rate of investment.

The use of aggregative national-income terms evidently reveals little of the process which is occurring. It is nevertheless useful to regard as a necessary but not sufficient condition for the take-off the fact that the proportion of net investment to national income (or net national product) rises from, say, 5% to over 10%, definitely outstripping the likely population pressure (since under the assumed take-off circumstances the capital/output ratio is low),* and yielding a distinct rise in real output *per capita.* Whether real consumption

---

* Capital/output ratio is the amount by which a given increase in investment increases the volume of output: a rough—very rough—measure of the productivity of capital investment; but since the arithmetic of economic growth requires some such concept, implicitly or explicitly, we had better refine the tool rather than abandon it. In the early stages of economic development two contrary forces operate on the capital/output ratio. On the one hand there is a vast requirement of basic overhead capital in transport, power, education etc. Here, due mainly to the long period over which investment yields its return, the apparent (short-run) capital/output ratio is high. On the other hand, there are generally large unexploited back-logs of known techniques and available natural resources to be put to work; and these back-logs make for a low capital/output ratio. We can assume formally a low capital/output ratio for the take-off period because we are assuming that the preconditions have been created, including a good deal of social overhead capital. In fact, the aggregate marginal capital/output ratio is likely to be kept up during the take-off by the requirement of continuing large outlays for overhead items which yield their returns only over long periods. Nevertheless, a ratio of 3:1 or 3·5:1 for the incremental capital/output ratio seems realistic as a rough bench-mark until we have learned more about capital/output ratios on a sectoral basis.

per capita rises depends on the pattern of income distribution and population pressure, as well as on the magnitude, character and productivity of investment itself.

As indicated in the accompanying table, we believe it possible to identify at least tentatively such take-off periods for a number of countries which have passed into the stage of growth.

TABLE I. *Some tentative, approximate take-off dates*

Country	Take-off	Country	Take-off
Great Britain	1783–1802	Russia	1890–1914
France	1830–60	Canada	1896–1914
Belgium	1833–60	Argentina‡	1935–
United States*	1843–60	Turkey§	1937–
Germany	1850–73	India‖	1952–
Sweden	1868–90	China‖	1952–
Japan†	1878–1900		

* The American take-off is here viewed as the upshot of two different periods of expansion: the first, that of the 1840's, marked by railway and manufacturing development, mainly confined to the East—this occurred while the West and South digested the extensive agricultural expansion of the previous decade; the second the great railway push into the Middle West during the 1850's marked by a heavy inflow of foreign capital. By the opening of the Civil War the American economy of North and West, with real momentum in its heavy-industry sector, is judged to have taken off.

† Lacking adequate data, there is some question about the timing of the Japanese take-off. Some part of the post-1868 period was certainly, by the present set of definitions, devoted to firming up the preconditions for take-off. By 1914 the Japanese economy had certainly taken off. The question is whether the period from about 1878 to the Sino-Japanese War in the mid-1890's is to be regarded as the completion of the preconditions or as take-off. On present evidence we incline to the latter view.

‡ In one sense the Argentine economy began its take-off during the First World War. But by and large, down to the pit of the post-1929 depression, the growth of its modern sector, stimulated during the war, tended to slacken; and, like a good part of the Western world, the Argentine sought during the 1920's to return to a pre-1914 normalcy. It was not until the mid-1930's that a sustained take-off was inaugurated, which by and large can now be judged to have been successful despite the structural vicissitudes of that economy.

§ Against the background of industrialization measures inaugurated in the mid-1930's the Turkish economy has exhibited remarkable momentum in the past five years founded in the increase in agricultural income and productivity. It still remains to be seen whether these two surges, conducted under quite different national policies, will constitute a transition to self-sustaining growth, and whether Turkey can overcome its current structural problems.

‖ As noted in the text it is still too soon to judge either the present Indian or Chinese Communist take-off efforts successful.

The take-off

The take-off is such a decisive transition in a society's history that it is important to examine the nature of our definition and the inner mechanism of take-off somewhat more closely.

There are several problems of choice involved in defining the take-off with precision. We might begin with one arbitrary definition and consider briefly the two major alternatives.

For the present purposes the take-off is defined as requiring all three of the following related conditions:

(1) a rise in the rate of productive investment from, say, 5% or less to over 10% of national income (or net national product (NNP));

(2) the development of one or more substantial manufacturing* sectors, with a high rate of growth;

(3) the existence or quick emergence of a political, social and institutional framework which exploits the impulses to expansion in the modern sector and the potential external economy effects of the take-off and gives to growth an on-going character.

The third condition implies a considerable capability to mobilize capital from domestic sources. Some take-offs have occurred with virtually no capital imports, for example, Britain and Japan. Some take-offs have had a high component of foreign capital, for example, the United States, Russia and Canada. But some countries have imported large quantities of foreign capital for long periods, which undoubtedly contributed to creating the preconditions for take-off without actually initiating take-off, for example the Argentine before 1914, Venezuela down to recent years, the Belgian Congo currently.

In short, whatever the role of capital imports, the preconditions for take-off include an initial ability to mobilize domestic savings productively, as well as a structure which subsequently permits a high marginal rate of savings.

This definition is designed to isolate the early stage when indus-

---

* In this context 'manufacturing' is taken to include the processing of agricultural products or raw materials by modern methods: for example, timber in Sweden, meat in Australia, dairy products in Denmark. The dual requirement of a 'manufacturing' sector is that its processes set in motion a chain of further modern sector requirements and that its expansion provides the potentiality of external economy effects, industrial in character.

trialization takes hold rather than the later stage when industrialization becomes a more massive and statistically more impressive phenomenon. In Britain, for example, there is no doubt that it was between 1815 and 1850 that industrialization fully took hold. If the criterion chosen for take-off was the period of most rapid overall industrial growth, or the period when large-scale industry matured, all our take-off dates would have to be set later; Britain, for example, to 1819–48; the United States, to 1868–93; Sweden, to 1890–1920; Japan, to 1900–20; Russia, to 1928–40. The earlier dating is chosen here because it is believed that the decisive transformations (including a decisive shift in the investment-rate) occur in the first industrial phases; and later industrial maturity can be directly traced back to foundations laid in these first phases.

This definition is also designed to rule out from the take-off the quite substantial economic progress which can occur in an economy before a truly self-reinforcing growth process gets under way. Consider, for example, British economic expansion between, say, 1750 and 1783; Russian economic expansion between, say, 1861 and 1890, Canadian economic expansion between 1867 and the mid-1890's. Such periods—for which there is an equivalent in the economic history of almost every growing economy—were marked by extremely important, even decisive, developments. The transport network expanded, and with it both internal and external commerce; a revolution in agricultural productivity was, at least, begun; new institutions for mobilizing savings were developed; a class of commercial and even industrial entrepreneurs began to emerge; industrial enterprise on a limited scale (or in limited sectors) grew. And yet, however essential these pre-take-off periods were for later development, their scale and momentum were insufficient to transform the economy radically or, in some cases, to outstrip population growth and to yield an increase in *per capita* output.

With a sense of the considerable violence done to economic history, we are here seeking to isolate a period when the scale of productive economic activity reaches a critical level and produces changes which lead to a massive and progressive structural transformation in economies and the societies of which they are a part, better viewed as changes in kind than merely in degree.

The take-off

The case for the concept of take-off hinges, in part, on quantitative evidence on the scale and productivity of investment in relation to population growth. Here we face a difficult problem; for investment data are not now generally available for early stages in economic history. Below is set out such a case as there is for regarding the shift from a productive investment-rate of about 5% of NNP to 10% or more as central to the process.

1. A prima facie case

If we take the marginal capital/output ratio for an economy in its early stages of economic development at 3·5:1 and if we assume, as is not abnormal, a population rise of 1–1·5% per annum it is clear that something between 3·5 and 5·25% of NNP must be regularly invested if NNP *per capita* is to be sustained. An increase of 2% per annum in NNP *per capita* requires, under these assumptions, that something between 10·5 and 12·5% of NNP be regularly invested. By definition and assumption, then, a transition from relatively stagnant to substantial, regular rise in NNP *per capita*, under typical population conditions, requires that the proportion of national product productively invested should move from somewhere in the vicinity of 5% to something in the vicinity of 10%.

2. The Swedish case

In the appendix to his paper on international differences in capital formation, Kuznets gives gross and net capital formation figures in relation to gross and net national product for a substantial group of countries where reasonably good statistical data exist. Excepting Sweden, these data do not go back clearly to pre-take-off stages.*

---

* The Danish data are on the margin. They begin with the decade 1870–9, probably the first decade of take-off itself. They show net and gross domestic capital formation rates well over 10%. In view of the sketch of the Danish economy presented in Kjeld Bjerke's 'Preliminary Estimates of the Danish National Product from 1870–1950' (preliminary paper mimeographed for 1953 Conference of the International Association for Research on Income and Wealth), pp. 32–4, it seems likely that further research would identify the years 1830–70 as a period when the preconditions were actively

The take-off

The Swedish data begin in the decade 1861-70; and the Swedish take-off is to be dated from the latter years of the decade, as shown in Table 2. (GCF: Gross Capital Formation; GNP: Gross National Product; NCF: Net Capital Formation; DGCF: Domestic GCF.)

TABLE 2. *Kuznets' table of calculations for Sweden*

Decade	Domestic GCF/GNP (%)	Domestic NCF/NNP (%)	Depreciation to DGCF (%)
1. 1861-70	5·8	3·5-	(42)
2. 1871-80	8·8	5·3	(42)
3. 1881-90	10·8	6·6	(42)
4. 1891-1900	13·7	8·1	43·9
5. 1901-10	18·0	11·6	40·0
6. 1911-20	20·2	13·5	38·3
7. 1921-30	19·0	11·4	45·2

Note (Kuznets'): Based on estimates in Eric Lindahl, *op. cit.*, parts I and II, particularly the details in Part II. These underlying totals of capital formation exclude changes in inventories. While gross totals are directly from the volumes referred to above, depreciation for the first three decades was not given. We assumed that it formed 42% of gross domestic capital formation.

3. *The Canadian case*

The data developed by O. J. Firestone* for Canada indicate a similar transition for net capital formation in its take-off (say,

established, 1870-1900 as a period of take-off. This view is supported by scattered and highly approximate estimates of Danish national wealth which exhibit a remarkable surge in capital formation between 1864 and 1884.

Estimates of National Wealth in Denmark

	1000 millions of kroner	Source
1864	3·5	Falbe-Hansen, *Danmarks statistik* (1885).
1884	6·5	Falbe-Hansen, *op. cit.*
1899	7·2	Tax-commission of 1903.
1909	10·0	Jens Warming, *Danmarks statistik* (1913).
1927	24·0	Jens Warming, *Danmarks erhvervs-or samfundsliv* (1930).
1939	28·8	Economic expert committee of 1943, *Økonomiske efterkrigsproblemer* (1945).
1950	54·5	N. Banke, N. P. Jacobsen and Vedel-Petersen, *Danske erhvervsliv* (1951).

(Furnished in correspondence by Einar Cohn and Kjeld Bjerke.) It should again be emphasized, however, that we are dealing with a hypothesis whose empirical foundations, on the side of statistics, are still fragmentary.

* O. J. Firestone, *Canada's Economic Development, 1867-1952, with Special Reference to Changes in the Country's National Product and National Wealth*, paper prepared for

1896–1914); but the gross investment proportion in the period from Confederation to the mid-1890's was higher than appears to have marked other periods when the preconditions were established, due to investment in the railway network (abnormally large for a nation of Canada's population), and to relatively heavy foreign investment, even before the great capital import boom of the pre-1914 decade (see Table 3).

TABLE 3. *Canada: gross and net investment in durable physical assets as percentage of gross and net national expenditure (for selected years)*

	GCF/GNP	NCF/NNP	Capital consumption as percentage of gross investment
1870	15·0	7·1	56·2
1900	13·1	4·0	72·5
1920	16·6	10·6	41·3
1929	23·0	12·1	53·3
1952	16·8	9·3	49·7

4. *The pattern of contemporary evidence in general**

In the years after 1945 the number of countries for which reasonably respectable national income (or product) data exist has grown; and with such data there have developed some tolerable savings and investment estimates for countries at different stages of the growth process. Within the category of nations usually grouped as 'underdeveloped' one can distinguish four types.†

the International Association for Research in Income and Wealth (1953), to which Mr Firestone has kindly furnished me certain revisions, shortly to be published. By 1900 Canada already had about 18,000 miles of railway line; but the territory served had been developed to a limited degree only. By 1900 Canada already had a net balance of foreign indebtedness of over $1 billion. Although this figure was almost quadrupled in the next two decades, capital imports represented an important increment to domestic capital sources from the period of Confederation down to the pre-1914 Canadian boom, which begins in the mid-1890's.

* I am indebted to Mr Everett Hagen for mobilizing the statistical data in this section, except where otherwise indicated.

† The percentages given are of net capital formation to net domestic product. The latter is the product net of depreciation of the geographic area. It includes the value of output produced in the area, regardless of whether the income flows abroad. Since indirect business taxes are not deducted, it tends to be larger than national income; hence the percentages are lower than if national income was used as the denominator in computing them.

(a) Pre-take-off economies, where the apparent savings and investment-rates, including limited net capital imports, probably come to under 5% of net national product. In general, data for such countries are not satisfactory, and one's judgment that capital formation is low must rest on fragmentary data and partially subjective judgment. Examples are Ethiopia, Kenya, Thailand, Cambodia, Afghanistan and perhaps Indonesia.*

(b) Economies attempting take-off, where the apparent savings and investment-rates, including limited net capital imports, have risen over 5% of net national product.† For example, Mexico (1950), Net Capital Formation/Net Domestic Product 7·2%; Chile (1950), NCF/NDP 9·5%; Panama (1950), NCF/NDP 7·5%; Philippines (1952), NCF/NDP 6·4%; Puerto Rico (1952), NCF (private)/NDP 7·6%; India (1953), NCF/NDP perhaps about 7%. Whether the take-off period will, in fact, be successful remains in most of these cases still to be seen; although Mexico, at least, would appear to have passed beyond this historical watershed.

(c) Growing economies, where the apparent savings and investment-rates, including limited net capital imports, have reached 10% or over; for example, Colombia (1950), NCF/NDP 16·3%.

(d) Enclave economies: (i) cases where the apparent savings and investment-rates, including substantial net capital imports, have reached 10% or over, but the domestic preconditions for sustained growth have not been achieved. These economies, associated with

---

* The Office of Intelligence Research of the Department of State, Washington, D.C., gives the following estimated ratios of investment (presumably gross) to GNP in its Report No. 6672 of 25 August 1954, p. 3, based on latest data available to that point, for countries which would probably fall in the pre-take-off category:

	%		%
Afghanistan	5	Pakistan	6
Ceylon	5	Indonesia	5

† The Department of State estimates (*ibid.*) for economies which are either attempting take-off or which have, perhaps, passed into a stage of regular growth include:

	%		%
Argentina	13	Colombia	14
Brazil	14	Philippines	8
Chile	11	Venezuela	23

Venezuela has been for some time an 'enclave economy', with a high investment-rate concentrated in a modern export sector whose growth did not generate general economic momentum in the Venezuelan economy; but in the past few years Venezuela may have moved over into the category of economies experiencing an authentic take-off.

major export industries, lack the third condition for take-off suggested above (p. 39). They include the Belgian Congo (1951), NCF/NDP 21·7%; Southern Rhodesia (1950), GCF/GDP 45·5%, (1952) GCF/GDP 45·4%.

(ii) Cases where net capital exports are large. For example, Burma (1938), NCF/NDP, 7·1%; net capital exports/NDP 11·5%; Nigeria (1950–1), NCF/NDP 5·1%; net capital exports/NDP 5·6%.

5. *The cases of India and Communist China*

The two outstanding contemporary cases of economies attempting purposefully to take off are India and Communist China, both operating under national plans. The Indian First Five Year Plan projected the growth-process envisaged under assumptions similar to those in paragraph 1, p. 41, above. The Indian Planning Commission estimated investment as 5% of NNP in the initial year of the plan, 1950–1.* Using a 3:1 marginal capital/output ratio, they envisaged a marginal savings rate of 20% for the First Five Year Plan, a 50% rate thereafter, down to 1968–9, when the average proportion of income invested would level off at 20% of NNP. As one would expect, the sectoral composition of this process is not fully worked out in the initial plan; but the Indian effort may well be remembered in economic history as the first take-off defined *ex ante* in national product terms.

So far as the aggregates are concerned, what we can say is that the Indian planned figures fall well within the range of prima facie hypothesis and historical experience, if India in fact fulfils the full requirements for take-off. The Chinese Communist figures are somewhat more ambitious in both agriculture and industry.

As of 1959, the momentum achieved over the past six years in China appears somewhat greater than that in India; but it will be some time before the accounts of progress in the two countries can be cast up with confidence—notably, with respect to agricultural development, which must play so large a role in each. What can be said is that the plans of both countries, in their overall investment

* Government of India, Planning Commission, *The First Five Year Plan* (1952), vol. 1, chapter 1.

goals and sectoral composition, are consistent with the take-off requirements; and, perhaps more important, the commitment of both societies to modernization appears too deep to permit more than temporary set-backs.

THE INNER STRUCTURE OF THE TAKE-OFF

Whatever the importance and virtue of viewing the take-off in aggregative terms—embracing national output, the proportion of output invested, and an aggregate marginal capital/output ratio—that approach tells us relatively little of what actually happens and of the causal processes at work in a take-off; nor is the investment-rate criterion conclusive.

Following the definition of take-off, we must consider not merely how a rise in the investment-rate is brought about, from both supply and demand perspectives, but how rapidly growing manufacturing sectors emerged and imparted their primary and secondary growth impulses to the economy.

Perhaps the most important thing to be said about the behaviour of these variables in historical cases of take-off is that they have assumed many different forms. There is no single pattern. The rate and productivity of investment can rise, and the consequences of this rise can be diffused into a self-reinforcing general growth process by many different technical and economic routes, under the aegis of many different political, social and cultural settings, driven along by a wide variety of human motivations.

The purpose of the following paragraphs is to suggest briefly, and by way of illustration only, certain elements of both uniformity and variety in the variables whose movement has determined the inner structure of the take-off.

THE SUPPLY OF LOANABLE FUNDS

By and large, the loanable funds required to finance the take-off have come from two types of source: from shifts in the control of income flows, including income-distribution changes and capital imports; and from the plough-back of profits in rapidly expanding particular sectors.

The notion of economic development occurring as a result of

income shifts from those who will spend (hoard* or lend) less productively to those who will spend (or lend) more productively is one of the oldest and most fundamental notions in economics. It is basic, for example, to the *Wealth of Nations*.†

Historically, income shifts conducive to economic development have assumed many forms. In Meiji Japan and also in Czarist Russia the substitution of government bonds for the great landholders' claims on the flow of rent payments led to a highly Smithian redistribution of income into the hands of those in the modern sector. In both cases the real value of the government bonds exchanged for land depreciated; and, in general, the feudal land-lords emerged with a less attractive arrangement than had first appeared to be offered. Aside from the confiscation effect, two posi-tive impulses arose from land reform: the State itself used the flow of payments from peasants, now diverted from landlords' hands, for activity which encouraged economic development; and a certain number of the more enterprising former landlords directly invested in commerce and industry. In contemporary India and China we can observe quite different degrees of income transfer by this route. India is relying to only a very limited extent on the elimination of large incomes unproductively spent by large landlords; although this element figures in a small way in its programme. Communist China has systematically transferred all non-governmental pools of capital into the hands of the State, in a series of undisguised or barely disguised capital levies; and it is drawing heavily for capital resources on the mass of middle and poor peasants who remain.‡

In addition to confiscatory and taxation devices, which can operate effectively when the State is spending more productively than the taxed individuals, inflation has been important to several take-offs.

---

* Hoarding can, of course, be helpful in the growth process by depressing consump-tion and freeing resources for investment, if, in fact, non-hoarding persons or institutions acquire the resources and possess the will to expand productive investment. A direct transfer of income is evidently not required.

† See, especially, Smith's observations on the 'perversion' of wealth by 'prodigality' —that is, unproductive consumption expenditures—and on the virtues of 'parsimony' which transfers income to those who will increase 'the fund which is destined for the maintenance of productive hands'. Routledge edition (London, 1890), pp. 259–60.

‡ W. W. Rostow *et al.*, *Prospects for Communist China* (New York and London, 1954), Part 4.

In Britain of the late 1790's, the United States of the 1850's, Japan of the 1870's there is no doubt that capital formation was aided by price inflation, which shifted resources away from consumption to profits.

The shift of income flows into more productive hands has, of course, been aided historically not only by government fiscal measures but also by banks and capital markets. Virtually without exception, the take-off periods have been marked by the extension of banking institutions which expanded the supply of working capital; and in most cases also by an expansion in the range of long-range financing done by a central, formally organized, capital market.

Although these familiar capital-supply functions of the State and private institutions have been important to the take-off, it is likely to prove the case, on close examination, that a necessary condition for take-off was the existence of one or more rapidly growing sectors whose entrepreneurs (private or public) ploughed back into new capacity a very high proportion of profits. Put another way, the demand side of the investment process, rather than the supply of loanable funds, may be the decisive element in the take-off, as opposed to the period of creating the preconditions, or of sustaining growth once it is under way. The distinction is, historically, sometimes difficult to make, notably when the State simultaneously acts both to mobilize supplies of finance and to undertake major entrepreneurial acts. There are, nevertheless, periods in economic history when quite substantial improvements in the machinery of capital supply do not, in themselves, initiate a take-off, but fall within the period when the preconditions are created: for example, British banking developments in the century before 1783 and Russian banking developments before 1890.

One extremely important version of the plough-back process has taken place through foreign trade. Developing economies have created from their natural resources major export industries; and the rapid expansion in exports has been used to finance the import of capital equipment and to service the foreign debt during the take-off. United States, Russian and Canadian grain fulfilled this function, Swedish timber and pulp, Japanese silk, etc. Currently Chinese exports to the Communist bloc, wrung at great administrative and human cost from the agricultural sector, play this decisive role. It should be noted that the development of such export sectors has not in itself guaranteed accelerated capital formation. Enlarged foreign-exchange proceeds have been used in many familiar cases to finance hoards (as in the famous case of Indian bullion imports) or unproductive consumption outlays.

One possible mechanism for inducing a high rate of plough-back into productive investment is a rapid expansion in the effective demand for domestically manufactured consumers' goods, which would direct into the hands of vigorous entrepreneurs an increasing proportion of income flows under circumstances which would lead them to expand their own capacity and to increase their requirements for industrial raw materials, semi-manufactured products and manufactured components.

A final element in the supply of loanable funds is, of course, capital imports. Foreign capital has played a major role in the take-off stage of many economies: for example the United States, Russia, Sweden, Canada. The cases of Britain and Japan indicate, however, that it cannot be regarded as an essential condition. Foreign capital was notably useful when the construction of railways or other large overhead capital items with a long period of gestation played an important role in the take-off or the late preconditions period. Whatever its strategic role, the proportion of investment required for growth which goes into industry is relatively small compared to that required for utilities, transport and the housing of enlarged urban populations. And foreign capital can be mightily useful in helping carry the burden of these overhead items either directly or indirectly.

What can we say, in general, then, about the supply of finance during the take-off period? First, as a precondition, it appears necessary that the community's surplus above the mass-consumption level does not flow into the hands of those who will sterilize it by hoarding, luxury consumption or low-productivity investment outlays. Second, as a precondition, it appears necessary that institutions be developed which provide cheap and adequate working capital. Third, as a necessary condition, it appears that one or more sectors of the community must grow rapidly, inducing a more general

49

industrialization process; and that the entrepreneurs in such sectors plough back a substantial proportion of their profits in further productive investment, one possible and recurrent version of the plough-back process being the investment of proceeds from a rapidly growing export sector.

The devices, confiscatory and fiscal, for ensuring the first and second preconditions have been historically various. And, as indicated below, the types of leading manufacturing sectors which have served to initiate the take-off have varied greatly. Finally, foreign capital flows have, in significant cases, proved extremely important to the take-off, notably when lumpy overhead capital construction of long gestation period was required; but take-offs have also occurred based almost wholly on domestic sources of finance.

THE SOURCES OF ENTREPRENEURSHIP

It is evident that the take-off requires the existence and the successful activity of some group in the society which is prepared to accept innovations. As noted above, the problem of entrepreneurship in the take-off has not been profound in a limited group of wealthy agricultural nations whose populations derived by emigration mainly from north-western Europe. There the problem of take-off was primarily economic; and when economic incentives for industrialization emerged commercial and banking groups moved over easily into industrial entrepreneurship. In many other countries, however, the development of adequate entrepreneurship was a more searching social process.

Under some human motivation or other, a group must come to perceive it to be both possible and good to undertake acts of capital investment; and, for their efforts to be tolerably successful, they must act with approximate rationality in selecting the directions toward which their enterprise is directed. They must not only produce growth but tolerably balanced growth. We cannot quite say that it is necessary for them to act as if they were trying to maximize profit; for the criteria for private-profit maximization do not necessarily converge with the criteria for an optimum rate and pattern of growth in various sectors. But in a growing economy, over periods longer than the business cycle, economic history is reasonably tolerant of deviations from rationality, in the sense that excess capacity is finally put to productive use. Leaving aside here the question of ultimate human motivation, and assuming that the major overhead items are generated, if necessary, by some form of State initiative (including subsidy), we can say as a first approximation that some group must successfully emerge which behaves as if it were moved by the profit motive, in a dynamic economy with changing production functions.

In this connexion it is increasingly conventional for economists to pay their respects to the Protestant ethic.* The historian should not be ungrateful for this light on the grey horizon of formal growth models. But the known cases of economic growth which theory must seek to explain take us beyond the orbit of Protestantism. In a world where Samurai, Parsees, Jews, North Italians, Turkish, Russian, and Chinese civil servants (as well as Huguenots, Scotsmen and British north-countrymen) have played the role of a leading élite in economic growth, John Calvin should not be made to bear quite this weight. More fundamentally, allusion to a positive scale of religious or other values conducive to profit-maximizing activities is an insufficient sociological basis for this important phenomenon. What appears to be required for the emergence of such élites is not merely an appropriate value system but two further conditions: first, the new élite must feel itself denied the conventional routes to prestige and power by the traditional less acquisitive society of which it is a part; second, the traditional society must be sufficiently flexible (or weak) to permit its members to seek material advance (or political power) as a route upwards alternative to conformity.

Although an élite entrepreneurial class appears to be required for take-off, with significant power over aggregate income flows and industrial investment decisions, most take-offs have been preceded or accompanied by radical change in agricultural techniques and market organization. By and large the agricultural entrepreneur has been the individual land-owning farmer. A requirement for take-off is, therefore, a class of farmers willing and able to respond

* See, for example, N. Kaldor, 'Economic Growth and Cyclical Fluctuations', *Economic Journal* (March 1954), p. 67.

to the possibilities opened up for them by new techniques, land-holding arrangements, transport facilities, and forms of market and credit organization. A small purposeful élite can go a long way in initiating economic growth; but, especially in agriculture (and to some extent in the industrial working force), a wider-based revolution in outlook must come about.

Whatever further empirical research may reveal about the motives which have led men to undertake the constructive entrepreneurial acts of the take-off period, this much appears sure: these motives have varied greatly, from one society to another; and they have rarely, if ever, been motives of an unmixed material character.

LEADING SECTORS IN THE TAKE-OFF

As suggested at the close of chapter 2, the overall rate of growth of an economy must be regarded in the first instance as the consequence of differing growth rates in particular sectors of the economy, such sectoral growth-rates being in part derived from certain overall demand factors (for example population, consumers' income, tastes etc.); in part, from the primary and secondary effects of changing supply factors, when these are effectively exploited.

On this view the sectors of an economy may be grouped in three categories:

(1) Primary growth sectors, where possibilities for innovation or for the exploitation of newly profitable or hitherto unexplored resources yield a high growth-rate and set in motion expansionary forces elsewhere in the economy.

(2) Supplementary growth sectors, where rapid advance occurs in direct response to—or as a requirement of—advance in the primary growth sectors; for example coal, iron and engineering in relation to railroads. These sectors may have to be tracked many stages back into the economy.

(3) Derived-growth sectors, where advance occurs in some fairly steady relation to the growth of total real income, population, industrial production or some other overall, modestly increasing variable. Food output in relation to population and housing in relation to family formation are classic derived relations of this order.

Leading sectors in the take-off

In the earlier stages of growth, primary and supplementary growth sectors derive their momentum essentially from the introduction and diffusion of changes in the cost–supply environment (in turn, of course, partially influenced by demand changes); while the derived-growth sectors are linked essentially to changes in demand (while subject also to continuing changes in production functions of a less dramatic character). In the age of high mass-consumption leading sectors become more dependent on demand factors than in the earlier stages, as considered in chapter 6.

At any period of time it appears to be true even in a mature and growing economy that forward momentum is maintained as the result of rapid expansion in a limited number of primary sectors, whose expansion has significant external economy and other secondary effects. From this perspective the behaviour of sectors during the take-off is merely a special version of the growth process in general; or, put another way, growth proceeds by repeating endlessly, in different patterns, with different leading sectors, the experience of the take-off. Like the take-off, long-term growth requires that the society not only generate vast quantities of capital for depreciation and maintenance, for housing and for a balanced complement of utilities and other overheads, but also a sequence of highly productive primary sectors, growing rapidly, based on new production functions. Only thus has the aggregate marginal capital/output ratio been kept low.

Once again history is full of variety: a considerable array of sectors appears to have played this key role in the take-off process. The development of a cotton-textile industry sufficient to meet domestic requirements has not generally imparted a sufficient impulse in itself to launch a self-sustaining growth process. The development of modern cotton-textile industries in substitution for imports has, more typically, marked the pre-take-off period, as for example in India, China and Mexico.

There is, however, the famous exception of Britain's industrial revolution. Baines's table* on raw-cotton imports and his comment on it are worth quoting, covering as they do the original leading sector in the first take-off (see Table 4).

* E. Baines, *History of the Cotton Manufacture* (London, 1835), p. 348.

53

TABLE 4. *Rate of increase in the import of cotton-wool,*
in periods of ten years from 1741 to 1831

	%		%
1741–51	81	1791–1801	67·5
1751–61	21·5	1801–11	39·5
1761–71	25·5	1811–21	93
1771–81	75·75	1821–31	85
1781–91	319·5		

From 1697 to 1741 the increase was trifling; between 1741 and 1751 the manufacture, though still insignificant in extent, made a considerable spring; during the next twenty years, the increase was moderate; from 1771 to 1781, owing to the invention of the jenny and the water-frame, a rapid increase took place: in the ten years from 1781 to 1791, being those which immediately followed the invention of the mule and the expiration of Arkwright's patent, the rate of advancement was prodigiously accelerated, being nearly 320%: and from that time to the present, and especially since the close of the war, the increase, though considerably moderated, has been rapid and steady far beyond all precedent in any other manufacture.

Why did the development of a modern factory system in cotton textiles lead on in Britain to a self-sustaining growth process, whereas it failed to do so in other cases? Part of the answer lies in the fact that by the late eighteenth century the preconditions for take-off in Britain were very fully developed. Progress in textiles, coal, iron and even steam power had been considerable throughout the eighteenth century; and the social and institutional environment was propitious. But two further technical elements helped determine the upshot. First, the British cotton-textile industry was large in relation to the total size of the economy. From its modern beginnings, but notably from the 1780's forward, a very high proportion of total cotton-textile output was directed abroad, reaching 60% by the 1820's.* The evolution of this industry was a more massive fact, with wider secondary repercussions, than if it were simply supplying the domestic market. Industrial enterprise on this scale had secondary reactions on the development of urban areas, the demand for coal, iron and machinery, the demand for working capital and ultimately the demand for cheap transport,

* The volume (official value) of British cotton-goods exports rose from £355,060 in 1780 to £7,624,505 in 1802 (Baines, *op. cit.* p. 350). See also the calculation of R. C. O. Matthews, *A Study in Trade Cycle History* (Cambridge, 1954), pp. 127–9.

which powerfully stimulated industrial development in other directions.*

Second, a source of effective demand for rapid expansion in British cotton textiles was supplied, in the first instance, by the sharp reduction in real costs and prices which accompanied the technological developments in manufacture and the cheapening real cost of raw cotton induced by the cotton-gin. In this Britain had an advantage not enjoyed by those who came later; for they merely substituted domestic for foreign-manufactured cotton textiles. The substitution undoubtedly had important secondary effects by introducing a modern industrial sector and releasing, on balance, a pool of foreign exchange for other purposes; but there was no sharp fall in the real cost of acquiring cotton textiles and no equivalent rise in real income.

The introduction of the railroad has been historically the most powerful single initiator of take-offs.† It was decisive in the United States, France, Germany, Canada, and Russia; it has played an extremely important part in the Swedish, Japanese and other cases.

The railroad has had three major kinds of impact on economic growth during the take-off period. First, it has lowered internal transport costs, brought new areas and products into commercial markets and, in general, performed the Smithian function of widening the market. Second, it has been a prerequisite in many cases to the development of a major new and rapidly enlarging export sector which, in turn, has served to generate capital for internal development, as, for example, the American railroads before 1914. Third, and perhaps most important for the take-off itself, the development of railways has led on to the development of modern coal, iron and engineering industries. In many countries the growth of modern basic industrial sectors can be traced in the most direct way to the requirements for building and, especially, for maintaining substantial railway systems. When a society has developed deeper institu-

* If we are prepared to treat New England of the first half of the nineteenth century as a separable economy, its take-off into sustained growth can be allocated to the period, roughly, 1820–50; and, again, a disproportionately large cotton-textile industry based substantially on exports (that is, from New England to the rest of the United States) is the regional foundation for sustained growth.

† For a detailed analysis of the routes of impact of the railroad on economic development see Paul H. Cootner, *Transport Innovation and Economic Development: The Case of the U.S. Steam Railroads* (1953), unpublished doctoral thesis, M.I.T. (Cambridge, Mass.).

tional, social and political prerequisites for take-off, the rapid growth of a railway system, with these powerful triple effects, has often served to lift it into self-sustained growth. Where the prerequisites have not existed, however, very substantial railway building has failed to initiate a take-off, as for example in India, China, pre-1895 Canada, pre-1914 Argentina, etc.

It is clear that an enlargement and modernization of armed forces could play the role of a leading sector in take-off. It was a factor in the Russian, Japanese and German take-offs; and it figures heavily in current Chinese Communist plans. But historically the role of modern armaments has been ancillary rather than central to the take-off.

Quite aside from their role in supplying foreign exchange for general capital-formation purposes, raw materials and food-stuffs can play the role of leading sectors in the take-off if they involve the application of modern processing techniques. The timber industry, built on the steam-saw, fulfilled this function in the first phase of Sweden's take-off, to be followed shortly by the pulp industry. Similarly, the shift of Denmark to meat and dairy products, after 1873, appears to have reinforced the development of a manufacturing sector in the economy, as well as providing a major source of foreign exchange. And as Lockwood notes, even the export of Japanese silk thread had important secondary effects which developed modern production techniques.*

To satisfy the demands of American weaving and hosiery mills for uniform, high-grade yarn, however, it was necessary to improve the quality of the product, from the silkworm egg on through to the bale of silk. In sericulture this meant the introduction of scientific methods of breeding and disease control; in reeling it stimulated the shift to large filatures equipped with machinery; in marketing it led to large-scale organization in the collection and sale of cocoons and raw silk…it exerted steady pressure in favour of the application of science, machinery, and modern business enterprise.

The role of leading sector has been assumed, finally, by the accelerated development of domestic manufacture of consumption goods over a wide range in substitution for imports, as, for example, in Australia, the Argentine and, perhaps, in contemporary Turkey.

* W. W. Lockwood, *The Economic Development of Japan* (Princeton, 1954), pp. 338–9.

What can we say, then, in general about these leading sectors? Historically, they have ranged from cotton textiles, through heavy-industry complexes based on railroads and military end-products, to timber, pulp, dairy products and finally a wide variety of consumers' goods. There is, clearly, no one sectoral sequence for take-off, no single sector which constitutes the magic key. There is no need for a growing society to recapitulate, for example, the structural sequence and pattern of Britain, the United States or Russia. Four basic factors must be present:

(1) There must be enlarged effective demand for the product or products of sectors which yield a foundation for a rapid rate of growth in output. Historically this has been brought about initially by the transfer of income from consumption or hoarding to productive investment; by capital imports; by a sharp increase in the productivity of current investment inputs, yielding an increase in consumers' real income expended on domestic manufactures; or by a combination of these routes.

(2) There must be an introduction into these sectors of new production functions as well as an expansion of capacity.

(3) The society must be capable of generating capital initially required to detonate the take-off in these key sectors; and especially there must be a high rate of plough-back by the (private or state) entrepreneurs controlling capacity and technique in these sectors and in the supplementary growth sectors they stimulated to expand.

(4) Finally, the leading sector or sectors must be such that their expansion and technical transformation induce a chain of requirements for increased capacity and the potentiality for new production functions in other sectors, to which the society, in fact, progressively responds.

THE TAKE-OFF IN PERSPECTIVE

This view of the take-off is, then, a return to a rather old-fashioned way of looking at economic development. The take-off is defined as an industrial revolution, tied directly to radical changes in methods of production, having their decisive consequence over a relatively short period of time.

This view would not deny the role of longer, slower changes in the whole process of economic growth. On the contrary, take-off requires the massive set of preconditions, going to the heart of a society's economic organization, its politics, and its effective scale of values, considered in chapter 3.

What this argument does assert is that the rapid growth of one or more new manufacturing sectors is a powerful and essential engine of economic transformation. Its power derives from the multiplicity of its forms of impact, when a society is prepared to respond positively to this impact. Growth in such sectors, with new production functions of high productivity, in itself tends to raise output per head; it places incomes in the hands of men who will not merely save a high proportion of an expanding income but who will plough it into highly productive investment; it sets up a chain of effective demand for other manufactured products; it sets up a requirement for enlarged urban areas, whose capital costs may be high, but whose population and market organization help to make industrialization an on-going process; and, finally, it opens up a range of external economy effects which, in the end, help to produce new leading sectors when the initial impulse of the take-off's leading sectors begins to wane.

In non-economic terms, the take-off usually witnesses a definitive social, political, and cultural victory of those who would modernize the economy over those who would either cling to the traditional society or seek other goals; but—because nationalism can be a social solvent as well as a diversionary force—the victory can assume forms of mutual accommodation, rather than the destruction of the traditional groups by the more modern; see, for example, the role of the Junkers in nascent industrial Germany, and the persistence of much in traditional Japan beyond 1880. By and large, the maintenance of momentum for a generation persuades the society to persist, and to concentrate its efforts on extending the tricks of modern technology beyond the sectors modernized during take-off.

CHAPTER 5

THE DRIVE TO MATURITY

DEFINITION AND TIMING

After take-off there follows what might be called the drive to maturity. There are a variety of ways a stage of economic maturity might be defined: but for these purposes we define it as the period when a society has effectively applied the range of (then) modern technology to the bulk of its resources.

In terms of sectoral development the drive to maturity sees the industrial process differentiated, with new leading sectors gathering momentum to supplant the older leading sectors of the take-off, where deceleration has increasingly slowed the pace of expansion. After the railway take-offs of the third quarter of the nineteenth century—with coal, iron, and heavy engineering at the centre of the growth process—it is steel, the new ships, chemicals, electricity, and the products of the modern machine-tool that come to dominate the economy and sustain the overall rate of growth. This is also, essentially, the case with the later Russian drive to maturity, after 1929. But in Sweden after 1890 it was the evolution from timber to wood-pulp and paper; from ore to high-grade steel and finely machined metal products. The leading sectors in the drive to maturity will be determined, then, not merely by the pool of technology but by the nature of resource endowments; by the character of the take-off, and the forces it sets in motion; and it may be shaped to a degree, as well, by the policies of governments.

Although much further detailed analysis would be required to apply this definition rigorously, we would offer the following sample as rough symbolic dates for technological maturity:*

Great Britain	1850	Sweden	1930
United States	1900	Japan	1940
Germany	1910	Russia	1950
France	1910	Canada	1950

* The reader may wonder why we have given only rounded, symbolic dates for arrival at maturity whereas more precise dates are offered in chapter 4 for the beginning

The oddity referred to in chapter 2 is to be noted again. These dates, independently derived, come more or less sixty years after the dates established, on quite different criteria, for the beginning of take-off. There is no body of argument or evidence we can now offer to make rational such a uniformity. But, as suggested earlier, it may be that when we explore the implications of some six decades of compound interest applied to the capital stock, in combination with three generations of men living under an environment of growth, elements of rationality will emerge.

SECTORAL PATTERNS OF MATURITY: RÁILWAYS AND THEIR AFTERMATH

In Great Britain the take-off had centred on the direct and indirect consequences of the rapid expansion in cotton textiles, including developments as distant from Lancashire as Eli Whitney's invention of the cotton-gin and such partially independent, but concurrent, developments as the refinement of the steam-engine and of an iron technology based on British ore and coke. The British road to maturity consisted not merely in the large-scale exploitation, after 1815, of the mutually reinforcing innovations of Arkwright, Watt and Whitney, but also in the railway booms of the 1830's and 1840's. These surges brought the British coal, iron, and heavy engineering industries to technical maturity by the mid-nineteenth century.

By, let us say, the Exhibition of 1851, Britain had mastered and extended over virtually the whole range of its resources all that the then modern science and technology had to offer an economy with

of take-off. The reason for this asymmetry derives from the fundamental theoretical basis of the stages-of-growth analysis, presented at the close of chapter 2. The stages-of-growth take their reality from rapid expansion phases in particular leading sectors. The initial dates for take-off are generally the moment when a clearly marked general expansion was launched based on rapid growth in particular industries. For the pre-1914 era, for example, the initial date for take-off often marks the beginning of a powerful cyclical expansion. As will emerge, arrival at maturity did not necessarily bring with it the prompt launching of the next stage, with new leading sectors. There was often an interval before the age of high mass-consumption was launched: an interval used to bring consumption up to the level necessary for this stage or passed in less wholesome ways, for example in relative stagnation or in military ventures. With the launching of the stage of high mass-consumption more precise dating again becomes possible; for new leading sectors again clearly emerge, with high momentum.

the resources (and the population-resource balance) of mid-nineteenth-century Britain. In various specific directions other nations exhibited something of a lead over Britain, even at mid-century: the Americans, for example, foreshadowing a virtuosity with labour-saving machinery—notably farm machinery; and the Germans, in chemicals. But at the Crystal Palace Britain was unique in reflecting a well-rounded mature economy.

Less than seventy years from the launching of the canal and cotton-textile boom of the 1780's, when the industrial revolution, narrowly defined, may be said to have begun, Britain had wholeheartedly transformed itself into an industrial nation—its commitment confirmed by the Repeal of the Corn Laws. Well ahead in most, but not in all sectors, with respect to the other societies whose pre-conditions had been well advanced during the eighteenth century, Britain was about to divert a substantial proportion of its capital and technical know-how in a quarter-century of diffusion abroad of the iron, heavy engineering, and construction technology on which railway building depended.

And, as noted in chapter 4, the take-offs of the United States, France, and Germany, all completed by 1873, were thus based squarely on railways rather than cotton textiles. For these nations the path to maturity lay in a complex of industries whose possibilities were, in part, unfolded by the nature of the railway take-off. For just as the railway boom in Britain was sparked by the success of the Manchester–Liverpool line, so the requirements of railway maintenance placed a high premium on the production of cheap and good steel, whose rails would not wear out as fast as the iron rails. It was largely from this incentive that the modern steel industry was built; in a sense steel flowed from the railroads, as the railroads had flowed from the requirements and consequences of modern cotton-textile industries. But once cheap, good steel was available, many further uses unfolded, including the efficient boiler and the modern steel ship; the machine-tool; new equipment for heavy chemical manufacture; and new forms of urban construction.

The history of the engineering profession thus tells in compressed form the story of the unfolding, leading sectors. Where its bases were not military, the modern engineering profession took its start in laying out roads and canals, in designing water-pumps for coal mines, and making textile machinery, including the means to power that machinery. Drawing on strands from all these early experiences the engineers moved on to railroads; and they then fanned out, in a process of differentiation, into mechanical, chemical, and electrical engineering specialities as well as such sub-specialities as naval construction and civil engineering. Of all the steps in the sequence of modern engineering the railway was, almost certainly, the most important. Just as the financing and management of the railroads set many patterns for large-scale industrialization on a wider front, so also, it was in the technical experience of building and operating the railways that a good part of the foundations were laid for the march of the Western world into maturity.

For the United States, Germany, and France, then, the post-take-off stage was concentrated on the development of post-railway technology, much of which was an elaboration of insights derived from earlier technical experience. The rise of steel—and all its uses, massive and refined—is certainly the central symbol of the post-railway movement to maturity on the continent of Western Europe and in the United States. And Britain, of course, joined fully in the elaboration and application of the post-railway technology.

But what of the later-comers of the nineteenth century? What, for example, of Sweden, of Japan, and Russia, whose take-offs begin between, say, 1870 and 1890?

SWEDEN

For Sweden the take-off of the 1870's and 1880's had been based primarily on a modern timber export industry and railway construction. The turning point into maturity comes in the early 1890's. And it comes in the form of a challenge: a depression marked by a sagging away of Sweden's export markets on which a good deal of its take-off had been built. This is a quite normal occurrence. The take-off is, structurally, a surge in output in a relatively few sectors. It is of the nature of the investment process that these sectoral surges should be overdone. Indeed, this is the essence of the trade cycle. Once having overshot the mark in the key sectors of a first take-off surge, it is necessary for the economy to regroup and re-allocate its resources for a resumption of growth in new leading sectors. Structurally this is the nature and the historic function of a trade depression. It has been normal, therefore, for the take-off to end with a trade depression; and one measure of take-off having been achieved is a society's ability to regroup its resources effectively and to accelerate expansion in a new set of leading sectors.

Sweden of the 1890's responded positively to this structural challenge. There was a shift from timber into wood-pulp, from the export of unplaned to planed board and matches. The Norrland ores began to be systematically exploited by modern methods. From pig-iron there was a surge into the highly refined steel and engineering industries. Hydro-electric sources of power were systematically exploited, laying the basis for an electric machinery industry of the highest skill, which was later to help the Swedish railways convert to electricity from coal. Even in agriculture there was a shift—in direction similar to that in Denmark—from grain to animal and dairy farming of higher productivity. And over a wide range Sweden began to produce at home manufactured commodities hitherto imported. In Lindahl's phrase, the 1890's marked for Sweden the beginnings of a phase of 'differentiation of production'* which continued down to 1914 and was, in fact, heightened by the requirements of Sweden's somewhat isolated neutrality of the First World War.

The essence of this transition was the systematic application to the rich but narrow mix of Swedish natural resources of the best methods modern technology could then offer. By the 1890's Swedish society had been transformed in such a way over the previous generation as to generate a corps of entrepreneurs and technicians sufficient to man this push along a wide front. So, by the end of the 1920's, Sweden had become a fully mature society, in terms of its own resources and of a modern technology to which it made significant contributions. It was ready for the welfare state and the gadgetry of the age of durable consumer goods.

JAPAN

From this perspective, the story of Japan in its broad outline—but timed with about a decade's lag—bears a family resemblance to that of Sweden; and this is so despite a population-resource balance

* *National Income of Sweden*, vol. I, especially pp. 122, 263–4, 281, and 314–15.

distinctly less advantageous than that of Sweden, and despite a cultural and political setting that, at first glance, could hardly be less similar. Japan, too, represents a remarkably purposeful surge to maturity, in which a relatively narrow array of natural resources was harnessed by a diligent, strongly motivated population to the best that modern technology could offer in a sixty-year surge: from, say, 1880 to 1940.

Just as the sectoral composition of the Japanese take-off differs from the Swedish case, so also does the mixture of industries which carried Japan to maturity in the 1930's.

The Japanese take-off was made possible by a series of prior and concurrent developments in agriculture that did the three essential things defined in chapter 3 as agriculture's mission in industrial development: from the side of supply, agriculture provided increased food and fibres for an enlarged population, for accelerated urbanization, and to earn foreign exchange; from the side of demand, the rise of productivity in rural areas provided Japanese industry with enlarged markets and encouragement for domestic industry; and finally, from the side of capital supply, the commutation of the feudal rents, and the diversion of this income stream to the government gave the Japanese modern sector an essential initial infusion of capital, until plough-back could take over a good part of industrial financing.

But despite the new technical and market skills that accompanied these agricultural developments, they alone could not have lifted Japan into take-off. In the 1880's and 1890's, a whole series of new industries took hold, initially sparked by government initiative, but increasingly turned over to private enterprise, as new men emerged ready to carry the responsibilities and risks of administration and ownership: the take-off—let us say between 1880 and 1900—was built on railways, on ship-building, on cotton manufacture (initially based on imported cotton), on silk cultivation and manufacture, on coal and pig-iron, and then, in the 1890's, on a surge of military outlays, that helped to build up the engineering industries.

In the 1890's, too, the beginnings of a modern chemical industry can be discerned. But the rise of chemicals, with their crucial role in Japanese agriculture, belongs with the process of industrial

64

differentiation—the advance on a broad front—which characterizes the first four decades of the twentieth century. For despite high growth-rates in the previous two decades, as of 1900 Japan was still a society whose modern industrial sector was small and, relatively, still dominated by textiles. It was between 1900 and 1920—notably stimulated by the First World War—that the Japanese industrial sector began to fan out into chemical fertilizers, steel, and electrical equipment.

Lockwood concludes in a formulation quite close to our definition of maturity: 'By the end of the 1920's...the processes of modernization and growth had extended in varying degrees to all sectors of the economy.' But it was only in the 1930's that the engineering industries came into their own, under the stimulus of the development of Manchuria and war outlays and preparations. It was only in this decade, for example, that the value of output in metals, machinery, and chemicals at last came to outrank textiles in their contribution to Japanese gross national production.*

Thus, starting its take-off about thirty years after the major nations of continental Europe, ten years after Sweden, Japan arrived at maturity just about in phase; that is, about three decades after France and Germany, a decade after Sweden.

RUSSIA

Now a few words about the Russian case, which is considered at greater length in chapter 7, in relation to that of the United States.

The Russian preconditions reach back, of course, a long way, at least to the time when Peter returned from the West with the conviction that Russia had to modernize; but the traditional society gave way slowly. It was shocked by Napoleon; and again by the Crimean War; and its bases were slowly eroded by the spreading knowledge of all that was going forward in the West, during the first half of the nineteenth century. With 1861, and the freeing of the serfs, the process of creating the preconditions for take-off accelerates: both technically—in the build-up of social overhead capital and the bases for modern industry—and in terms of the

* K. Ohkawa *et al.*, *The Growth Rate of the Japanese Economy since 1878* (Tokyo, 1957), pp. 81–3.

ideas, attitudes, and aspirations of various groups of Russians. Then, by 1890 or so, the Russian take-off begins.

Like the concurrent Canadian take-off, the Russian take-off was aided by the rise in grain prices and the export demand for grain which occurred in the mid-1890's; for it was this rise that made attractive the laying of vast railway nets in the two countries, just as, in the 1840's, the potato famine in Ireland, and the pressure on Western Europe grain acreage in general, set the stage for the rail-roadization of the American mid-West in the 1850's. And it was the railway, with its multiple impact on growth, that took Russia into its take-off by the outbreak of the First World War. Coal, iron, and engineering surged ahead, as well as a modern cotton-textile industry to meet the expanded demand at home. In addition, the Baku petroleum industry expanded to its natural limit; and the Ukrainian coal–iron complex was brought to life as were the Ruhr, and the Pennsylvanian and mid-Western American complexes a half-century or so earlier.

By 1914 Russia was producing something like five million tons of pig-iron, four million tons of iron and steel, forty million tons of coal, ten million tons of petroleum and a food-grain export surplus of about twelve million tons. Despite its ultimate internal collapse and defeat, during the First World War, Russia was able to mount, supply, and sustain for three years of terrible casualties an enormous army, in modern combat, including artillery and aircraft of considerable sophistication.

The Communists inherited, then, an economy that had taken off; and one which had developed a substantial export surplus in agriculture.

It took about a decade for Lenin and his successors to reorganize this system to their taste, and to get it back to its previous peak output; and then came the series of Five Year Plans. They are to be understood not as a take-off but as a drive to maturity: the process of industrial differentiation, the advance to modernization on a wide front.

Stalin was the architect not of the modernization of a backward country, but of the completion of its modernization. Stalin was Witte's successor in a quite direct and technical sense.

Russia

With certain specific differences stemming from the objectives of the Communist leadership, the broad pattern of Soviet economic growth between 1929 and, say, Stalin's death is similar to that of Western Europe and the United States of the pre-1914 decades: this was the post-railway age in Russia, the age of steel, machine tools, chemicals, and electricity. The Russian surge to maturity came, however, at a time when the back-log of accumulated technological possibilities included developments (notably in electronics, aeronautics, and atomic energy) which were not available a few generations earlier, so that as Russia drew technologically level, it was level at a different range of technology from that of the powers which had reached maturity by 1914.

In its broad shape and timing, then, there is nothing about the Russian sequence of preconditions, take-off, and drive to technological maturity that does not fall within the general pattern; although like all other national stories it has unique features, which will be considered in later chapters.

SOME PROBLEMS IN DEFINING MATURITY

The meaning of this technological definition of maturity—and its limits—may be better perceived by considering briefly a few specific problems posed by the particular dates here chosen for maturity.

Is France, for example, on the eve of the First World War, to be regarded as technologically mature, despite its large, comfortable but technologically backward peasantry and its tendency to export large amounts of capital, despite certain technologically lagging industrial sectors? The case can, of course, be argued either way; but it does dramatize the need to allow, within the present definition, for regions of a nation or sectors of the economy to resist—for whatever reason—the full application of the range of modern technology. And this turns out to be generally true of nations which, by and large, one would judge mature. The United States of 1900 contained, after all, the South, whose take-off can be dated only from the 1930's; and contemporary mature Canada contains the still-lagging province of Quebec. The technological definition of maturity must, then, be an approximation, when applied to a whole national society.

Japan as of 1940 poses a somewhat different problem. Can one rate as mature an economy with so labour-intensive an agricultural sector? The answer is affirmative only if one is prepared to take as given—outside the definition of maturity—a society's decision about its population size. Within the Japanese population-resource balance, its agriculture, with extraordinary refinement in the use of both water and chemical fertilizers, does indeed reflect a high form of modern technological achievement, even if modern farm machinery, designed to save labour, is capable of only limited use.

What about contemporary Russia, with more than 40% of the working force still in agriculture and much modern technology still unapplied in textiles and other consumers' goods industries? Here again, the present definition of maturity would not predetermine how a society chooses to allocate its technological capabilities. By and large contemporary Russia is to be judged a mature economy despite the fact that its leaders have chosen for political reasons to bear the costs of a low-productivity agriculture and have chosen to concentrate capital and technology in sectors other than manufactured consumption goods. Put another way, the obstacles to full modernization of the Russian economic structure do not lie in the supply of capital, entrepreneurial administrators, or technicians.

Finally, there is the case of Britain, mature on this definition as early, say, as the Crystal Palace Exhibition. How is one to deal with the long interval between the stage of its maturity, in terms of the effective application of mid-nineteenth-century technology, and the next stage of growth: the age of high mass-consumption, when the radical improvements in housing and durable consumers' goods and services become the economy's leading sectors?

The reasons for the gap in the British sequence lie in the nature of this next stage. The age of high mass-consumption represents a direction of development a society may choose when it has achieved both technological maturity and a certain level of real income per head. Although income per head—and usually consumption per head—will rise in the drive to maturity, it is evident that there is no fixed connexion between technological maturity and any particular level of real consumption per head. The course of these variables after take-off will depend primarily on the society's population-resource balance and on its income distribution policy. The process of growth, by definition, raises income per head, but it does not necessarily lead to uniformity of *per capita* income among nations or, even, among regions within nations; and, in Canada and certain other cases, we even have societies which have entered into the stage of high mass-consumption before technological maturity was attained.

There are—and there are likely to be—technologically mature societies that are, so to speak, both rich and poor. When historical data on national income are developed to permit systematic comparison, we are likely to find that incomes per head, at maturity, vary over a considerable range. Mid-century Britain would, presumably, stand low in that range. The improvements in real income and consumption per head that occurred in the second half of the nineteenth century took the form of improvements in diet, housing, urban overhead capital, and other forms of increased welfare which, while substantial, did not create within Britain new leading industrial sectors—at least down to the bicycle boom of the 1890's.*

* In a different perspective, it is possible to dismiss the gap between mid-nineteenth century British technological maturity and twentieth-century high mass-consumption as a simple product of technological history; that is, the technology of modern transportation, suburban housing, and household gadgetry did not exist in, say, the third quarter of the nineteenth century. And for many purposes that is a quite satisfactory way to look at the matter.

On the other hand, three considerations argue that it is also, for other purposes, worth regarding the British sequence in the second half of the nineteenth century as involving a gap. First, technology itself is, in its widest sense, not an independent variable (W. W. Rostow, *Process of Economic Growth*, especially pp. 83–6). If the level of British incomes and consumption had been high enough, incentives might have existed which would have yielded a quite different evolution of technology. Second, the phenomenon of a gap in time between the attainment of technological maturity and the age of high mass-consumption—the existence of relatively poor as well as rich mature societies—is more general than the British case. And a view of Britain in the second half of the nineteenth century as in the process of closing the gap may, for certain purposes, be linked suggestively to similar transitions in other societies. Third, much in British social, political (and, even, entrepreneurial) history in the second half of the nineteenth century is typical of transformations in attitude and policy which have occurred in other societies after technological maturity has been attained: the beginnings of serious welfare legislation, with the Ten Hours Bill; the pressures and reflexions which led the society to accept the Second and Third Reform Bills; the emergence of political coalitions which damped the power of industrial interests; the mounting intellectual attention and public sentiment focused on problems of social reform, laying the bases for the pre-1914 Liberal measures and the emergence of the Labour Party. In short, even narrowly examined, much in British history in the period 1850–1900 is illuminated by the notion that this was a society which took its technological virtuosity as given and, at decorous rate, proceeded to explore, at the margin, objectives beyond.

The drive to maturity

And so Britain, after Crystal Palace, moved onward in growth at a modest pace, using its capital and entrepreneurship substantially to help acquire resources with which it was not sufficiently endowed and to help build the preconditions and assist the take-offs of other societies, suffering along the way some of the costs of having led in the process of industrialization, to enter the new century with most of its initial lead gone. Put another way, the achievement of maturity by Western Europe and the United States early in the twentieth century, at the then existing level of technology, found Britain in a roughly equivalent position: while the newer nations had moved from take-off to maturity in the sixty years before the First World War, Britain had moved, in terms of income levels, from being a relatively poor mature society to being a relatively rich mature society.

MATURITY IN PERSPECTIVE

Now a few words about the non-economic aspects of the drive to maturity. Look backwards a moment.

The period of preconditions is the time in the life of a society when the traditional structure is undermined piecemeal, while important dimensions of the old system remain. Just before and during the take-off, the new modern elements, values, and objectives achieve a definitive break-through; and they come to control the society's institutions; and then, having made their point, with their opponents in retreat or disarray they drive to carry the process of modernization to its logical conclusion. Post-1815 Britain, post-Civil War America, Bismarck's Germany after 1870 and slower-moving France, too, in the same period, Japan from 1900 to 1920, Stalin's Russia of the Five Year Plans—these were all societies run by men who knew where they were going. They were caught up in the power of compound interest and in the possibilities of transforming one sector after another of the society by extending the tricks of modern technology. By and large these were confident periods in the life of societies, where there were big palpable jobs to be done; where the results could quickly be seen; and the society, reluctantly or otherwise, gave its industrial leaders—who were also sometimes politicians—their head. The course of real wages for the urban and agricultural worker, and his fate in a larger sense, varied as among these societies during the drive to maturity—from comfortable Sweden to Stalin's forced-labour society; but generally speaking the power of those who controlled capital and technology was not seriously opposed. The traditional society was defeated; and those groups and interests who would interpose values other than the extension of modern techniques had not formed up and made themselves effective.

Nevertheless the path to maturity had within it the seeds not of its undoing—for this analysis is neither Hegelian, nor Marxist—but the seeds of its own modification.

Specifically, three things happened as maturity moved towards its close.

First, the working force changed. It changed in its composition, its real wage, its outlook, and in its skills. Before take-off perhaps 75% of the working force is in agriculture, living on a low, if not merely survival, real wage; by the end of take-off the figure may drop to 40%; and by maturity, it has in many cases fallen to 20%. But maturity means not only that the urban population grows, but that the number of office and semi-skilled workers increases, and the number of highly trained technicians and professionals as well. This is not merely—or even necessarily—a shift from unskilled to skilled labour. Sometimes the contrary is the case. It is a shift to those who design or handle complex machines, keep office records and manage big bureaucracies, rather than lay railway tracks or puddle steel, or handle rather crudely masses of unskilled labour. These people are not fresh in from the countryside. They are the increasingly literate and knowledgeable children of the city and the world of technology. Moreover the real wages of workers are not only likely to be rising but the workers are also likely to perceive that, if they organize and make their presence felt in the society, they can probably achieve even higher wages and greater security of employment and welfare.

In short, the process of moving to maturity lays the basis for the kind of political and social pressures that led to that long succession of humane modifications starting with the factory legislation of the 1840's in Britain down through Bismarck's concessions, Lloyd

George's reforms, the American Progressive era; and, if you like, to the concessions made to the Russian consumer, technician, and bureaucrat since 1953.

Second, the character of the leadership changes; from the buccaneering cotton-, railway-, steel- and oil-baron to the efficient professional manager of a highly bureaucratized and differentiated machine.*

Third, related to but transcending the first two changes, the society as a whole becomes a little bored with the miracle of industrialization. Just as Soviet society has protested against the imposition upon it of endless novels in which a man's love for his tractor or machine-tool is the central theme, so in many subtle ways the Western world articulated, late in the nineteenth century, its second thoughts about industrialization as a unique and overriding objective: via the Fabians and the muck-rakers, the Continental social democrats, Ibsen and Shaw and Dreiser and, indeed, via Mill and Marshall. It is here, too, as a protestant against the human costs of the drive to maturity, that Marx fits as well, as we shall see in chapter 10.

These changes in the real income, structure, ambitions, and outlook of the society, as maturity comes to be achieved, pose a searching problem of balance and choice around the question: how shall this mature industrial machine, with compound interest built into it, be used? To offer increased security, welfare and perhaps leisure for the citizens as a whole? To offer enlarged real incomes, including the manufactured gadgets of consumption, to those who can earn them? To assert the stature of the new mature society on the world scene? For, as we shall see in chapter 8, maturity is a dangerous time as well as one which offers new, promising choices.

* Few exercises are likely to be more fruitful for the understanding of modern economic history than a comparison of the first three generations of leadership in growing economies; the relatively modest, creative fellows who get the growth started; the hard-handed task-masters who, perceiving the scale of possibilities, drive the society to maturity, if necessary despite itself; and the comfortable, cautious committee-men who inherit and manage the economy as a profession while the society seeks objectives which include but transcend the application of modern technology to its resources.

CHAPTER 6

THE AGE OF
HIGH MASS-CONSUMPTION

THE THREE-WAY CHOICE

Chapter 5 argues that, as technical maturity was approached, men began to take for granted what they were born to, in this case a well advanced industrial society; and their minds turned increasingly to reconsider the ends to which the mature economy might be put.

In a quite technical sense, the balance of attention of the society, as it approached and went beyond maturity, shifted from supply to demand, from problems of production to problems of consumption, and of welfare in the widest sense.

In this post-maturity stage there have been three major objectives which, to some degree, have competed for resources and political support, three directions in which welfare, in this wide sense, might be increased.

First, the national pursuit of external power and influence, that is, the allocation of increased resources to military and foreign policy. It has been a quite consistent feature of modern history for some groups to look out beyond their borders for new worlds to conquer, as their societies approached technical maturity. And in some cases, by one route or another, they gained effective political control over national policy.

A second direction for the use of the resources of a mature economy we can call the welfare state; that is, the use of the powers of the State, including the power to redistribute income through progressive taxation, to achieve human and social objectives (including increased leisure) which the free-market process, in its less adulterated form, did not achieve. During the take-off and in the drive to maturity, those elements in what Lionel Robbins calls the individualist-utilitarian creed which did not lead to a maximization of output were, relatively, suppressed, the degree of their suppression varying from

73

society to society. As maturity approached, these more humane objectives asserted themselves with increased force. Men were prepared, in a sense, to take risks with the level of output—and the incentives in the private sector—in order to cushion the hardships of the trade-cycle; in order to increase social security; in order to redistribute income; in order to shorten the working day; and, generally, to soften the harshness of a society hitherto geared primarily to maximizing industrial output and the spread of modern technology.

The third possible direction opened up by the achievement of maturity was the expansion of consumption levels beyond basic food, shelter, and clothing, not only to better food, shelter, and clothing but into the range of mass consumption of durable consumers' goods and services, which the mature economies of the twentieth century can provide.

Each society which has created for itself the possibility and necessity of making a choice among these objectives—by attaining technological maturity—has struck a different balance, unique in degree, at least. The uniqueness of the balance was determined in each case by geography, the old culture, resources, values, and the political leadership which dominated it at various intervals beyond maturity. A good deal of American and Western European history since about 1900, Japanese history since the 1930's, and even Russian history since Stalin's death, can be told in terms of the problem of choice posed by the attainment of maturity and in terms of the different balances struck among these three objectives, at different times.

Since the United States was the first of the world's societies to move sharply from maturity into the age of high mass-consumption we shall begin by tracing briefly and schematically how the balance among these alternatives was struck, in the sequence of American history over the past half-century. We shall examine this sequence in four phases: the progressive period, the 1920's, the great depression of the 1930's, and the post-war boom of 1946–56.

74

The age of high mass-consumption

Phase One: The Progressive Period, 1901–16

First, a few words about the progressive period; that is, the period from, roughly, the accession of Theodore Roosevelt in 1901 to the engulfment of Woodrow Wilson's administration in the problems of the First World War.

Although McKinley had easily won the election of 1900, with a stance that looked backward to the sequence of Republican administrations which had dominated the drive to maturity after the Civil War, American life in a wider sense had been actively preparing itself for a shift in the balance of its objectives; and this was revealed by the popularity of Theodore Roosevelt's style and rhetoric, as well as by the clear-cut bipartisan defeat of Taft, and all he then appeared to represent, in the election of 1912.

The progressive objectives had, then, fifteen years of relative dominance over domestic policy; and they left their mark. By 1916 the United States had accepted the most revolutionary of all forms of economic policy, the progressive income-tax; it had created a climate in which big business curbed itself or was, to a degree, curbed; the unions were given explicitly the right to organize, outside the Anti-Trust Act; a Federal Reserve System was created, in part to permit a degree of public control to be exercised over the trade cycle. In some of the states even more powerful measures of social control were introduced. But the progressive period was more a matter of mood and the direction of policy than of drastic re-allocation of resources.

In these years Americans made another significant decision about the direction of national affairs. In the 1890's a widespread mood was generating that the United States had, in some sense, become a mature world power, and that it was time for it to play a major role on the world scene; to move out from behind the protective barrier represented by the Monroe Doctrine and the implicit deal with the British, in which the British navy shielded the United States from the vicissitudes of the Eurasian balance-of-power game. And Theodore Roosevelt, architect of the seizure of the Philippines and hero of the Spanish-American War, pressed forward this sense of emergence and, to a degree, of assertion on the world scene in his two administrations.

But the so-called 'large view' symbolized by Theodore Roosevelt failed to take hold. The Philippines were kept; but Americans, having been tempted, and fallen a bit from what they conceived to be isolationist grace, in the end turned their backs on the acquisition of empire. In foreign policy they opted for a version of the British Liberal rather than the British Conservative tradition, in the progressive period—quite explicitly so in the figure of Wilson.

American resources, then, did not flow in significantly increased volume either to social services or to military outlays; although the progressive legislation, the Great White Fleet, and the increased role of government in American society were facts.

American resources did, however, flow increasingly into the third post-maturity alternative—into new dimensions of consumption: a trend damped by the rise in urban living costs down to 1920, but palpable in the next major phase, that is, in the boom of the 1920's.

Phase Two: The 1920's

The American 1920's are generally now studied as a period of tragic isolation; as the prelude to severe depression; or as a bizarre social era of bath-tub gin, jazz, mah jong, glamorous athletes, distinguished novelists, and the Charleston.

But that decade is also to be understood as the first protracted period in which a society absorbed the fruits and consequences of the age of durable consumers' goods and services.

Let us examine now a few figures which suggest the character of the change proceeding in American society, and in its economy, over this era of high mass-consumption of which the 1920's is the centre-piece.

First, there was the rise of a new middle class. Between 1900 and 1940 the number of farmers in the United States declined. Those in manufacture, construction, and transport—including skilled workers—rose about in proportion to the total rise in the working force. But semi-skilled workers increased more than twice as rapidly as the working force as a whole; professional people and office workers three times as rapidly as the working force as a whole. The era of the professional technician, and of the skilled and semi-skilled worker had come; and this trend in the structure of the working force has proved virtually universal to all post-maturity societies.

Now where did this population, oriented increasingly towards the provision and enjoyment of consumers' goods and services, live? The answer is that the population was not only increasingly urban, but increasingly suburban. In the 1920's the American population as a whole increased by 16%. Those living in the centres of cities increased by 22%. But those living in the satellite areas— the suburbs—increased by 44%.

What then happened to manufacturing output? Fabricant has arrayed the increases in physical output in the United States between 1899 and 1937 by order of increase. Automobiles lead the list with an increase of 180,100%; cigarettes, petroleum, milk, beet-sugar are all over 1000%; cement, canned fruits and vegetables are only a little under 1000%.*

What does all this add up to? The United States took to wheels. This was quite truly the age of the mass automobile. With the automobile the United States began a vast inner migration into newly constructed, single-family houses in the suburbs; and these new houses were filled increasingly with radios, refrigerators, and the other household gadgetry of a society whose social mobility and productivity had all but wiped out personal service. Within these houses Americans shifted their food consumption to higher-grade foods, increasingly purchased in cans—or, later, frozen.

Automobiles, single-family houses, roads, household durables, mass markets in higher-grade foods—these tell a good deal of the story of the transformation of American society in the 1920's, a transformation which supported the boom of the 1920's and which altered the whole style of a continent's life, down to its courting habits.

Phase Three: The Great Depression

Then came, of course, a decade's severe and protracted depression. We shall not consider at length here the causes of the onset of depression or the reasons for its extraordinary depth, except to

---

* S. Fabricant, *The Output of Manufacturing Industries, 1899–1937* (New York, 1940), p. 89.

say this much: in its onset, the depression of 1929 was a perfectly normal cyclical down-turn; the leading sectors of the boom were wearing a little thin, notably in housing, stimulated by the housing back-log built up during the First World War, but weakened by the deceleration in population growth and family formation. The depression went abnormally deep because the institutions of credit, at home and abroad, broke down, like a series of collapsing floors, grinding the cycle at each stage of collapse to a lower point, through its effects on income, confidence, and expectations.

The length of the depression in the United States—as opposed to its depth—deserves rather more comment; for it relates directly to the stage of growth, to the era of high mass-consumption, into which the United States had entered.

Although many ancillary forces undoubtedly played a part, the central reason for the intractability of the American depression, which still left 17% unemployed on the eve of the Second World War, was that the leading sectors of this phase of American growth required full employment and an atmosphere of confidence before they could become activated again.

What were those leading sectors in the American age of high consumption? They were, once again, the automobile, suburban home-building, road-building, and the progressive extension of the automobile and other durable consumers' goods to more and more families. When, in earlier historical stages, the momentum of growth hinged on the continued extension of railroads, or on the introduction of other cost-reducing industrial processes—on the side of supply—investment could be judged profitable at relatively low levels of current consumers' demand. But when investment comes to be centred around industries and services based on expanding consumption, full employment is needed, in a sense, to sustain full employment; for unless consumption levels press outward, capacity in consumers' goods industries and those supplying them with inputs will be under-used, and the impulse to invest will be weak. The horizons of American industry lowered radically in the 1930's, and appeared almost to stabilize at a low level.

When, in the nineteenth century, steel went mainly into railways or the new steel ships, the demand for steel was a reflex of what some economists like to call exogenous investment; in the age of high consumption, when the demand for steel is, let us say, from the automobile firms and canning industries, the demand for steel becomes a reflex of endogenous investment—of the rise of incomes, of the accelerator, one may say.

On this view the Second World War was a sort of *deus ex machina* which brought the United States back up to full employment; and in the context of the post-war world—its institutional arrangements drastically altered by the New Deal and such legislation as that put through for veterans' housing—the United States went on to round out the durable consumers' goods revolution in a decade of chronic full employment between, say, 1946 and 1956.

During the depression, American society did more, of course, than merely experience a depression. When the engine of growth based on the automobile, suburbia, and durable consumers' goods broke down, the United States threw its weight hard towards a post-maturity alternative, that is, to increased allocations for social welfare purposes. And the contours of the welfare state were rounded out under Franklin Roosevelt to remain an accepted part of the American scene, down to the present.

Phase Four: The Post-War Boom

The fourth phase—the great post-war boom of 1946–56—can be regarded as a resumption of the boom of the 1920's. The march to the outer suburbs continued after a marked deceleration in the 1930's. In 1948 54% of American families owned their own cars; a decade later, 73%. In 1946, 69% of houses wired for electricity had electric refrigerators; a decade later the figure was 96%; and the figures for other electric gadgets—for example, the vacuum cleaner and electric washer—are similar. Television was installed in 86% of such homes by 1956.

And although the deep-freeze and air conditioning are just beginning to take hold in American households it is clear that American growth can no longer continue to be based so heavily on the extension to a higher and higher proportion of the community of the suburban house, the automobile, and the standard mix of electric-powered gadgets. In some items output began to fall off absolutely

79

before the recent recession when the automobile industry, seized of *hybris* in its recent models, over-reached itself and was suddenly forced to learn that all sectoral growth curves are subject to long-run deceleration.*

Phase Five: Where next?

What then does the future hold? Are Americans, having fashioned this suburban, mobile civilization going to settle down to tidy it up a little, and enjoy the benefits of affluence? Is it the four-day work week and the three-day weekend which is coming soon? Some think it is; and it is still too soon dogmatically to deny their judgment.

But it is clear that something new and important did happen in American society as the age of durable consumers' goods moved towards its logical conclusion; and this process again follows the Buddenbrooks' dynamics. As the durable consumers' goods revolution was moving to a point where the rate of diffusion had to slow down, American society made a most extraordinary and unexpected decision. Americans began to behave as if they preferred the extra baby to the extra unit of consumption.

During the war years the birth-rate rose from 18 per 1000 to about 22. This was judged at the time—and to a large degree it certainly was—a phenomenon of resumed full employment and early wartime marriages. In the post-war years, however, the level of births moved up and stayed at about 25 per 1000, yielding a rise in the population, as well as changes in the age-structure of the population and in the rate of family formation, of major economic significance. An official forecast of American population made in 1946 estimated that the American population would reach 165 million in 1990; that figure was, in fact, passed within a decade. At the moment American population is increasing at a rate of more than 1·5% *per annum*, and is predicted to be some 240 million by 1980.

* This transition poses, incidentally, an interesting problem for the United States; for it occurs at just the time when Western Europe, Japan, and—some distance behind—Russia, are entering a rapid growth stage in durable consumers' goods. Some important part of the American export advantage in recent times has been based on its pioneering status in these light-engineering commodities. Now they are being mass-produced efficiently in many countries, where lower wage-rates prevail. Is Detroit repeating a version of what British manufacturers of cotton goods and rail iron went through in the more distant past?

The American case

This reimposition of Malthusianism in American society, in all its consequences, combined with other circumstances—notably the cumulative deficit in social overhead capital and the cost of the arms race, if it should continue—are likely to make the next decade in American history one of vigorous expansion of output, touched at the level of private consumption by a degree of austerity.

To make this notion of strain on private consumption more concrete consider an estimate of the 'dependency ratio' recently calculated in a study of American population by Conrad and Irene Taeuber.* That ratio measures the relation between the working population and those outside the working-force age limits—in the United States those under 20 and over 65. It is calculated in the form of the number of dependent persons 100 members of the working force must support. Historically that ratio has been falling; that is, each member of the working force has had to support fewer and fewer persons outside. In 1915 it was 84; in 1935, as low as 74; but by 1955 it had risen back to 81; and on the basis of present population structure and birth-rates it will be of the order of 98 in 1975.

In short, by its own choice, American society as of 1959 is not quite as affluent as it looks. It is too soon for a four-day week and for tolerance of substantial levels of unemployment, if only the unemployment benefits are large enough—as Professor Galbraith has counselled. A society like the United States, structurally committed to a high-consumption way of life; committed also to maintain the decencies that go with adequate social overhead capital; committed by its own interests and the interests of those dependent upon it or allied to it to deal with a treacherous and extremely expensive world environment; committed additionally, out of its own internal dynamics, to a rapidly enlarging population and to a working force which must support more old and more young... such a society must use its resources fully, productively, and wisely. The problem of choice and allocation—the problem of scarcity—has not yet been lifted from it.

* C. Taeuber and I. B. Taeuber, *The Changing Population of the United States* (New York, 1958), p. 325.

The question now arises: why did not Western Europe, which had also attained maturity by the First World War, join the United States in the age of high mass-consumption in the 1920's? Or, put another way, what has been the sequence of choices made by Western Europe in its post-maturity phase, among the post-maturity alternatives?

Pre-1914

Before 1914, as the pressures to balance out and soften the harshness of an industrial society mounted, the societies of Western Europe moved more sharply towards the welfare state than the United States. This was probably because they were less agrarian in their political balance; but there were other elements as well, notably the greater weight of Socialist doctrines and ideals within the industrial working force and among intellectual leaders. The government was called upon to provide a higher proportion of total consumption than in the United States; and as the recent comparisons between the O.E.E.C. countries and the United States, directed by Milton Gilbert, indicate, Western Europe has continued down to 1955 to look to the State for a higher proportion of consumption (excluding defence) than the United States.* The rise of urban consumption in Western Europe was also, as in the United States, under severe restraint in the pre-1914 decade, due to the rise in the cost of living.† And, to a degree, such movements as Lloyd George's Liberal Reform are to be understood partially as a turning to politics to redress with ballots the unfair allocations of the market-place, much as the New Deal was the response of a society frustrated by severe and chronic unemployment.

The 1920's

What can we say about the 1920's in Western Europe?

In the immediate post-war years Western Europe faced, of course, more severe problems of reconstruction and more difficult problems of re-adjustment than the United States. Western Europe did not

* Milton Gilbert *et al.*, *Comparative National Products and Price Levels* (O.E.E.C., Paris, 1958), especially Table 28, p. 82.

† See, notably, A. R. Prest, *Consumers' Expenditure in the United Kingdom, 1900–1918* (Cambridge, 1954), pp. 5–10.

proceed straight away into the age of durable consumers' goods as did the United States.

Here the story of the European national economies differs a good deal. What we can say in general is that in the 1920's there were for most of Europe only about four years of relatively normal prosperity, 1925–9; and these only brought Western Europe back to something like—or slightly above—1913 levels of output. While American growth carried forward, lifted by the new phase of suburban housing, the automobile, and consumers' durables, Europe relatively fell behind in the 1920's. If the present analysis is correct, the reason was that European societies, in the widest sense, failed to move on to what is logically—in terms of the apparent income-elasticities of demand of a free economy—the normal stage-of-growth beyond maturity.

The 1930's

The story of the 1930's tends to confirm this hypothesis, to a degree. Leaving rearmament aside, it was housing and some acceleration in the automobile and durable consumers' sectors that helped create a degree of Western European prosperity in the 1930's. Or, put another way, when the policies of European governments began to create an environment of greater prosperity in the 1930's, income-elasticities of demand expressed themselves in a disproportionate rise in demand for durable consumers' goods and services—including housing.

Consider, for a moment, the relative production of motor vehicles, private and commercial, as they moved between 1929 and 1938 in Western Europe and the United States. Svennilson calculates that the four major European nations produced in 1929 702,000 private and commercial vehicles, whereas the United States produced 5·4 million in that year. After a decade of protracted depression in the United States and a considerably greater degree of European recovery, the figures for 1938 were quite different. For Europe 1·1 million; for the United States, 2·5 million. The gap was narrowed from a European figure 13% of the American in 1929 to a European figure 44% of the American on the eve of the Second World War.*

* Ingvar Svennilson, *Growth and Stagnation in the European Economy* (U.N., E.C.E., Geneva, 1954), pp. 144–52.

Diffusion of the private automobile

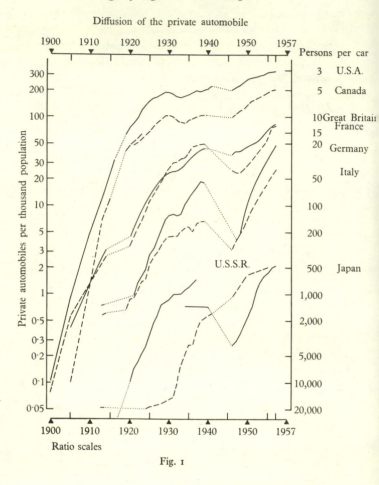

Fig. 1

Figs. 1, 2 and 3 suggest over a longer period the relative diffusion of the private automobile in the post-maturity societies.

A number of technical and geographic factors bear on Europe's relatively slower shift to the road: the vast capital needed for road-building; the monopolistic power of the railways and the governments behind them; the earlier start of the United States in the concept of the mass-produced car for a mass market; the greater distances in the United States and the greater availability of cheap suburban land for housing development. In the end it must be added, however, that American society, with its egalitarian bias, its traditional high wages and high workers' living standards, took

Diffusion of the private automobile

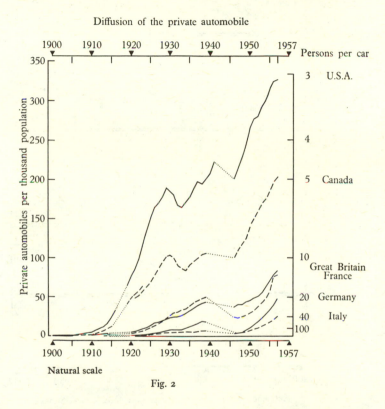

Fig. 2

more easily to the concept of high consumption on a mass basis than did the more hierarchical societies of Europe. It has taken the European worker a little while to accept the notion that the gadgets of the machine age, travel, and the other services a mature economy can afford are really for him and his family. And this fact helps, in part, to account for the relative stagnation of the European economy during the inter-war years.

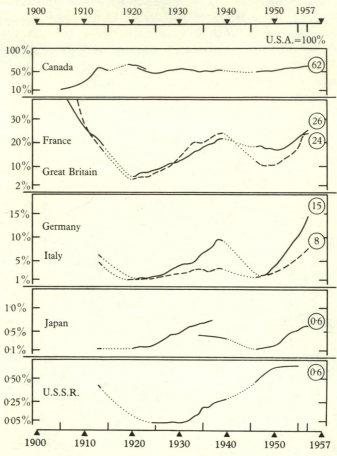

Automobiles per head in comparison with the United States
U.S.A.=100% throughout

Fig. 3

But, of course, another factor also helped determine the outcome. The great depression after 1929 broke the hold of a generation of political leaders in almost every mature society, whose outlook had been dominated by a desire to re-create a kind of pre-1914 normalcy. In the United States the depression led to an opposition coming to power which installed an American version of the welfare state. In Britain it led to a National and then to a Conservative Government that built prosperity of a sort on housing, devaluation, and Empire Preference; in France it led to a Popular Front Government. But in Germany and Japan, the break-down—economic, diplomatic, military and psychological—of the system implicit in the Versailles settlement led to regimes which opted for a quite different use of the potentialities of mature economies: military expansion. And once Hitler and the Japanese militarists were in power, the competitive arena of power imposed a quite different set of imperatives on all other societies. In the short run rearmament became a factor in the European recovery of the 1930's, diverting resources from the expansion of mass consumption; and in the not-so-long-run there was a major war.

Post-1945

In the post-war years, an interval of reconstruction followed. But this time Western Europe broke out into the phase of durable consumers' goods and services. As the United States was pushing the era of high consumption to a kind of logical conclusion, and beginning to alter its contours by opting for larger families, Western Europe and Japan began to diffuse to their populations, in different degree, the kinds of goods and services which a mature industrial system can supply. Between 1950 and 1955 the gap between American and Western European proportionate outlays in consumers' durables began to narrow; and the Gilbert study shows that in the post-war years the differences in outlay on consumption between the United States and Western Europe, and as among the Western European countries, can be almost wholly explained in terms of relative incomes and relative prices. The area to be explained by what economists call 'differences in taste' becomes remarkably narrow.

All the post-war mature societies of the West and Japan are behaving in a remarkably 'American' manner, except the Americans, with their curious new obsession with family life, privacy, do-it-yourself, getting away on trailers and in motor boats, writing impiously about the Organization Man.

The level of real income and consumption per head in Japan is, of course, lower than in most Western European countries. Nevertheless, the remarkable post-war rise in tertiary industry, and the evidences of a diffusion of consumers' goods and services on a new scale, even to the peasantry, suggest that, with appropriate modifications, the Japanese are also experiencing a typical post-maturity surge of growth based in good part on expanding levels of mass consumption.* Western Europe and Japan have then—in their own ways—entered whole-heartedly into the American 1920's: without, however, the peculiarly American aberration of Prohibition.

It is important to be clear that for Western Europe this shift of leading sectors to the areas of high mass-consumption is not a strictly post-war development. The Great West Road, the rise of Coventry, and the Morris works at Oxford are earlier phenomena; and the Volkswagen—as a conception—is a product of Hitler's Germany, and of pressures for a kind of consumption to which the German government of the late 1930's felt the need to respond, even if only by gesture. But it is only in the post-war years that the obstacles—technical, political, and sociological—were cleared away. There is no doubt that the momentum of the post-war economies of Western Europe is to be explained substantially by a widespread boom in consumers' goods and services: the acceptance and absorption of the age of high mass-consumption.

THE TERMS OF TRADE AFTER TWO WARS

But there is still a problem to be explained. In considering the United States in the 1930's you will recall the emphasis on the role of full employment as an initial force—almost a prior necessary condition—for getting the engine of diffusion under way. The dictum was, roughly, that for high consumption to serve as a leading sector, one had to attain full employment, so that pressure to expand investment in the consumption sectors would be felt.

Here one must explain how it came about that the societies of Western Europe had such difficulty attaining full employment after the First World War and why it was, relatively, so easy after the Second.

---

* See, notably, K. Ohkawa, *The Growth Rate of the Japanese Economy since 1878*, pp. 231–43.

With all due respect to the Keynesian Revolution, the sea-change in democratic politics with respect to full employment is not a sufficient explanation; for while the politicians would have been inexorably pressed to create conditions of full employment, if unemployment had proved to be the major post-1945 problem—that was not their situation down to 1956. Their dilemma has centred on inflation and on balance-of-payments difficulties. Their central problem has been how to mobilize sufficient resources for other essential purposes—military and foreign policy, exports and investment—in the face of a powerful drive to extend the area and scale of mass consumption.

In good part the reason for the outcome lies in a radical difference between the world after 1920 and that after 1945. In 1920 the prices of food-stuffs and raw materials broke sharply with respect to indus-trial products, making for extremely favourable terms of trade for the urban areas of the world, but weakening the rural demand for manufactured products. Thus the export markets of Europe suf-fered.* In Britain, and to a lesser degree elsewhere, the advantages of favourable terms of trade were largely dissipated in the inter-war years in the form of chronic unemployment in the export sectors and in those industries dependent upon them, such as coal. For a decade after the Second World War the situation was exactly reversed. The cities—and such nations as Britain—were hard-pressed by unfavourable terms of trade; but the demand for exports was high, full employment relatively easy to obtain. And if one adds to chronic full employment such structural changes as the stimulus of the Second World War to the light-engineering industries—which could be converted efficiently to many lines of consumers' durables and capital goods; the wartime determination of European populations to assert themselves politically and socially; the demonstration effect of American G.I.'s smoking cigars and distributing the largess of the P.X.'s to the local girls; you have the basis for the new era in Western European and Japanese economic, social, and political history, which we can now observe.

* Britain, and other large exporters to food-stuff- and raw material-producing areas, have experienced a mild version of the terms of trade dilemma in 1958-9. In the con-temporary world, however, the pressures to maintain the incomes of importers of manufactured goods—via capital exports—are vastly more powerful than in the 1920's.

BEYOND HIGH MASS-CONSUMPTION

Now, let us stand back a bit, and seek a wider perspective.

The argument of this book has been that, once man conceived of his physical environment as subject to knowable consistent laws, he began to manipulate it to his economic advantage; and once it was demonstrated that growth was possible, the consequences of growth and modernization, notably its military consequences, unhinged one traditional society after another, pushed it into the treacherous period of preconditions, from which many, but not all the world's societies have now emerged into self-sustained growth through the take-off mechanism described in chapter 4.

This revolutionary state of affairs did not decree a single pattern of evolution to which each society has conformed; but it did, at each stage, pose a similar set of choices for each society, framed by the problems and possibilities of the growth process itself.

In successive chapters we have looked at the problems, possibilities, and choices of the preconditions period, of the take-off, of maturity, and of the era of high mass-consumption.

The era of high mass-consumption has by no means come to an end, even in the United States; and it is still gathering momentum in many parts of Western Europe and in Japan as well. We can be sure that there will be variety in the patterns of consumption that will emerge as compound interest grinds on and the income-elasticities of demand, in their widest sense, reveal themselves in different societies. For example, there is no need for other societies to invest as much as the United States in the automobile; to set up the suburbs as far away from the centres of the cities; and to impose on themselves the kinds of problems the United States now faces with the reconstruction of the old city centres, the building of new continental and metropolitan road networks, and the provision of parking space. Indeed, there are grave geographic and physical limitations on other nations repeating this pattern, except, perhaps, Russia. We can be confident, however, that to the degree that consumer sovereignty is respected and real incomes increase we will see similar—but not identical—income-elasticities of demand and, therefore, similar patterns of structural evolution in different societies as they go through the high-consumption phase.

Now, leave aside the arms race and the threat of war, and consider this question: what lies beyond? What will happen to societies when income provides such good food for virtually all that it raises questions of public health by its very richness; where housing is of an order that people are not tempted to exert themselves much to improve it; where clothing is similarly adequate; where a Lambretta or Volkswagen is within the grasp of virtually all—if not necessarily a twin-tailed American monster? This stage has not yet been fully attained; but it has been attained by enough of the American and Northern European population to pose, as a serious and meaningful problem, the nature of the next stage.

After all, the life of most human beings since the beginning of time has been mainly taken up with gaining food, shelter and clothing for themselves and their families. What will happen when the Budden-brooks' dynamics moves another notch forward, and diminishing relative marginal utility sets in, on a mass basis, for real income itself?

Will man fall into secular spiritual stagnation, finding no worthy outlet for the expression of his energies, talents, and instinct to reach for immortality? Will he follow the Americans and reimpose the strenuous life by raising the birth-rate? Will the devil make work for idle hands? Will men learn how to conduct wars with just enough violence to be good sport—and to accelerate capital depreciation—without blowing up the planet? Will the exploration of outer space offer an adequately interesting and expensive outlet for resources and ambitions? Or will man, converted *en masse* into a suburban version of an eighteenth-century country gentleman, find in some mixture of the equivalent of hunting, shooting and fishing, the life of the mind and the spirit, and the minimum drama of carrying forward the human race, sufficient frontiers to keep for life its savour. (Parenthetically, we doubt that half the human race—that is to say, women—will recognize the reality of the problem; for the raising of children in a society where personal service is virtually gone is a quite ample human agenda, durable consumers' goods or no. The problem of boredom is a man's problem, at least until the children have grown up.)

Nevertheless this is a real enough question. Salvador de Madariaga has recently posed the question thus, in writing of the Scandinavian and Anglo-Saxon democracies.*

All these countries enjoy two advantages which give them a certain prestige: the standard of living of their populations is relatively high; and their political life is undisturbed by any serious incidents. Internal peace and prosperity are such obvious benefits that other peoples contemplating them might perhaps let themselves be carried away by envy and admiration, to the extent of not observing certain counter-balancing aspects of the lives of Anglo-Saxons and Scandinavians.

The most striking of these is without doubt boredom. Well governed and well administered people are bored to death.

We are not prepared to accept this judgment wholly; but still it poses the question: are poverty and civil strife a necessary condition for a lively human existence?

We shall return to this theme in the final chapter, in comparing Marx's nirvana of Communism with our own view of the long-run implications of compound interest. But we need not brood excessively over this matter. For the moment—for this generation and probably the next—there is a quite substantial pair of lions in the path. First, the existence of modern weapons of mass destruction which, if not tamed and controlled, could solve this and all other problems of the human race, once and for all. Second, the fact that the whole southern half of the globe plus China is caught up actively in the stage of preconditions for take-off or in the take-off itself. They have a reasonably long way to go; but their foreseeable maturity raises this question: shall we see, in a little while, a new sequence of political leaders enticed to aggression by their new-found technical maturity; or shall we see a global reconciliation of the human race. Between them these two problems—of the arms race and the new aspiring nations—problems closely related in the world of contemporary diplomacy—pose, for the technically more mature northern societies, a most searching agenda to which, despite the blandishments of durable consumers' goods and services and, even, larger families, we had better turn our minds if we are to have the chance to see whether secular spiritual stagnation—or boredom—can be conquered.

* S. de Madariaga, *Democracy versus Liberty?* (London, 1958), p. 17.

CHAPTER 7

RUSSIAN AND AMERICAN GROWTH

A REMARKABLE PARALLEL

Before turning, in chapters 8 and 9, to the relevance of the stages-of-growth to issues of war and peace, it may be useful to examine briefly a matter of both historical and contemporary interest: the nature and meaning of the relative paths of growth of Russia and the United States.

When we think journalistically of Russian economic development a number of images may come to mind: an image of a nation surging, under Communism, into a long-delayed status as an industrial power of the first order—symbolized by the Russian success in launching the first earth and solar satellites; an image of a pace of industrial growth unique in modern experience, held at forced draught by a system of state controls that constrains consumption, maintains unexampled rates of investment, and avoids lapses from full employment; an image of a planned economy so different in its method and institutions as to require forms of analysis different from those applicable in the West. In short, the conventional image is of a story apart.

There are, of course, profound special elements in the story of the evolution of modern Russian society and of its economy; and, before we finish, we shall try to identify the nature of its uniqueness. But the first point to grasp is that Russian economic development over the past century is remarkably similar to that of the United States, with a lag of about thirty-five years in the level of industrial output and a lag of about a half-century in *per capita* output in industry. Moreover, the Russian case, linking the Czarist and Communist experiences, falls, like the case of the United States, well within the broad framework of the stages-of-growth analysis.

Now, first, consider Figure 4, reproduced from the work of G. Warren Nutter, showing industrial production per head of population for Russia from 1880 to 1955 and for the United States from

1870 to 1955.* Note, particularly, that Nutter's chart converts industrial output per head into an index, with 1913 equal to 100. It shows, therefore, comparative rates of growth in output per head, not absolute figures; and it should be read with an awareness that the median lag in 1955, for the thirty-seven industries involved, is fifty-six years of growth: in short the whole Soviet curve is set below the American by an amount that does not vary greatly, in terms of time-lag.

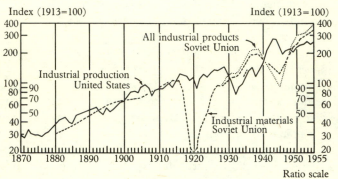

Fig. 4

What emerges is that, between the 1880's and the First World War, Russia, relatively, came forward during its take-off; it fell behind, in the 1920's, when the United States enjoyed a boom, and Russia reorganized slowly after war and revolution; it came forward relatively during the first Five Year Plans of the 1930's, when the United States was gripped in a slump; and in its post-1945 phase Russia again came forward relatively, at a time when Russian output was more heavily concentrated in industry and American

* G. Warren Nutter, 'Soviet Economic Developments: Some Observations on Soviet Industrial Growth', *The American Economic Review*, May 1957. See also 'Measuring Production in the U.S.S.R.: Industrial Growth in the Soviet Union', *A.E.R.*, May 1958. A similar analysis of Russian and American economic growth, yielding similar conclusions, is that of Oscar Honkalehto, *Some Sectoral Growth Patterns in Russian Economic Development*, a thesis submitted for the degree of Master of Science, M.I.T., Cambridge, Mass., February 1955. It is evident that Nutter's more massive statistical investigations are wholly independent of Honkalehto's more limited pioneer effort. See also Gregory Grossman, 'Thirty Years of Soviet Industrialization', *Soviet Survey*, No. 26 (October–December 1958).

output was shifting structurally to housing and non-manufactured services.

Now consider the Tables, based on absolute levels of output (5) and output *per capita* (6). Broadly speaking, the relative position, in terms of years of lag, remains in 1955 surprisingly what it was in 1913. The lags are, of course, not uniform: in output they are under twenty years in iron ore, chemical fertilizers and dyes; well over fifty years in certain consumers' goods: soap, for example, woollens, and beer. But if one takes the growth sequence as the basis for comparison, rather than other possible criteria, Nutter is correct in his four conclusions:

Soviet industry seems still to be roughly three and a half decades behind the United States in levels of output and about five and a half decades in levels of *per capita* output....Second,...the development of Soviet industry is roughly equivalent to what took place (in the United States) in the four decades bracketing the turn of the century—in *per capita* terms, to an even earlier period ending around the turn of the century. Third, over the Soviet era as a whole, Soviet industries have generally lost historical ground to their American counterparts—the lags have generally increased—in terms of both total and *per capita* output....Fourth, while Soviet industries have tended in recent years to gain ground in terms of total output, they have continued to lose ground in terms of *per capita* output.

All of this is, in a sense, a statistical way of stating that the Russian take-off was under way by the 1890's, whereas the American take-off was completed by 1860. After take-off both societies suffered severe vicissitudes: the United States in the Civil War and the protracted depression of the 1930's, Russia in two World Wars which brought devastation from which the United States was spared. But the progress of industry, after take-off, was remarkably similar in the two cases, in terms of output; and in terms of productivity per man, the initial American population-resource balance advantage was, down to 1955, roughly maintained. And the similarities include the fact that the Russian take-off was also a railway take-off, bringing to life new modern coal, iron, and heavy-engineering industries; and these railway take-offs were also each followed by a stage dominated by the spread of technology to steel fabrication, chemicals and electricity.

TABLE 5. *Lag of the Soviet Union behind the United States in output, bench mark dates, 37 industries*

	Lag (number of years)			Increase (+) or decrease (−) in lag		
	1913	1937	1955	1913–37	1937–55	1913–55
Iron ore	28	36	15	8	−21	−13
Pig-iron	30	36	39	6	3	9
Steel ingots	21	32	29	11	−3	8
Rolled steel	27	35	29	8	−6	2
Primary blister copper	33	50	51	17	1	18
Lead	94	60	52	−34	−8	−42
Zinc	46	43	46	−3	3	0
Electric power	13	21	16	8	−5	3
Coal	45	49	47	4	−2	2
Coke	31	36	30	5	−6	−1
Crude petroleum	14	26	34	12	8	20
Natural gas	32	51	52	19	1	20
Soda ash	22	31	24	9	−7	2
Mineral fertilizer	43+	27	14	−16+	−13	−29+
Synthetic dyes	2	15	12	13	−3	10
Caustic soda	17	25	24	8	−1	7
Paper	44	46	54	2	8	10
Sawn wood	61	73	62	12	−11	1
Cement	19	33	32	14	−1	13
Window glass	13	0	*	−13	—	−13+
Rails	42	57	54	15	−3	12
Railroad passenger cars	21	46	53	25	7	32
Railroad freight cars	33	51	69	18	18	36
Butter	21	38	35	17	−3	14
Vegetable oils	5	26	29	21	3	24
Sausages	24+	36	38	—	2	—
Fish catch	−11	4	*	15	−4+	—
Soap	34+	52	52	—	0	—
Sugar	6	17	27	11	10	21
Canned food	43+	45	45	—	0	—
Beer	42	66	73	24	7	31
Cigarettes	−1	11	14	12	3	15
Boots and shoes	23+	44	44	—	0	—
Rubber footwear	14+	19	*	—	−19+	−14+
Cotton fabrics	28	44	48	16	4	20
Silk and synthetic fabrics	23	44	25	21	−19	2
Woollen and worsted fabrics	43+	67+	69	—	—	—
Median	28	36	35	11	−1	9

Note: A Soviet lead is indicated by a negative sign in the first three columns. Where U.S. data do not go back far enough to give the full lag, the calculable lag is followed by a plus sign. Dash (−) indicates insufficient data. Asterisk (*) indicates Soviet output exceeds U.S. output up to present.

From: G. Warren Nutter

TABLE 6. *Lag of the Soviet Union behind the United States in* per capita *output, bench mark dates, 37 industries*

	Lag (number of years)			Increase or decrease (−) in lag		
	1913	1937	1955	1913–37	1937–55	1913–55
Iron ore	53 +	52	54	—	2	—
Pig-iron	48	52	56	4	4	8
Steel ingots	30	40	49	10	9	19
Rolled steel	24 +	48 +	52	—	—	—
Primary blister copper	53	58	66	5	8	13
Lead	105 +	109	76	—	− 33	− 29 +
Zinc	53	57	59	4	2	6
Electric power	14	26	25	12	− 1	11
Coal	66	69	69	3	0	3
Coke	33 +	49	56	—	7	—
Crude petroleum	27	34	41	7	7	14
Natural gas	32 +	52	70	—	18	—
Soda ash	27	43	45	16	2	18
Mineral fertilizer	43 +	40	30	− 3 +	− 10	− 13 +
Synthetic dyes	14 +	20	22	—	2	—
Caustic soda	19	40	35	21	− 5	16
Paper	54 +	67	71	—	4	—
Sawn wood	114 +	102	111	− 12 +	9	− 3 +
Cement	30	38	47	8	9	17
Window glass	34 +	− 2	15	− 36 +	17	− 19 +
Rails	46 +	70	85	—	15	—
Railroad passenger cars	27	57	69	30	12	42
Railroad freight cars	33 +	57 +	75 +	—	—	—
Butter	30	50	58	20	8	28
Vegetable oils	16	40	44	24	4	28
Sausages	24 +	48 +	61	—	—	—
Fish catch	33 +	57 +	19	—	− 38 +	− 14 +
Soap	34 +	58 +	76 +	—	—	—
Sugar	12	32	47	20	15	35
Canned food	43 +	62	60	—	− 2	—
Beer	43 +	67 +	85 +	—	—	—
Cigarettes	0	15	19	15	4	19
Boots and shoes	23 +	47 +	65 +	—	—	—
Rubber footwear	14 +	38 +	56 +	—	—	—
Cotton fabrics	43 +	67 +	85 +	—	—	—
Silk and synthetic fabrics	34	58	42	24	− 16	8
Woollen and worsted fabrics	43 +	67 +	85 +	—	—	—
Median	—	—	56	10	4	13

Note: See Table 5.

From: G. Warren Nutter

Having established this rough but important framework of uniformity of experience now let us catalogue some of the major differences between Russia and the United States.

First, the creation of the preconditions for take-off was, in its non-economic dimensions, a quite different process in Russia. Russia was deeply enmeshed in its own version of a traditional society, with well-installed institutions of Church and State as well as intractable problems of land tenure, an illiterate serfdom, over-population on the land, the lack of a free-wheeling commercial middle class, a culture which initially placed a low premium on modern productive economic activity. The United States, again to use Hartz' phrase, was 'born free'—with vigorous, independent land-owning farmers, and an ample supply of enterprising men of commerce, as well as a social and political system that took easily to industrialization, outside the South. Thus, whereas Russia had to overcome a traditional society, the United States had only to overcome the high attractions of continuing to be a supplier of food-stuffs and raw materials—as well, if you like, as the damper of a milder colonialism.

Second, throughout this sequence, American consumption per head, at each stage of growth, was higher than in Russia. We have, as in other cases, a high degree of uniformity in the timing of the spread of technology, taking place within a considerable spread in income and consumption *per capita*. Basically, this is a matter of population-resource balances; but the tendency was reinforced in both Czarist and Soviet Russia by constraints imposed by the State on the level of mass consumption.

Third, the drive to maturity took place in the United States, after the Civil War, in a setting of relative political freedom—outside the South—in a society tightly linked to the international economy, at a time of peace, and, generally, with rising standards of consumption per head. In Russia it occurred in the three decades after 1928, in a virtually closed economy, against a background of war and preparations for war, which did not slow the spread of technology, but which did limit the rise of consumption; and it occurred with something over 10 million members of the working force regularly in forced labour down to very recent years.

Fourth, the Soviet drive to maturity took place not only with constraints on consumption in general but severe restraints in two major sectors of the economy, not fully represented in these industrial production indexes: agriculture and housing. In housing the Soviet Union lived substantially off the Czarist capital stock down to recent years, minimizing housing outlays, letting space per family shrink; in agriculture it invested heavily, but within a framework of collectivization that kept productivity pathologically low, once Lenin's 'New Economic Policy' was abandoned in 1929. In addition, Russia has invested very little indeed in a modern road-system, which has drawn so much American capital.

Thus, the equality in historical pace between Soviet and American industrialization has been achieved by a radically higher proportion of Soviet investment in the heavy and metal-working industries than in the United States, imparting a major statistical advantage to Russia in comparison of indexes of industrial growth. And this difference in the pattern of investment was reinforced by the following two further quite real technical factors enjoyed by any late-comer: the ratio of net to gross investment during the industrialization drive was higher in Russia than in the United States; and the pool of unapplied technological possibilities was greater than in the United States.* Both of these latter advantages are, essentially, transient; that is, as Russia has come to maturity, it must allocate increased relative proportions of its resources to meet depreciation; and, as it catches up with modern technology over the full range of its resources, it can enjoy, like the United States and the other mature economies, only the annual increment to technology, as it were, rather than a large unapplied back-log.

But one apparent advantage remains to the Soviet Union in the statistics of the growth race, and this we had better examine a little further; that is, the concentration of its investment in heavy industry related to military potential, as opposed to the American diffusion of investment over heavy and light industry, consumers' goods and

* See, especially, Norman M. Kaplan, 'Capital Formation and Allocation', in A. Bergson (ed.), *Soviet Economic Growth* (Evanston and N.Y., 1953).

services. It is essentially this difference in the pattern of the outlays above the level of consumption which defines technically the major differences between the Soviet and American economies and which poses, in a sense, the question of whether future Soviet economic growth is a danger to the Western world.

To approach this question rationally it is necessary to separate sharply two questions: the question of military outlays; and the question of the Soviet rate and pattern of economic growth.

THE MILITARY QUESTION

First the military question. In recent years the Soviet Union has been allocating about 20% of GNP to military purposes. The most recent Soviet budget figures suggest some decline in the proportion, but not in the absolute level of allocation to military purposes. The United States has been allocating about 10% of GNP to military purposes. Correcting for relative levels of GNP and relative prices it is probably true that in real terms the total Soviet military effort is about equivalent to the American. It is, however, quite different in composition. Russia has plunged somewhat ahead in medium- and long-range ballistic missiles and is in a stage of production rather than research and development which uses up, almost certainly, a higher proportion of its budget; and Russia has maintained a large army. The United States has, on the other hand, larger naval and air-force allocations.

The nature of the Soviet military threat lies, then, not in the scale of its military outlays relative to the United States but in whether its particular military dispositions are likely to yield one of the two following situations: first, a lead in missiles sufficiently great to take out Western retaliatory power at a blow. If this result were to be achieved, it would derive not from the scale of the Soviet effort, but from a forehanded superior concentration of its best scientific talents on a new weapons system: just as the Battle of France was lost in 1940 not because of the scale of the German effort relative to that of France and Britain but because the blitz-krieg technique was built on mobile tank warfare backed by the dive-bomber. The second danger is that Russia will find a situation where it can effectively counter the American air and naval strength with its missile threat and bring to bear its superior ground forces in a successful limited war in some important area.

There is also a third danger, of a mixed military and diplomatic character; namely, that in a test of will Moscow will succeed in forcing a Western diplomatic retreat, in a specific area, due to fear that holding fast will risk major war.

It happens to be the author's view that American military efforts should be larger than they now are; but the danger lies not in the relative scale of Soviet versus American and Western military out-lays; nor does it lie in some generalized Soviet superiority in growth-rate of GNP; the danger lies in the composition of the Soviet military effort relative to that of its potential opponents, and in the ways the Soviet leadership might contrive to bring it to bear.

This general point can be made more concrete by an illustration. After the first Soviet sputnik was launched there was some quite widespread soul-searching in the United States on whether that country was producing too few engineers and scientists. In some quarters the argument assumed the form of a kind of numbers racket in which charts were drawn up of the output of engineers in both countries, with the curves ominously crossing. This approach missed the point. The point is that Russia has concentrated a much higher proportion of its existing engineers and, especially, its first-class break-through scientists in military affairs; and it concentrated them to a much higher degree on the missiles problem. It is in allocation rather than in number that Russia has moved forward—in missiles, and in military power generally.* It has created first-class military status from an economic base which, in scale and productivity, is some distance behind that of the United States, grossly behind that of the United States and Western Europe combined. In this sense, it has repeated what Germany and Japan did in the 1930's. We would not, for one moment, deprecate the meaning or the threat of this Russian performance. But this selective and purposeful performance should not be confused with the question of growth-rates and their meaning.

* This argument would not, of course, imply that the size of the total pool of scientists and engineers is irrelevant to a society's military capabilities. For example, Russia and the United States with their 'large battalions' can explore simultaneously a number of possible solutions to bottleneck problems; whereas Britain and France, for example, must gamble on a prima facie choice among possible solutions.

THE ECONOMIC QUESTION

That leaves us with the second question: the danger—or, better, the meaning—of the current higher rate of increase in Soviet GNP. Are we to quaver because in Russia GNP moves forward now at something just under 6%; whereas it has averaged only 3 or 4% in the post-1945 United States? Although, of course, the Western world would lose power and influence in many directions if its output should continue to stagnate, there is no cause for panic in the light of aggregative Soviet statistics. Why not? Will not the curves soon cross? Will not Russia soon achieve world economic primacy in some meaningful sense?

First, it is necessary to beware of linear projections. A variety of forces at work in Russia, already evident in her projected figures for expansion, are making for deceleration. The *E.C.E. Survey of Europe in 1957* (published in 1958) presented, for example, the official projected rates of growth in key sectors of Russian industry shown in Table 7.*

TABLE 7. *Rates of growth in Russian industry* (%)

Annual average rate of increase	Coal	Oil	Pig-iron	Steel	Electric power	Cement
1955–60	8·6	13·6	10·0	8·5	13·5	19·5
1957–72	2·8	9·4	5·3	5·3	9·7	8·6

There is little doubt, for example, that the absolute figures of Soviet steel output will approach the level of those in the United States. As Nutter has said: 'each son will ultimately catch up to his father in height, and brothers of different age will differ less and less in height as they get older'. But retardation in growth-rate is already under way in many Soviet sectors; and while the absolute figures of the two nations will get closer, and, in time, the historic productivity lags should also diminish...what of it? Why should Russia not have an industrial establishment equal to or even greater than the United States, if its population and population-resource balances permit?

---

* These longer-term figures are not markedly inconsistent with the 1965 goals presented by Khrushchev to the 21st Congress of the Soviet Communist Party in January 1959.

Second, if the West copes with the military and foreign policy menace represented by the ambitions and dilemmas of Russia—along some such lines as are suggested in chapter 9—then the composition of Russian output is of little concern to us.

Moreover, the composition of Russian output must certainly change. The present higher Soviet rate of increase in GNP is the product substantially of a peculiar concentration of investment in certain sectors. If steel is not to be used for military purposes, what will it be used for? An enormous heavy industry, growing at high rates, is not a goal in itself; nor is it an intrinsic international advantage. This is gradually being reflected in Soviet allocations: in agriculture, for example, where the pressure to increase the supply of higher grade food is a major domestic goal; to a degree in housing; to a degree in other forms of consumers' goods—for example, television. Slowly, ever so slowly, the creep of washing machines, refrigerators, motor-cycles, bicycles, and even automobiles has begun—and the first Russian satellite town is under construction.* As these pressures grow, and the structure of the Soviet economy moves closer to that of the high-consumption economies of the West, we can expect the growth-rates to become more alike, as well. But the fundamental point is this: we should not be taken in by the fallacy of misplaced concreteness. An economy is an instrument for a larger purpose. When that economy is turned to purposes which endanger us—as in the Soviet pattern and scale of military outlays—we must respond by making aggression steadily unattractive. Otherwise, the test of our own economies—and of the non-Communist world as a whole—lies not in the Soviet economic performance, but in our ability to fulfil the ambitions of our own peoples.

THE LOCUS OF THE CHALLENGE

Here is the rub and the challenge. Commenting on Nutter's exposition late in 1957 Hans Heymann, Jr, said: ' ...the reduction in Soviet growth that is likely to have occurred would hardly appear to be a cause of jubilation on our part, particularly when viewed against the background of the trend in U.S. manufacturing output,

* See, notably, *Economic Survey of Europe in 1957* (E.C.E., Geneva, 1958), chapter 1, pp. 14 and 22.

which has grown not at all over the last two years.'* If American and Western output stagnates, we shall not be able to mount adequate programmes of military defence or of assistance to under-developed areas; and we shall not be able to meet the pressures for increased private consumption and social overhead capital arising from our enlarging populations. It is evident, for example, that democratic societies must learn to solve the problem of inflation by means other than constraint on the level of employment and output. While the American and Western European rates of growth, in themselves, are not the key question, it is only against the back-ground of adequate rates of increase in both output and productivity that the democratic process is likely to yield a composition of output which will both protect our societies and maintain their inner quality.

The lesson of all this is, then, that there is nothing mysterious about the evolution of modern Russia. It is a great nation, well endowed by nature and history to create a modern economy and a modern society. In the course of its take-off it was struck by a major war, in which the precarious and changing balance between traditional and democratic political elements collapsed in the face of defeat and disorder; and a particular form of modern societal organization took over control of a revolutionary situation it did not create. Its domestic imperatives and external ambitions have produced a version of the common growth experience, abnormally centred in heavy industry and military potential. Its political leadership is now trying to exploit the margins of resources opened up by arrival at maturity to seek a radical expansion of Soviet power on the world scene, by damping the rate of expansion of consumption. But neither in scale, nor in allocation, nor in momentum do Russian dispositions present a menace beyond American and Western resources to deal with; nor, peering farther ahead, are there reasons to believe the Russian experience will transcend familiar limits.

The problem posed by contemporary Russia lies not in the unique-ness of its story of modernization, but in whether the United States and the West can mobilize their ample resources to do the jobs that

* *American Economic Review, Papers and Proceedings,* May 1958, p. 424.

must be done—resources of spirit, intellect, will and insight quite as much as steel and electronic gadgets; and jobs which extend not only to missile arsenals and the further diffusion of welfare at home, but to the Indian second and third Five Year Plans and the far reaches of Asia, the Middle East, Africa, and Latin America.

The problem lies not in the mysterious East, but in the inscrutable West.

CHAPTER 8

RELATIVE STAGES-OF-GROWTH AND AGGRESSION*

WAR IN MODERN HISTORY

In this chapter we turn to the problem of war. Indeed, it cannot be evaded in a system of thought designed to make some kind of order of the transition from traditional to modern societies. For the progression we have considered thus far—from traditional societies to societies of high mass-consumption—has, as a matter of simple historical fact, been shot through with violence organized on a national basis. Men and the societies they have constructed have not climbed smoothly up the stages-of-growth, once the world of modern science was understood and began to be applied. They did not create, unfold and diffuse the layers of technology and let consumers' sovereignty and its income- and price-elasticities of demand determine the contours of growth. War has drawn resources, shattered or altered societies, and changed the options open to men and to the societies of which they were a part.

Quite aside from the brute historical fact of armed conflict there are three quite particular reasons why this book must deal with the problem of war.

First, the theory of the preconditions period—of the undoing of the traditional society and its supplanting with one form or another of modern society—hinges substantially on the demonstration effect of the relation between modernization and military power.

Second, if this system is to challenge and supplant Marxism as a way of looking at modern history it must answer, in its own way, the question posed under the rubric of 'imperialism' by the Marxist analysis, as elaborated by Marx's successors.

And finally, if this system is to provide a useful partial perspective on the times in which we live, it must throw some light on the nature

* For an interesting and fresh analysis of the causes of war, different from this in structure but similar in spirit, see Raymond Aron, *War and Industrial Society*, London, Oxford University Press, 1958.

of our dangers, in a time of precarious nuclear stalemate; and it should help in some small way to suggest how the lions which stand in our path—that is, the arms race and the organization of a world containing many new mature nations—can be removed or safely by-passed.

THE PROBLEM OF NATIONAL SOVEREIGNTY

We start with a fact given from outside this analysis. The fact is that the whole transition we are examining took place historically within a system of nation states and of national sovereignty. National sovereignty means that nations retain the ultimate right—a right sanctioned by law, custom, and what decent men judge to be legitimacy—the right to kill people of other nations in defence or pursuit of what they judge to be their national interest. The concepts of nationhood, of national sovereignty, and of the legitimacy of war as a reserved instrument of national policy are inherited, then, from the world of traditional societies; they antedate the sequence of post-traditional stages we are examining in this book. They are not to be explained by the processes set in motion by the transformation of traditional to modern societies; nor are they to be explained by special features or compulsions of any particular stage-of-growth.

Nevertheless, the wars fought by nations since the process of modernization got under way have certain distinctive characteristics. And while the fact of war is not to be explained with reference to the stages-of-growth, the character of wars can be usefully related to these stages.

THREE KINDS OF WARS

Specifically, it is possible to distinguish rather sharply three kinds of wars which have been fought in, say, the past three centuries, since Western Europe began to develop endogenously the pre-conditions for take-off.

First, colonial wars. Here we bring together the conflicts arising from the initial intrusion of a colonial power on a traditional society; from the effort to transfer power from one colonial power to another; and conflicts arising from the effort of colonial peoples to assert their independence of the metropolitan power.

A second kind of war can be defined as regional aggression. This type of limited war arose from the dilemmas and the exuberance of newly formed national states, as they looked backward to past humiliation and forward to new opportunity, while confronting the choices open to them in the early stages of modernization.

Finally, there have been the massive wars of this century centred on the struggles to achieve—or to prevent others from achieving—a definitive grasp on the Eurasian balance of power: a grasp that was tantamount, in the first half of the twentieth century, to world power.

We shall now consider separately each of these types of military conflict as they relate to the stages-of-growth. Again, it should be borne in mind that what we have to say cannot be a full explanation of war; for the hypothesis is that war, ultimately, arises from the existence and acceptance of the concept of national sovereignty; and the nature and origins of nationalism lie outside this way of looking at things. We shall consider merely how certain types of wars can be related to the relative stages-of-growth among sovereign nations, as they pursued what they conceived to be their interests in the highly competitive, but also highly oligopolistic circumstances in which they have found themselves.

COLONIALISM

We turn first, then, to conflicts arising from colonialism. Colonialism arose, in part, of course, because from the fifteenth century on, a world arena of power existed in which the European nation states competed in various overseas areas for trade; for bases of military advantage; and for what was then military potential: that is, for bullion, naval stores, and the like. As Charles Wilson points out, in his essay on *Mercantilism*, Josiah Child counselled that 'Profit and Power ought', in such circumstances, 'jointly to be considered'.

The element of power, however, was initially often remote and derivative so far as the day-to-day business of the then major powers was concerned. The proximate goal—for example, in the famous Anglo-Dutch competition of the seventeenth century—was trade; and, especially, it was that form of trade which was highly regarded by the major nations of the seventeenth and eighteenth centuries:

that is, trade which permitted the import of bullion and raw materials and a favourable balance of exports—if possible, the export of manufactures. The favourable trade balances such commerce was designed to foster did relate, in contemporary thought, to relative national power; but the operating goal was trade.

Why, then, was not trade conducted without the creation of colonies? The answer to this fundamental question has two elements that need to be sharply distinguished; although they tend to get intermixed in the flow of history.

First, the struggle for trade took place in a framework where the major powers were postured, by the nature of history, as competitors. It is no accident that the major wars of the eighteenth century were wars of succession. The nations were caught up, by historical inheritance, so to speak, in an inherently competitive system of power—not, in the first instance, economic power, but military and political power. And in part the wars in the colonies derived from those larger competitive compulsions: the compulsion not merely to advance a national interest positively, but to advance a national interest negatively by denying a source of power to another nation. The creation of a trade monopoly in a colonial area was one way to do this, once the new areas were discovered or old areas rediscovered.

But there was a second reason, as well, for the application of military power in the colonies; and this second reason relates not to the power structure of Europe, but to the societal condition of the colonial areas themselves. Colonies were often established initially not to execute a major objective of national policy, nor even to exclude a rival economic power, but to fill a vacuum; that is, to organize a traditional society incapable of self-organization (or unwilling to organize itself) for modern import and export activity, including production for export. Normal trade between equals would often have fulfilled the initial motivation of the intruding power, and a large part of its continuing motivation; for the traditional society had nothing but raw materials to export. And normal trade would have been in many cases tidier, more rational, and even, less costly. In the four centuries preceding 1900, however, the native societies of America, Asia, Africa, and the Middle East were, at various stages, structured and motivated neither to do business with Western Europe nor to protect themselves against Western European arms; and so they were taken over and organized.

Colonies were founded, then, not mainly as a purposeful goal of national policy in pursuit of power, but for two more oblique reasons. First, as a reflex of the power struggle built into the European arena. Second, colonies were founded because of the following sequence: because some economic group wanted to expand its purchases or sales; it encountered difficulty in arranging the conditions for efficient business; it encountered also gross military weakness; and it persuaded a government which looked kindly on its efforts to take responsibility for organizing a suitable political framework to ensure, at little cost, the benefits of expanded trade.

Once colonial responsibility was accepted by the nation concerned, however, the whole affair was transformed. It moved from the essentially peaceful terrain of business to the area of national prestige and power where more primitive and general national interests and motives held sway.

Two specific consequences flowed from this transfer from the world of book-keeping to that of the flag. First, certain non-colonial powers came, as a matter of prestige and style, to desire colonial possessions as a symbol of their coming of age. For example, nothing in the capital markets of the Atlantic world or in their trading patterns justified much ado about colonies, on strictly economic grounds, from, say, 1873 to 1914.* A little more could be said for certain colonial positions on military or strategic grounds in the nineteenth century. But the competition for colonies was conducted for reasons that were unilaterally rational on neither economic nor military grounds: the competition occurred essentially because com-

---

* There was, incidentally, a somewhat more rational economic case for colonies in the seventeenth and eighteenth centuries, before the industrial revolution took hold in Europe, than in the late nineteenth century. Before the industrial revolution the total supply of food-stuffs and raw materials (or the total supply of colonies) could be regarded, in a sense, as fixed and finite; that is, what one nation had was intrinsically a denial to others. Once the flow of modern technology was under way, under nineteenth-century conditions, where supplies could be drawn in trade with sovereign nations (for example, the United States), the possibility existed of using applied technology to substitute for imports (for example, chemical fertilizers), or to generate exports which would permit their economical acquisition from accessible foreign markets.

petitive nationalism was the rule of the world arena and colonies were an accepted symbol of status and power within that arena.

As the United States discovered, for example, when it found itself to its surprise and discomfiture owning the Philippines after the Spanish–American War, there was no way of relinquishing a colony which had not modernized its society, without turning it over to another colonial power. The colonial game had thus become a reflex not of economic imperatives, but of inherently competitive sovereignties. This kind of mixture of profit and power—which Josiah Child probably had in mind—holds for the pre-1914 imperialist competition, as well as for that of the seventeenth and eighteenth centuries.

But there was a second kind of mix-up of profit and power which Child may not have perceived, because it was only to become fully apparent in later times. The second consequence of shifting colonies from a limited economic to major symbolic status, in an oligopolistic arena of power, was that withdrawal from a colony became a matter of national prestige, and thus extremely difficult. Almost without exception colonial positions were acquired at relatively little cost, at the behest of limited interests which might not have commanded national support if much blood and treasure had been initially required for the enterprise. Even when wars were fought to transfer the control of sovereignty over colonies they were generally limited wars. But the exit from imperial status, with a few exceptions, took the form of bitter, bloody war, or it was accompanied by major political and diplomatic crises at home. The experience of colonial administration created not merely ties of economic advantage but human memories of cumulative effort, and achievement and status— as well as of national power and prestige—extraordinarily difficult to sever: as Britain, France, and the Netherlands have all found since 1945.

So far as colonial wars are concerned, then, the stages-of-growth offer only a partial and limited insight. On the one hand they were partially a reflex of competitive nationalism which led nations to take the plunge into colonies as part of dynastic or other power competition; and this link of colonialism to non-economic dimensions of nationalism helps explain the psychological pain of withdrawal.

In part, however, it was of the nature of the initial relation between a traditional and a more advanced society that the doing of efficient business required a type of administration the traditional society could not supply. But once the commitment to administer was made, a host of non-economic motives became mixed up in the affair which, again, made withdrawal difficult.

The ability of the colonial peoples to force withdrawal is, however, more directly related to the stages-of-growth. As pointed out in chapter 3, although imperial powers usually set up administrations and pursued policies which did not optimize the creation of the preconditions for take-off, they could not avoid bringing about transformations in thought, knowledge, and institutions—as well as in trade and in the supply of social overhead capital—which moved the colonial society along the path towards take-off; and the colonial powers often included modernization of a sort as one object of colonial policy. By positive and negative demonstration effects a version of the preconditions period was thus set in motion. Above all a concept of nationalism, transcending the old ties to clan or region, inevitably crystallized around an accumulating resentment of colonial rule.

In the end, out of these semi-modernized settings, local coalitions emerged which generated political and, in some cases, military pressure capable of forcing withdrawal. The wars of independence which dot colonial history, from 1776 in America to 1959 in Algeria, are thus, to a degree, related to the stages-of-growth. Specifically, they are related to the dynamics of the preconditions period.

REGIONAL AGGRESSION

And it is directly from the dynamics of the preconditions period that a second type of war has arisen: regional aggression. For the coalitions and policies appropriate for achieving independence rarely suit the subsequent needs for completing the preconditions and launching the take-off. It is out of the dilemmas and opportunities of men, risen to power on the banners of independence, trained as politicians or soldiers, but now facing responsibility for a turbulent transitional society, that this second kind of war has tended to occur.

Recall again, one of the central themes of chapter 3. It is argued there that a reactive nationalism was likely to be an initial unifying element, making for a purposeful effort to supplant the traditional society, binding up quite disparate elements into an *ad hoc* coalition. Once the new coalition had attained power against the older traditional groups, the colonial power, or both, it faced a choice among three lines of policy; or, more accurately, a problem of striking a balance among them. Specifically, the new leaders faced this question: should nationalism be turned to assert power and dignity on the world scene; should an effort be made to consolidate the power of the central government over the residual traditional forces in the regions; or should economic and social modernization be the primary objective? From late eighteenth-century America to the contemporary scene in Asia, the Middle East, and Africa the universality of this problem of choice and balance among the three possible directions of nationalist endeavour can be established.

Historically, it has proved extremely tempting for a part of the new nationalism to be diverted on to external objectives, notably if these objectives looked to be accessible at little real cost or risk. These early aggressive exercises were generally limited in objective, aimed at territories close to the new nation's own borders—within its region—rather than directly at the balance of Eurasian power: thus, the American effort to steal Canada during the French wars; Bismarck's neat military operations against Denmark, Austria, and France from 1864 to 1871; the Japanese acquisition of primacy in Korea in 1895; and the Russian drive through Manchuria to Vladivostok, leading to the test of strength with resurgent Japan in 1904–5. And, from this perspective, the wars of the French Revolution became the greatest of all examples of regional aggression, arising from an unresolved transitional process, during the preconditions period.

These adventures in regional aggression often have substantial political support, in part because an ebullient nationalism is widespread, irrespective of economic or social interests; in part because special interests believe they will directly benefit from the new territorial acquisitions. But, above all, such regional aggression, based on a 'bloody shirt' politics which recalls past humiliation, can help maintain cohesion in a society where the concrete tasks of modernization raise difficult and schismatic domestic issues, which the leader of the coalition would seek to evade if possible. The gropings for a unifying national policy of, say, Nasser and Sukarno in the period 1955–8, represent a version of an old problem and a familiar response. The battle-cries centred on West Irian, Kashmir, Israel, and the tendency of bedevilled politicians in transitional societies to cling to the anti-colonial banner should be no surprise. And we should be in reasonably good heart about this phase. For these early, limited external adventures, associated with late pre-conditions or early take-off periods, appear generally to have given way to a phase of absorption in the adventure of modernizing the economy and the society as a whole. Post-civil-war America, post-1873 Germany, post-1905 Japan, even post-1920 Russia were, for several decades at least, so absorbed at home with the extension of modern technique that they did not assert themselves dangerously on the world scene. Historically the next dangerous age comes with the approach of economic maturity, when one of the options open is to concentrate the resources of the mature economy on a more ambitious expansion of external power.

STRUGGLES FOR THE EURASIAN POWER BALANCE

The differential timing of the approach to economic maturity helps, specifically, to illuminate the three great military struggles of the twentieth century: the First World War, the Second World War, and the Cold War, at which we shall draw an arbitrary line in June 1951, with the beginning of the Korean truce negotiations.

But to understand the problem of power and major conflict in the first half of the twentieth century we must, first, look backward and ask why there were no major international wars in the century after Napoleon's defeat.

Britain emerged a victor from the Napoleonic Wars in part because its take-off into industrialization, based largely on cotton textiles, helped (along with the monopoly in West Indian trade) to provide the foreign exchange to sustain its alliances and to minimize Napoleon's continental blockade. In any case, Britain's economic status at the time of Napoleon's defeat was unique, when viewed from the perspective of stages-of-growth; and its military strength—centred in the navy—was unchallengeable in the arena of power as it then existed.

Why did the settlement of 1815 produce this relatively happy result? The settlement of 1815 worked because, at one end of Eurasia, neither Germany nor Russia felt able (or was permitted) to acquire the territories held within the Austro-Hungarian Empire; and because, at the other end of Eurasia, Japan and China, as well as the bulk of Africa, the Middle East, and South-East Asia, were essentially out of the power game.

The world that Britain held in balance thus consisted mainly of Western and Central Europe and the maritime fringes of Asia, the Middle East, and Africa. Russia, it is true, lurched from one side of its Eurasian cage to the other, first to the west, then to the east; but, in the nineteenth century, it could be held within that cage with reasonable economy of amphibious force, as the Crimean and Russo-Japanese Wars indicated. And the Western Hemisphere emerged as a special sphere, closely related to—but still separated from—the major power game by the Monroe Doctrine and the complex implicit understanding with Britain which gave it vitality.

In the three decades after the Civil War, the four great areas—Germany, Japan, Russia, and the United States—whose coming to maturity was to determine the world's balance of power in the first half of the twentieth century—were at stages which did not lead to major aggression. The world balance of power which emerged after 1815 was being rapidly undermined; but this fact could largely be concealed, except from those professionally concerned with the problem of force and potential force. After the Franco-Prussian War, Germany settled down under Bismarck to consolidate its political position and to move from a remarkable take-off into economic maturity; Japan, after the Meiji restoration, took about a decade to consolidate the preconditions for take-off, and, less dramatically than Germany, moved into the first stages of sustained economic growth. Russia also slowly completed its preconditions and moved, from the 1890's, forward into a take-off bearing a family resemblance to that of the United States a half-century earlier.

The twentieth-century arena, clearly beginning to form up in the latter decades of the nineteenth century, assumed, then, this form; stretching east from Britain were new major industrial powers in Germany, Russia, and Japan, with Germany achieving maturity by about 1910—the most advanced among them. In the face of this phenomenon, Britain and France were moving uncertainly into coalition, with Britain beginning to look West for further support. And, poised uncertainly on the rim of the world arena, groping to define a stance consistent with both its isolationist tradition and its new sense of world status, was the United States, like Germany also moving into technical maturity.

But the sweep of industrialization across northern Eurasia was not uniform. Eastern Europe and China did not move into take-off in the early decades of the twentieth century. They were still caught up in the early, turbulent, transitional phases of the preconditions; and they were to provide peculiar difficulty.

Why should this have been so? Why were Eastern Europe and China the cause of so much trouble? Each of these two regions, if attached to any major power, had the geographic location, the population, and the long-run potential capable of shifting radically the Eurasian power balance; but lagging their neighbours as they did in the growth sequence, they lacked the political coherence and economic strength to assert that potential independently or to avoid, throughout the first half of the twentieth century, a high degree of dependence.

It was this differential alteration in the power balance, traceable to differences in the timing of the stages of economic growth, that was to provide a terrible temptation to Germany in Eastern Europe and to Japan in China; it was to serve alternately as a source of fear and temptation to Russia, in both regions; and it was to offer chronic danger to France, Britain and the United States, whose strategic status was radically and permanently altered by both consequences of the spread of industrialization—that is, both by the creation of a single, interacting arena of power across the northern half of the globe and by the emergence of soft spots within it which made the pursuit of Eurasian hegemony appear possible and attractive, at various stages, to Germany, Russia, and Japan.

Struggles for the Eurasian power balance

In the end, it was the relative weakness of Eastern Europe and China—their vulnerability to military, political, and economic intrusion in their protracted stage of preconditions—that provided the occasion for the First World War, the Second World War, and the Cold War in its first phase.

The ambiguity about the future control of Eastern Europe—and the large implications for Eurasian and world power of who did control it—set the stage for the struggle of 1914–18. The possibilities of joining Japan's hegemony in China with a German victory in the West, made conceivable by prior German dominance of Eastern Europe, set the stage for the struggle with the Axis of 1939–45. Stalin's vision (and, later, Mao's) of pressing beyond the advanced positions acquired in Eastern Europe and China to achieve a definitive Communist victory, set the stage for the Communist duel with Truman. This third Eurasian struggle ended in at least interim stalemate with the success of the Berlin airlift in the West in the spring of 1949, and in the East, with the defensive victories of the reorganized United Nations forces in April–May 1951, which set the stage for the truce negotiations whose beginning was signalled by Malik in June.

Thus, as the world expanded out across Eurasia to replace the world of 1815 and after, new major powers emerged. The old rivalry of Britain and France was replaced by a new awareness of defensive common interest; and the United States, sharing at one remove this common interest, became the strategic reserve of the West. In that role the United States was twice called on to help rescue the West from military defeat, being required to intervene earlier, with greater weight, in the Second than in the First World War, but still relying on time, distance, and allies to see it through. In 1945–6, the United States showed every indication of seeking again a degree of withdrawal, although more limited than in 1919–20; but the inability of Britain to sustain Greece and Turkey, the general deterioration of the Western economic and political position in 1947, and the collapse of Nationalist China, brought it back forthwith to bear directly the brunt of the third muted Eurasian struggle, in which Truman duelled successfully with Stalin and Mao to prevent a definitive loss of the Eurasian power balance—a duel accomplished without substantial warfare in the West, but at the cost of the Korean War in the East.

We are asserting, then, that there is an inner continuity in the three great struggles to be observed between 1914 and 1951. This continuity arises from the successive temptation of three powers—Germany, Japan, and Russia—to exploit their newly achieved maturity and the vulnerability of the still transitional societies of Eastern Europe and China, to attempt to seize control of the Eurasian arena which emerged from the spread of industrialization over the previous century. Each effort failed because a fourth power had simultaneously come to maturity—the United States—which shared with Western Europe an interest in frustrating such a unilateral dominance of Eurasia, and which in the end successfully made common cause with the older mature powers, most notably with Great Britain.

THE CHOICE OF AGGRESSION

This argument has thus far by-passed the deeper reasons for certain societies having succumbed to the temptations and fears offered by the state of the Eurasian arena as they approached maturity; and it has by-passed also the reason for the failure of the United States and the West to take the forehanded steps necessary to make the choice of aggression unattractive. The stages-of-growth analysis does not pretend to explain all of history: there are factors at work, relating to the onset of the great wars and power struggles of the twentieth century, which are quite independent of the analysis presented in this book. Nevertheless, the stages-of-growth throw some light on these more profound questions.

So far as the First World War is concerned there is a kind of stumbling of men into a conflict whose dimensions and consequences they did not understand or correctly measure. Nevertheless, at its basis was the fact that the Austro-Hungarian Empire was in an early preconditions stage, a rural-based traditional society breaking up, which could not cope with or harness constructively the surging nationalism of the Eastern European peoples stirred by what was going on in Russia, Germany, and still further to the West. That nationalism asserted itself in such a way as to set up in the East the threats and attractions of either Russian or German domination; and so the setting of the First World War was created.

But, it is fair to ask, why did Germany not concern itself exclusively with the expansion of consumption, as it moved into and beyond maturity? The short answer is that the grip of the Kaiser, and those around him, made impossible an immediate concentration of German resources and energy on creating an age of high mass-consumption. Why, then, were such men in control of Germany? To answer this question one must go back to the origins of modern German nationalism and to the concept emphasized in chapter 3; namely, that in many cases—including Germany—a reactive ambitious nationalism lay initially at the basis of modernization, or was a very strong force within it. Modern Germany has had to pass through much travail before the marks of its birth, in the diversion and capture of the liberal Revolution of 1848, were substantially removed; and we cannot yet be wholly sure of the outcome. A part of the answer to the question of why Germany succumbed to the temptations of power in 1914—rather than to the blandishments of high mass-consumption—lies, then, in the nature of the motivations which launched Germany on the path to modernization.

So far as the Second World War is concerned we must first look at what happened between the wars in the United States and the West, if we are to find a connexion with the stages-of-growth. The United States fell into a depression which, if we are correct, was peculiarly intractable because of the nature of the full-employmen problem in the era of high mass-consumption; and with the depression of the 1930's on its hands many liberal Democrats as well as traditionally isolationist Republicans were, in effect, isolationists. Down to the Fall of France in 1940, there was an isolationist majority in the United States, in part—but only in part—because of an obsession with domestic affairs related to a breakdown in the dynamics of the growth stages.

In Western Europe, if our view of inter-war stagnation is correct, Britain and France failed to maintain momentum—and inner con fidence—because the nature of their societies and their public policies failed to permit a quick and decisive movement into the age of high mass-consumption. Their leaders—and in a sense, their peoples as a whole—had their eyes fastened on a return to a normalcy defined in terms of memories of the world that was before 1914.

The sluggishness that resulted—a sense of waning powers, accompanied by distracting domestic conflicts and problems—contributed to (no more than that) the grave diplomatic failure to halt German and Japanese aggression at a sufficiently early stage.

In Japan, as in Germany, the most powerful opposition to the Western-oriented, relatively pacific politicians of the 1920's came not from men determined to carry the Japanese economy into the age of high mass-consumption, but from men whose roots and ambitions reached back to the origins of Japanese modernization in a reactive nationalism, full of fear and hope. And so, when the depression came, and the fragile international system reconstructed after Versailles collapsed, throwing each nation back on its own resources, policies, and heritage, they took over and had their fling.

Something of the same can be said of Stalin's choice probably made definitively at the end of 1945 or early in 1946. There was a widespread hope within Soviet society as well as outside, at the end of the Second World War, that Russia, having survived destruction and emerged as a Great Power—its government and peoples having, in the end, performed in a great national tradition—would turn its resources and attention primarily to reconstruction and to the welfare of the Russian peoples, accepting the concept of Big Three unity offered in evident good faith during and immediately after the war. Here again the distractions of the United States and the West at home—leading, for example, to helter-skelter American disarmament and a vacuum in Eastern Europe—combined with the evident opportunities for Communism in China—proved too great a temptation. The world supplied an extraordinarily attractive setting for Soviet expansion in the immediate post-war years.

But what about the demand side of the equation? Why did Stalin —like the Germans and the Japanese before him—decide not to turn to domestic welfare as a primary goal? Why did he not set aside the temptation to expand Soviet power unilaterally? Again one must look back to the reactive nationalism which helped create modern Russia, and which became woven into the peculiar imperatives of Communist ideology and domestic policy, a problem considered in chapter 10. What is clear—as a simple matter of fact—

is that Stalin was not prepared in the post-war years to accept and face all the domestic consequences of the age of high mass-consumption. He gave a high priority to expanding Soviet power in the world arena.

The stages-of-growth do, then, throw some light on—but they do not pretend to explain fully—the great power struggles of the twentieth century. But that, after all, is one of the major conclusions of this book—that economic forces and motives are not a unique and overriding determinant of the course of history.

Our concern here is, then, rather narrow. It is to make clear that, to the extent that the great struggles for power of the twentieth century have an economic basis, that basis does not lie in imperialism, or in compulsions arising from an alleged monopoly stage of capitalism; nor does that basis lie even in an automatic oligopolistic competition over colonies: it lies in the contours of the Eurasian arena of power, as determined by relative stages-of-growth and of military potential. And quite particularly it lies in the temptations and fears of certain new mature powers with respect to the transitional societies that lay close by, in Eastern Europe and in China, societies that were by-passed in the series of take-offs that got under way in, roughly, the third quarter of the nineteenth century, which destroyed the world of 1815 and after.

THE NEXT PHASE: NUCLEAR WEAPONS AND THE FURTHER SPREAD OF INDUSTRIALIZATION

It may seem odd that this analysis is broken off in 1951. The struggle between the Communist world and the West by no means ended with the Korean truce, as any day's newspaper reveals. Nevertheless, some time in the early 1950's the shape of that struggle altered its character due, on the one hand, to the full emergence of the new weapons, notably the H-bomb; and, on the other hand, to the gathering implications of the growth process at many points in the world.

Historians are thus likely to recognize the existence of a watershed in the early 1950's which quite sharply distinguishes, say, the first six post-war years from the problems and events that have followed.

Relative stages-of-growth and aggression

In any case, we turn in chapter 9 to examine the problems and prospects that confront us now that man has pressed his control over his physical environment to the point where the destruction of organized life on the planet is technically possible, in a setting where the stages-of-growth move forward not only in the northern half of the globe, whose story dominates the history of the past two centuries, but in the southern half of the globe, and in China as well.

CHAPTER 9

THE RELATIVE STAGES-OF-GROWTH AND THE PROBLEM OF PEACE

In this chapter we leave the relatively safe world of history to examine the implications for the future of the onward march of compound interest in the various parts of the world when combined with a not wholly unrelated fact; that is, the existence of modern weapons of mass destruction. And having stated, in terms of the stages-of-growth, where it is that the nations stand and appear to be going, we shall suggest briefly and in broad terms how we might go about solving our great common problem—the problem of reasonably stable and secure peace.

THE REVOLUTION IN WEAPONS

First, the weapons and what they have done and are doing to the world arena of power.

There is the story of an American negro community, set in a southern farming area, which was beset with drought. Finally, under the guidance of their pastor, they turned to prayer. For a time they prayed; but the sun continued to shine with a bright cruelty; and the corn stalks were stunted and beginning to wither at the edges; and the cracks multiplied in the dry ground. Then, at last, it rained. At first they wondered at the miracle and were grateful. But as the rain persisted, day and night, beginning to wash away the stunted growths, they grew restive; until the pastor, feeling a special responsibility, resumed the monologue: 'Lord,' he said, 'we suffered from drought; we prayed; and we asked for rain. But what you've given us is plumb ridiculous.'

For the United States and its allies in the Second World War, haunted since 1939 by the sure knowledge that somewhere in Germany lay all the scientific clues to atomic weapons, the common achievement of the first atomic weapons was, indeed, providential. But this extension of man's ability to manipulate his environment— the ultimate military achievement of the Newtonian outlook, by non-Newtonian physics—has produced a military situation which is, truly, plumb ridiculous.

On the one hand, the Soviet Union, the United States, and Britain have in their hands—and soon France and others will have in their hands—instruments which grossly surpass in their destructive power anything that has gone before; but their use, now the monopoly is broken, presents the risk of triggering circumstances, if not a direct response, which will destroy the user and us all.

In a technical sense, what has happened is that the proportionality between industrial potential and usable military force—a proportionality which had existed for about a century and a half—has now been violated. The destructive capabilities of science and technology have gone on increasing at an accelerated pace; but the surface of the globe is fixed in size and can be blanketed. The powers of destruction have thus passed into the area of decreasing marginal productivity—if not negative productivity. It is true that the Great Powers, or those who wish to exercise a degree of influence in the muted chess game of the atomic arms race, continue to concentrate vast resources, including a high proportion of their scarcest creative talents, on the production of weapons, means of delivery, and means of defence. But the circumstances in which these weapons can be rationally used become progressively more narrow. Indeed, as the number of powers merely possessing the weapons expands—as we move from duopoly out to nuclear oligopoly—the uncertainty and danger arising from their very existence increases, quite apart from the danger of their use.

Of course, a lead by any one power sufficiently great to destroy the retaliatory capacity of all others at a blow would render world domination—for what it might be worth—a possible short-term objective, if that power were to undertake the risks before God and man of initiating such an attack (called antiseptically, in the military literature, a pre-emptive attack).* A great deal of effort and resource

* Strictly speaking, a pre-emptive attack in, for example, Soviet military literature, is to be launched only when it is judged that the other party is preparing to initiate major war, but has not yet struck his initial blow. But with two powers geared to the possibilities of launching pre-emptive attack, the possibilities of a spiralling tension leading to an initiation of major war are evident enough. Moreover, preparations for pre-emptive attack would serve also for an attack launched when Moscow might become convinced that its lead in weapons, means of delivery, and means of defence was sufficiently great to justify rationally the initiation of a decisive blow.

is now flowing in the Western world to avoid offering that awful temptation to Moscow. And this effort is wholly justified: in my view it is not sufficiently large.

But aside from the logic of deterrence, it would almost seem that some cosmic joke has been played on man: he has been permitted to create weapons which concentrate tremendous power in the hands of a few technologically mature societies; but the net effect is to reduce rather than to increase the ability of those favoured societies to apply military force rationally.

Whatever the nature and source of the paradox, the fact is surely this: the military and foreign policies of the major powers are now being conducted at two distinct and only tenuously related levels: one the level of mutual deterrence—of mutual frustration with mass weapons; the other, the softer level of diplomacy, economic policy, and conventional weapons of a low order where the main business of the world goes on.* In this softer struggle the major powers from day to day operate under great restraint with respect to powers whose military potential in no way approximates their own.

Setting aside the arms race among the industrial giants—which fills our minds with images of a bi-polar or barely oligopolistic world—the fact is that effective power has been rapidly diffused since 1945. The paradox of atomic weapons has permitted the lesser powers degrees of bargaining freedom they would not have if military force had not taken so violent and discontinuous a technical leap.

Tito began the exploitation of this paradox, in a sense, with his successful defiance of Stalin in 1948; but in different ways on different issues Nehru, Nasser, Ben-Gurion, Adenauer and many others have found ways of exploiting this paradox within the non-Communist world; and Mao and Gomulka as well as Tito have done it within the Communist bloc. The lesser power cannot always pull it off, as the young Hungarians in Budapest discovered in October and November of 1956; but they were not defeated with atomic weapons. They were defeated in a police action, by the

* The two levels of activity are linked by the method of nuclear blackmail, in which the threat of nuclear attack is evoked to strengthen a move in which softer weapons are applied; for example, the Soviet threats in the context of the Suez, Lebanon, and Berlin crises of 1956–9.

crudest kind of infantry and tank combat, in a victory for which Moscow had to pay a high price in the other area of struggle; that is, the non-military struggle of diplomacy and ideology.

In short, societies still in the preconditions period, like Egypt, or in the early stages of take-off, like India and China and Yugoslavia, have been able to behave in world diplomacy on a significant range of issues—not on all issues, but over a significant range—as the equivalent of major powers; and this is due to the paradoxical character of the new weapons and the diffusion of effective power they have brought about, in the setting of nuclear stalemate.

THE DIFFUSION OF POWER IN THE LONGER RUN

What we can observe in the past decade foreshadows a long-run trend; for in the longer run, the diffusion of power will acquire a firmer base, even, than the paradoxical impact of the new weaponry.

Just as the forward march of the stages-of-growth in the latter half of the nineteenth century shaped the world arena of the first half of the twentieth—bringing Japan, Russia, Germany, France, and the United States into the arena as major powers—so sequences of change, long at work, and gathering momentum in the post-1945 years, are determining the somewhat different world arena now coming to life.

For the central fact about the future of world power is the acceleration of the preconditions or the beginnings of take-off in the southern half of the world: South-East Asia, the Middle East, Africa, and Latin America. In addition, key areas in Eastern Europe (notably Yugoslavia and Poland), and, of course, China, are hardening up, as their take-offs occur; and while they remain vulnerable to military conquest and occupation (like, say, mature Denmark) they have lost or are losing their old spongy character as societies in awkward transition from traditional to modern, regularly growing status. The arena over which the First and Second World Wars were fought and the first phase of the Cold War as well, no longer exists.

Put more precisely, the take-offs of China and India have begun. Pakistan, Egypt, Iraq, Indonesia and other states are likely to be less than a decade behind—or at least not much more, given the acute pressures to modernize now operating on and within their societies.

And in Latin America the take-off has been completed in two major cases (Mexico and Argentina); and it is under way in others, for example, in Brazil and Venezuela.

In short, looking ahead some sixty years it can be said with reasonable confidence that the world will contain many new nations which have achieved maturity. They may not be rich in terms of consumption per head; they may not yet be prepared by the turn of this century to plunge into the age of high mass-consumption; but they will have the capacity to apply to their resources the full capabilities of (then) modern science and technology.

To make this notion still narrower and more concrete, it is fairly safe to predict that, by 2000 or 2010—which is not all that far away—India and China, with about two billion souls between them, will be, in our sense, mature powers. They may not be ready for the age of the mass automobile; and it is by no means assured that Communism will then dominate China, and democracy India. China and India face many difficult choices and vicissitudes in the years and decades ahead. But it is reasonably clear that compound interest has come to be built into those two massive societies; and three generations of an environment of growth should produce maturity—perhaps less than that, if China maintains forced draft and solves the food problem.

Compound interest will, of course, continue to operate in the societies which have already achieved or passed beyond maturity. Their gross national products will almost certainly rise—unless they opt radically for leisure—and their virtuosity in modern weaponry will increase, if the arms race continues. But so long as the military stalemate is maintained, this process is likely to add little to their capacity rationally to use military force. Meanwhile, unless an effective system of arms control is introduced, the newer powers are likely to acquire, in one way or another, a sufficient atomic weapons capability to enter into and to complicate the chess game of the arms race, if not to dominate it; and within the limits set by the arms race, they will be in a position to assert their interests with increasing effect.

It is true that some increase in rationally usable force may emerge, as limited war capabilities develop and the antagonists feel their way towards common-law rules that permit some clashes of force to occur without spiralling into an unwanted exchange of all-out nuclear attack. But so long as each side is believed capable of shielding a substantial delivery capability from sudden decisive nuclear attack, the use of force by the major industrial powers is likely to remain rational only over a narrow range. And beyond the requirements of security policy, the bulk of the increase in output is likely to be channelled into consumption, even in the presently Communist states.

Thus, the most likely prospect—ruling out both major war and the organization of an effective system of arms control—is for the newer industrial states to narrow the gap between their own military capabilities and those of the existing industrial powers.

The central fact to which all nations must foreseeably accommodate their policies, then, is the likelihood that the arena of power will enlarge to become, for the first time in history, truly global; and that the centres of effective power within it will increase. The image of a bi-polar world, in which all but Washington and Moscow are spectators, is inaccurate now, and it will become progressively more inaccurate with the passage of time. Although still gripped in an essentially bi-polar arms race, we are, in fact, approaching an age of diffused power, in which the image of Eurasian hegemony— fearful and enticing—will lose its reality, and world domination will become an increasingly unrealistic objective—assuming, always, maintenance of nuclear stalemate.

THE PROBLEM OF PEACE

This is the setting in which the problem of peace is confronted. Technically, the problem of peace consists in the installation of a system of arms control and inspection within a level of armaments agreement, which would offer all powers greater security than that now afforded by an arms race of mutual deterrence. Given the nature of modern weapons and the opportunities for their concealment, this, in turn, requires that all societies be opened up to inspectors who would have, in effect, bank inspectors' privileges: that is, they could go anywhere, at any time, without notice.

The presence of a corps of such knowledgeable, mobile inspectors (backed by free, mutual aerial surveillance) could not absolutely guarantee that no atomic weapons were retained, contrary to agreement; it could not absolutely guarantee that a surprise attack could not be mounted; but it could produce a situation vastly less dangerous than that with which we now live from day to day.

Moreover, despite honest and well-founded doubts and worries the governments of the United States—and of the West as a whole—would accept such a drastic alteration in national sovereignty if they were convinced that the inspection privileges within the Communist bloc were bona fide.

Finally, it is reasonably clear that if Soviet policy were governed solely by criteria of national interest similar to those which govern the policy of the United States and the West, such an agreement would now be made.

THE RUSSIAN NATIONAL INTEREST

Why should Russia now join in an effective system of arms control, on national grounds?

Having failed in the immediate post-war bid to convert the confusions of Europe and Asia into a prompt Eurasian hegemony for Communism dominated from Moscow, and ruling out a successful sudden nuclear attack—based on the achievement of radically superior technical capabilities—what is the prospect for Russia? The prospect for Russia is to see vast new nations come into the world arena which Russia cannot control. Moreover, as atomic weapons capabilities spread, these new nations will be in a position to take actions which might precipitate a war disastrous to Russian interests. The basic Russian national interest, with respect to both the new weapons and the rise to maturity of new nations, is a defensive interest, essentially similar to that of the United States, Western Europe, and Japan.

The one great option open to Russia, at this moment in history, when it shares Great Power nuclear status with the United States and Britain, among the older nations of the north, is to create an effective system of arms control; and to concentrate its efforts, along with those of others, on making the system work. The common objective would be to make the system of arms control so solid and secure over the coming decades, that, as these massive new nations—

China and those of the south—come into maturity they enter a world of orderly politics rather than one where the power struggle persists with weapons of mass destruction still one of the pawns. In the face of the diffusion of power being brought about by a new series of take-offs, the Russian national interest shifts closer to that of the United States and the West. The old Eurasian struggle, based on the vulnerability to intrusion of Eastern Europe and China in their preconditions period, is a part of the past.

It is evident that some perception of this problem already exists in Moscow. It certainly lies behind the emphasis on ending H-bomb tests, which would, in effect, freeze atomic weapons capabilities more or less where they are. But this approach cannot hold up, unless it is soon followed by the real thing: an effective international system of arms control. Put another way, the newer powers (China, for example) and some of the older powers (France, Germany, and Japan—and even Sweden and Switzerland) are unlikely to permit weapons capabilities to be limited to the Big Three, while the Cold War goes on in its old terms, merely without H-bomb tests.

In short, it is not a realistic option to conceive of a continued bilateral or trilateral world of atomic powers blocking the others out, but continuing the competitive game of Cold War; nor is it a realistic option to conceive of a world controlled by Washington, Moscow, or both. But the present Great Powers do have one realistic option: it does lie within their grasp to make the terms and the setting within which power will be diffused, as new nations take off and march to maturity; but that is the historical limit of their powers, except, of course, to blow the whole world up.

The diffusion of power can be rendered relatively safe or very dangerous; but it cannot be prevented. The process of growth and the stages at which various nations now stand rule out equally the notion of an American century, a German century, a Japanese century, or a Russian century.

The rational policy for a nationalistic Russia would be, then, to exercise this moment of option to join the United States in imposing mutually on one another and on the world the one thing the world would accept from the two Great Powers; that is, an effective international system of arms control.

It may have been considerations of this kind which shaped President Eisenhower's peroration, when he spoke—evidently to Moscow—at the United Nations Assembly during the Middle East debate of 13 August 1958, as follows:

As I look out on this Assembly, with many of you representing new nations, one thought above all impresses me. The world that is being remade on our planet is going to be a world of many mature nations. As one after another of these nations moves through the difficult transition to modernization and learns the methods of growth, from this travail new levels of prosperity and productivity will emerge.

This world of individual nations is not going to be controlled by any one power or group of powers. It is not going to be committed to any one ideology. Please believe me when I say that the dream of world domination by any one power or of world conformity is an impossible dream. The nature of today's weapons, the nature of modern communications, and the widening circle of new nations make it plain that we must, in the end, be a world community of open societies. And the concept of the open society is the key to a system of arms control we can all trust.

MOSCOW'S PROBLEM OF ACCEPTANCE

But the acceptance of some such proposition means that Moscow would have to abandon the notion of world domination and accept explicit status as a major, responsible nation-state in a world of powerful nation-states, all of whom had largely abandoned the right to kill other peoples in the pursuit of the national interest.

It is extremely difficult for Moscow to act on this perception about the diffusion of power—which is probably growing among Russians—because in two fundamental respects Soviet policy is not determined by conventional criteria of the national interest.

First, externally, the Soviet government is committed to strive in the direction of world hegemony for Communism. In fact, since shortly after the November Revolution, this has been interpreted operationally as an effort to maximize the effective power exercised from Moscow, rather than in simple ideological terms. Tito was not the first Communist to discover that when a clash existed between the degree of power exercised from Moscow and the spread of Communism as an ideology, Moscow would opt for the former.

Put another way, if the problem were merely external commitment of Moscow to Communism, it would not be too difficult to resolve it by a *de facto* acceptance of national status for the Soviet Union accompanied by a maintenance of the rhetoric of the old-time world-domination religion. A nation's rhetoric can persist for a long time, as familiar, comforting, background music, after it has lost its relationship to reality.

It is the second, domestic dimension of the problem which makes it so searching and serious for Russia and for the world. For the acceptance of conventional national status, within an effective arms control system, would require not merely a change in Russia's relation to the world, but also basic and revolutionary changes in the relation of the Russian state to the Russian peoples.

For forty years now men have been told in Russia that fixed laws of history decree that the external world is implacably hostile and must ultimately be conquered; that this inescapable struggle justifies and requires a high degree of secret-police control within the Soviet Union; and that this inescapable struggle requires extraordinarily high allocations to investment and military purposes. On these three propositions—external hostility, internal police-state control, and austerity—the whole of Soviet policy has been based for two generations; the institutions of the Soviet state; and Soviet political economy as well. Each would be shattered if an effective system of arms control were to be installed within the Soviet bloc.

Why is this so? It is so because an effective system of arms control would, in effect, create an open society in Russia. How could the police state—whose rationale down to today rests on the assumption of spying, sabotaging foreigners—how could the police state be justified when the Russian peoples were informed that Russian security rested on an exchange of men with bank inspectors' privileges; and westerners were turning up any time, anywhere, throughout Russia, without notice to Russian officials? And how could Russia avoid the age of durable consumers' goods and services, if something like 20% of GNP—which now goes into the Soviet military budget—were released from military to civil outlays? In short, the case for hostility, for the secret police, and for austerity would be broken; the case for democracy and welfare would be overwhelming, if an effective international arms control system were installed.

It is this set of converging revolutionary consequences for Soviet domestic rule that makes the problem of peace so difficult; for whether the Russian price- and income-elasticities of demand prove to be similar to those of the United States and Western Europe, it is clear that the open society and age of high mass-consumption implicit in effective control of armaments would require drastic revisions in the conceptions and institutions of the Soviet Union of a kind that working politicians will go a long way to avoid.

At the moment the Soviet Union is a society technically ready for the age of high mass-consumption; it is structurally ready in terms of the education and skills of its working force; it is psychologically ready and anxious, as evidenced by Soviet literature, by Soviet politics, and, indeed, by trends in the Soviet economy, where the demands for housing and durable consumers' goods are beginning to assert themselves; but the regime is straining to hold the dam, to control the bulk of the increment to annual income for military and investment purposes.

In terms of the stages-of-growth, Russia is a nation seeking to convert its maturity into world primacy by postponing or damping the advent of the age of high mass-consumption. But it is doing so not because the prospects for a temporary victory over the West are all that good; not because Russian security could not be more cheaply and effectively insured; not because it is in the Russian national interest to continue the arms race—for the contrary is the case—but because Communism is a curious form of modern society appropriate only to the supply side of the growth problem: perhaps for take-off, although this is still to be proved, given Communism's inherent difficulties in agriculture; but certainly it can drive a society from take-off to industrial maturity—as Stalin demonstrated—once its controls are clamped upon that society. But in its essence Communism is likely to wither in the age of high mass-consumption; and this, almost certainly, is well understood in Moscow.

THE GREAT ACT OF PERSUASION

How, then, are we going to persuade the Russians to face up to the fact of the diffusion of power on the world scene; to accept the consequences of peace and the age of high consumption; so that they can go forward with the rest of the human race in the great struggle to find new peaceful frontiers for the human experience? Essentially we in the non-Communist world must demonstrate three things.

We must demonstrate that we shall not permit them to get far enough ahead to make a temporary military resolution rational.

We must demonstrate that the underdeveloped nations—now the main focus of Communist hopes—can move successfully through the preconditions into a well established take-off within the orbit of the democratic world, resisting the blandishments and temptations of Communism. This is, I believe, the most important single item on the Western agenda.

And we must demonstrate to Russians that there is an interesting and lively alternative for Russia on the world scene to either an arms race or unconditional surrender.

But the great act of persuasion has an extra dimension: and that extra dimension is time. For this searching problem of transformation Russians must solve for themselves; and it will take time for them to do it. The rest of the world can make it easier rather than more difficult for the Russians: by creating a setting which rules out the apparently cheap solution of either military or political victory; and by articulating persuasively a vision of where we would like everyone to fetch up, sufficiently precise so that Russians can soberly weigh the advantages against the costs of an arms control system. But it will take time for Russians to accept and absorb the implications of the new world of diffused power. It will take time for Russians to accept that their only rational destiny is to join the great mature powers of the north in a common effort to ensure that the arrival at maturity of the south and of China will not wrack the world as the arrival at maturity of Japan, Germany, and Russia itself did at an earlier time; for with nuclear weapons, that old national self-indulgence—seeing how far you can go towards world power when you reach maturity—this sport of the Kaiser and Hitler and the Japanese militarists and Stalin—can no longer be safely afforded.

Specifically, it is likely that the Buddenbrooks' dynamics will operate in Russia, if given time and a strong Western policy that rules out as unrealistic Soviet policies of expansion—whether hard, soft, or mixed. Recall, if you will, how Stalin created and supported a generation of modern technicians, to supplant the old Bolsheviks, whose skills in the dialectic and in conspiratorial politics no longer suited the Russian age of steel and machine tools and modern armies. The cadres of the 1930's—the second Soviet generation—are now, or soon will be, the men who 'decide everything'; but their children —taking a modern industrial system for granted—are reaching out for things that the mature society created by Stalin cannot supply. What is it we can detect moving in Soviet society? An increased assertion of the right of the individual to dignity and to privacy; an increased assertion of the dignity of Russia—as a nation and a national culture—on the world scene; an increased assertion of the will to enjoy higher levels of consumption, not some time in the future, but now; an increased appreciation of the way that modern science has altered the problem of power, including certain old and treasured military maxims, both Russian and Communist in their origins.

These trends, pushing Russia broadly in the directions of national-ism and welfare which are required to make the great act of persua-sion work, have certainly not yet triumphed in Soviet society or in Soviet policy. Moreover, there is no reason to believe that these underlying trends will automatically work themselves out smoothly and peacefully. On the other hand we should be aware that the dynamics of the generations within Soviet society—and notably the trends in the first post-maturity generation—combined with the diffusion of power on the world scene, could, in time, solve the problem of peace, if the West does its job.

The kinds of issues now in contention have, in the long sweep of the past, normally led to war; namely, a tangling of issues of both power and ideology. Generally men have preferred to go down in the style to which they had become accustomed rather than to change their ways of thinking and of looking at the world. There are no grounds for viewing the future with easy optimism; but, when combined with the operation of the Buddenbrooks' dynamics, the existence of the new weapons and the sequence of take-offs in Asia, the Middle East, Africa, and Latin America may permit us to get through by posing for Russia prospects judged, in the end, even more dangerous than the acceptance of the age of the mass automobile, the suburban one-family house, and free mutual inspection.

The concept of the stages-of-growth does, then, throw a little light on the shape of the future and the problem of peace. It helps prepare our minds—and, one would hope, our nations' policies—for the world of diffused power into which we shall enter, and into which we have to a degree been prematurely plunged by the paradox of the new weapons. It helps give a rough time-dimension to the emergence of China and the nations of the south to maturity; that is, if it is agreed that many of the new nations, Africa apart, which have not yet entered into take-off are likely to do so within about a decade. It throws some light on the nature of Moscow's difficult problem of accepting the diffusion of power abroad, and of accepting at home the primacy of welfare and an end to the police state. And it helps define the area of hope in the quite technical sense developed in chapter 7; that is, we can see a possibility of forces within Soviet society which might opt for a different balance among the three major directions in which the capabilities of a post-maturity economy may be turned: in this case, away from the pursuit of power towards enlarged consumption and human welfare in the widest sense.

BEYOND PEACE

History and danger to the peace will, of course, not end with the Soviet acceptance of the age of durable consumers' goods, even when accompanied by acceptance of an effective international inspection system. It is quite true that societies caught up in the process of translating industrial potential into the satisfaction of consumers' wants and diffusing the new goods and services on a widening basis are likely to generate powerful checks against aggression and an increased willingness to accept dilutions of sovereignty to preserve a reasonably comfortable *status quo*. But it is contrary to the whole spirit of this analysis to make a simple mechanical association of this kind between peace and high mass-consumption. This is an analysis which presents, not iron-clad imperatives, but choices for men.

And, moreover, there is much history that lies beyond the watershed we are all trying to attain. For example, to name two great issues beyond the control of armaments, there will certainly be the problem of north–south relations, on a global basis, when all societies are modernized, in many ways a racial problem; and there will be the not simple problem of maintaining an arms control system for a long period, once it is established.

THE SIGNIFICANCE OF THE DIFFUSION OF POWER FOR WESTERN EUROPE

A word, now, about a particular aspect of this analysis: namely, its implications for the present and future role and status of Great Britain and, indeed, of Western Europe as a whole, in the world arena of power.

In March 1958 *Punch* published a poem which contained these lines:

> When Britain first at Heaven's command
> Arose from out the azure main
> She scarcely foresaw how NATO planned
> To plunge her right back in again.
>> Cool, Britannia, beneath the nuclear wave;
>> While the bigger, bigger nations misbehave.*

If the picture drawn in this chapter of the implications for the future of the stages-of-growth is a roughly correct picture, the implications of this poem—and the mood that underlies it—are excessively pessimistic. Of course, the 'bigger, bigger nations' may in fact blow us all up; but, in terms of the jobs that need to be done in a world of diffusing power there is ample scope for Britain and Western Europe to play roles of dignity, initiative, and responsibility. The arms race tends to mislead us as to what really is going on and what most needs to be done.

For example, Britain and Western Europe have the resources and the pool of technical assistance to play a major—even a decisive—role in making sure the underdeveloped areas of the non-Communist world move through the preconditions and through take-off without succumbing to that peculiar and intractable form of modern societal organization called Communism. And the British Commonwealth structure offers a basis and pattern on which the alternative to colonialism can be built with will and resources. There is no reason

* Paul Dehn, *Punch*, 19 March 1958.

in the world, for example, why Britain should not lift its eyes from fair shares and hire-purchase and focus, as a major national enterprise, on making a success of the Indian third Five Year Plan on which, operationally, the future of the Commonwealth so largely depends. Western Europe has a major role to play, as well, in the more constructive aspects of the great act of persuasion—in the process of initiative, communication, and negotiations with the Communist world. And these nations can even make—as Britain is now making—a significant military contribution to the deterrence of war, both nuclear and limited.

There will be, of course, no return to the old-fashioned empires, of the kind that were created and built in the pre-1914 era. The traditional societies have moved too far into the preconditions for take-off for that to be possible. On the other hand, if our minds are cleared of the illusory notion that total power has somehow passed from Western Europe to Moscow and Washington; if we look at the world as it is, and as it is becoming; if we look at its possibilities as well as its dangers, it becomes clear that we are trying to create and organize a world of middling powers who, foreseeably, will share all the tricks of modern technology. In fact it is only on a very narrow range of issues that, even now, Washington and Moscow can behave as anything else but middling powers.

In this perspective there is little cause for excessive Western European nostalgia or self-pity. And there is danger for us all in the Little England, Little Europe policies this mood generates; for there is a great deal, of first-rate importance, for Britain and Western Europe to do to bring about the outcome we all seek which will not and cannot be done unless they do it. The task is to isolate these new challenges to make a new agenda; and then to wrest from the enlarging resources of Western Europe a sufficient margin—despite the pressures of the age of high mass-consumption—to do what can and should be done. With certain limited exceptions in the arms race itself, there is no contribution that the United States could and should make to its own and the world's future that Britain and Western Europe could not also make, on at least a proportionate scale.

The significance of the diffusion of power for Western Europe

The lesson of the stages-of-growth for the peoples of Britain and Western Europe is that their fate is about as much in their own hands as it has ever been—or, at least, it is no less so than for the other peoples of the planet.

TAKE-OFFS, PAST AND PRESENT

The argument of this book—and, particularly, of this chapter—has thus far assumed that it is useful, as well as roughly accurate, to regard the process of development now going forward in Asia, the Middle East, Africa, and Latin America as analogous to the stages of preconditions and take-off of other societies, in the late eighteenth, nineteenth, and early twentieth centuries. It is now time to ask: is this analogy fair? Or, more particularly, what are the similarities; what are the differences; and what implications flow from the differences?

Similarities

The similarities are straightforward enough. With respect to the sectors, we can observe many problems and patterns familiar from the past. Most of the presently underdeveloped nations, in the stage of preconditions or early take-off, must allocate much of their resources to building up and modernizing the three non-industrial sectors required as the matrix for industrial growth: social overhead capital; agriculture; and foreign-exchange-earning sectors, rooted in the improved exploitation of natural resources. In addition, they must begin to find areas of modern processing or manufacture where the application of modern technique (combined with high income- or price-elasticities of demand) are likely to permit rapid growth-rates, with a high rate of plough-back of profits.

Many are also caught up in the problems of capital formation in general, examined in chapter 4, where the inner mechanics of the take-off is considered. They must seek ways to tap off into the modern sector income above consumption levels hitherto sterilized by the arrangements controlling traditional agriculture. They must seek to shift men of enterprise from trade and money-lending to industry. And to these ends patterns of fiscal, monetary, and other policies (including education policies) must be applied, similar to those developed and applied in the past.

Moreover, the non-economic problems of these areas bear a resemblance to those of the past which needs no forcing. At the level of politics we can observe a spectrum of positions, with respect to modernization, ranging from die-hard traditionalists to those prepared to force the pace of modernization at any cost; and these positions contend against each other. Moreover, the problem of balance between external and internal expression of nationalist ambition is present—acutely present—in almost every case. Above all, there is continuity in the role of reactive nationalism, as an engine of modernization, linked effectively to or at cross-purposes with other motives for remaking the traditionalist society.

And more narrowly, the contemporary catalogue of necessary social change is familiar to the historian: how to persuade the peasant to change his methods and shift to producing for wider markets; how to build up a corps of technicians, capable of manipulating the new techniques; how to create a corps of entrepreneurs, oriented not towards large profit margins at existing levels of output and technique, but to expanded output, under a regime of regular technological change and obsolescence; how to create a modern professional civil and military service, reasonably content with their salaries, oriented to the welfare of the nation and to standards of efficient performance, rather than to graft and to ties of family, clan, or region.

Some Relative Differences

But there are differences as well, some making the contemporary task of moving into a successful take-off more difficult, others making it easier than in the past.

The most profound difficulty flows directly from a fact which also provides the most profound current advantage; namely, the presently underdeveloped areas have available to them an enormous back-log of technology which includes the technology of public health. Modern public health and medical techniques are extremely effective and prompt in lowering death-rates; they require relatively low capital outlays; and they meet relatively little social and political resistance. Thus, the rates of population increase in the presently underdeveloped areas are higher than those that generally obtained in the stage of preconditions in the past.

Historically, population rates of increase during the take-off decades were generally under 1·5% per annum. France was as low as 0·5%; Germany, Japan, and Sweden, about 1%; Britain as high as 1·4% only in the two decades preceding 1820. Nineteenth-century United States (over 2·5%) and pre-1914 Russia (over 1·5%) are the great exceptions; but in both cases these rates occurred in societies rapidly expanding the area under cultivation. Aggregated annual rates for the major underdeveloped regions of the contemporary world are about as follows: Latin America, 2·5%; South Asia, 1·5%; the Middle East, 2·3%; the Far East, 1·8%; Africa, 1·7%.

These higher rates of population increase impose a strain and a challenge in both aggregative terms and, more narrowly, in terms of the pace of the technological revolution in agriculture. Aggregatively, if we take the marginal capital/output ratio at, say, 3, then an extra 3% of national income must be invested simply to counter the margin of an extra 1% increase in population. But given the structure of consumption in these poor areas, the more significant strain comes to rest on the problem of food supply, where a more rapid diffusion of modern agricultural techniques is required than in the past if the whole development process is not to risk frustration.

Politically and socially, the high rates of population increase impose strain in other directions; for they raise the question of chronic unemployment or partial unemployment. Unemployment takes on a peculiar urgency, as a problem of policy, since the populations of these areas, notably their urban populations, live in a setting of international communications which makes their frustration, perhaps, more strongly felt than in comparable situations in the past. The gap between existing levels of consumption and those which might become possible—or which are thought to be possible—is extremely vivid; and a sense of the gap is spreading fast.

Finally, the Cold War, which constitutes a part of the international setting of the transitional process, affects its contours in various ways. On the one hand, the pull and haul of Communist and non-Communist security interests tends to divert attention, talent, and resources away from domestic tasks of development, in certain of the areas, notably those located close upon the borders of the

Communist bloc. On the other hand, the ideological dimensions of the Cold War heighten a sense of choice concerning the appropriate political and social techniques for modernization, raising in particular the question of whether the Communist method should be followed. More than that, the existence of the international Communist movement, with its explicit objective of take-over within the under-developed areas, draws some portion of the literate élite away from the current tasks of development and creates a special dimension of schism which is costly to the national effort.

Some Relative Advantages

But the contemporary transitional areas also enjoy two substantial advantages which were not available, in equal degree, in the past. First, the pool of unapplied and relevant technology is larger than it has ever been. Second, international aid in the form of technical assistance, soft loans or grants—including flows of surplus food and fibres—are a unique feature of the modern scene. In the past, of course, transitional nations could come into the private international capital markets to float bonds, notably for the building of social overhead capital; and it was not unknown for them to soften their loans by the somewhat crude device of default. But changes in the structure of the markets, combined with the inherent instability of their situation, have to a degree diminished the conventional flows of private capital for social overhead purposes. The willingness of the governments of industrialized nations to contemplate enlarged soft loans and grants constitutes, thus, a potential compensation for the diversionary and disruptive consequences of the Cold War.

THREE MAJOR IMPLICATIONS FOR POLICY

While the relative difficulties faced by contemporary transitional nations are pressing hard upon them, the relative advantages are being only indifferently exploited. Specifically, this rough balance-sheet suggests three broad areas for concerted action, if the transitional nations are to move through the preconditions and take-off while maintaining the possibility of a progressively more democratic political and social development.

First, the potentialities of known technology capable of raising the productivity of agriculture must be brought to bear more purposefully and rapidly than at present. Although, evidently, the earliest possible decline in birth-rates would ease the development process, the known potentialities of irrigation, chemical fertilizers, and improved seeds are capable of providing for some time an increase in food consumption per head, even in the face of current rates of population increase. The limitation lies mainly in the size and competence of the pool of technicians willing and able to go into the countryside to demonstrate patiently the advantages of the newer methods. The danger to the level of welfare in contemporary transitional societies does not lie in any inherent tendency for the acceleration of investment to constrain consumption; for the tricks of agricultural productivity are highly productive and prompt in their effect. The danger lies in the sluggishness of the leadership in facing squarely the problem of agricultural productivity and organizing the human and material resources necessary to accelerate the diffusion of well-known techniques.

Second, the potentialities of external assistance must be organized on an enlarged and, especially, on a more stable basis. With current levels of population increase and current levels of both domestic capital formation and external aid, an increase of the order of some $4 billion in annual external aid would be required to lift all of Asia, the Middle East, Africa, and Latin America into regular growth, at an increase of *per capita* income of, say, 1·5% per annum. In many areas the preconditions process is not sufficiently advanced to permit external capital to be productively absorbed on the scale implicit in such an aggregative estimate.* Realistic figures for increased international aid are lower. What is clear is that the present level of external assistance is substantially inadequate to the task of out-racing the rate of population increase in many key regions where capital might be productively absorbed. But even more important than the question of enlarged scale is the issue of continuity of aid. The analysis of the preconditions process in chapter 3 emphasized the crucial importance of the political decision within a transitional society to focus a high proportion of energy, talents,

---

* For the calculations and assumptions yielding this estimate see M. F. Millikan and W. W. Rostow, *A Proposal* (New York, 1957).

and resources on domestic development as opposed to alternative expressions of nationalism. If the local political leaders are to commit their fortunes to this course, they must do so with the maximum confidence that over their horizon of policy-making (say, five years) they can know that a reasonable level of assistance will be sustained. Absorptive capacity itself is, in large part, a product of the extent to which governments mobilize their own resources around the development problem. Thus, the amount of capital productively absorbable in transitional societies partially depends on the scale and continuity of the offer of external assistance.

In the end, however, the task of development must be done by those on the spot. The non-Communist literate élites in these transitional societies bear a heavy responsibility for the future of their peoples. They have the right to expect the world of advanced democracies to help on an enlarged scale, with greater continuity; but it is they who must overcome the difficulties posed by the rapid diffusion of modern medicine, and ensure that the humane decision to save lives does not lead to an inhumane society. It is they who must focus their minds on the tasks of development, despite the temptations to press nationalism in other directions and to surrender to the distractions of the Cold War. It is they who, having helped achieve independence, under the banners of human freedom, appealing to those values in the West which they share, must now accept a large part of the responsibility for making those values come to life, in terms of their own societies and cultures, as they complete the preconditions and launch themselves into self-sustained growth.

The upshot for those who live in contemporary transitional societies is clearly not pre-determined either by the patterns of history or by the nature of the technical tasks of growth or by the balance of the Cold War. The historical stage at which their societies stand, the pool of unapplied and relevant technology, and the world setting in which they find themselves set the limits and the possibilities of their problems. But like other peoples at great moments of decision, their fate still lies substantially within their own hands.

CHAPTER 10

MARXISM, COMMUNISM, AND THE STAGES-OF-GROWTH

This final chapter considers how the stages-of-growth analysis compares with Marxism; for, in its essence, Marxism is also a theory of how traditional societies came to build compound interest into their structures by learning the tricks of modern industrial technology; and of the stages that will follow until they reach that ultimate stage of affluence which, in Marx's view, was not Socialism, under the dictatorship of the proletariat, but true Communism. As against our stages—the traditional society; the preconditions; take-off; maturity; and high mass-consumption—we are setting, then, Marx's feudalism; bourgeois capitalism; Socialism; and Communism.

We shall proceed by first summarizing the essence of Marx's propositions. We shall then note the similarities between his analysis and the stages-of-growth; and the differences between the two systems of thought, stage by stage. This will provide a way of defining the status and meaning of Marxism, as seen from the perspective of the stages-of-growth sequence. Finally, we shall look briefly at the evolution of Marxist thought and Communist policy, from Lenin forward; and draw some conclusions.

THE SEVEN MARXIST PROPOSITIONS

Marxist thought can be summarized in seven propositions, as follows.

First, the political, social and cultural characteristics of societies are a function of how the economic process is conducted. And, basically, the political, social and cultural behaviour of men is a function of their economic interests. All that follows in Marx derives from this proposition until the stage of Communism is reached, when the burden of scarcity is to be lifted from men and their other more humane motives and aspirations come to dominance.*

* The exact form of the function relating economic interest to non-economic behaviour varies in Marx's writings and in the subsequent Marxist literature. Much in the original texts—and virtually all the operational conclusions derived from them—depend

Second, history moves forward by a series of class struggles, in which men assert their inevitably conflicting economic interests in a setting of scarcity.

Third, feudal societies—in our phrase, traditional societies*— were destroyed because they permitted to grow up within their framework a middle class, whose economic interests depended on the expansion of trade and modern manufactures; for this middle class successfully contended against the traditional society and succeeded in imposing a new political, social, and cultural superstructure, conducive to the pursuit of profit by those who commanded the new modern means of production.

Fourth, similarly, capitalist industrial societies would, Marx predicted, create the conditions for their destruction because of two inherent characteristics: because they created a mainly unskilled working force, to which they continued to allocate only a minimum survival real wage; and because the pursuit of profit would lead to a progressive enlargement of industrial capacity, leading to a competitive struggle for markets, since the purchasing power of labour would be an inadequate source of demand for potential output.

Fifth, this innate contradiction of capitalism—relatively stagnant real wages for labour and the build-up of pressure to find markets for expanding capacity—would produce the following specific mechanism

---

on a simple and direct function relating economic interest to social and political behaviour. In some parts of the Marxist literature, however, the function is developed in a more sophisticated form. Non-economic behaviour is seen as related not immediately and directly to economic self-interest but to the ideology and loyalties of class. Since, however, class interests and ideologies are presented as, essentially, a function of the techniques of production and the social relationships arising from them, this indirect formulation yields much the same results as the more primitive statement of connexion. In the main stream of Marxist literature, from beginning to end, it is only in seeking, protecting and enlarging property and income that men are really serious. Finally, there are a few passages in Marx—and more in Engels—which reveal a perception that human behaviour is affected by motives which need not be related to or converge with economic self-interest. This perception, if systematically elaborated, would have altered radically the whole flow of the Marxist argument and its conclusions. Marx, Engels, and their successors have turned their backs on this perception, in ideological formulations; although, as suggested later in this chapter, Lenin and his successors in Communist politics have acted vigorously on this perception.

* Marx's concept of feudalism is too restrictive to cover all the traditional societies, a number of which did not develop a class of nobility, linked to the Crown, owning large tracts of land. Marxist analyses of traditional China, for example, have been strained on this point.

of self-destruction: an increasingly self-conscious and assertive proletariat goaded, at last, to seize the means of production in the face
of increasingly severe crises of unemployment. The seizure would be
made easier because, as the competition for markets mounted, in the
most mature stage of capitalism, monopolies would be formed; and
the setting for transfer of ownership to the State would be created.

Sixth—this is a Leninist extension of Marxism—the mechanism
of capitalism's downfall would consist not only in successive crises
of increasingly severe unemployment, but also in imperialist wars,
as the competition for trade and outlets for capital, induced by
markets inadequate to capacity, led on not only to monopolies but
also to a world-wide colonial struggle among the national monopolies
of the capitalist world. The working class would thus seize power
and install socialism not only in a setting of chronic, severe unemployment but also of disruption caused by imperialist wars, to which the
capitalist world would be driven in order to avoid unemployment
and to evade and divert the growing assertiveness of an increasingly
mobilized and class-conscious proletariat, led and educated by the
Communists within its ranks.

Seventh, once power is seized by the Socialist state, acting on
behalf of the industrial proletariat—in the phase called 'the dictatorship of the proletariat'—production would be driven steadily forward,
without crises; and real income would expand to the point where
true Communism would become possible. This would happen because
Socialism would remove the inner contradictions of capitalism. Let
me quote Marx's vision of the end of the process: 'In a higher phase
of Communist society, after the enslaving subordination of individuals under the division of labour, and therefore also the anti-
thesis between mental and physical labour has vanished; after labour,
from a mere means of life has of itself become the prime necessity of
life; after the productive resources have also increased with the all-
round development of the individual and all the springs of co-operative
wealth flow more abundantly—only then can the narrow horizon of the
bourgeois law be fully left behind and society inscribe on its banners:
from each according to his ability, to each according to his needs.'*

* Quoted from 'Critique of the Gotha Programme', in J. Eaton, *Political Economy*,
a Marxist Textbook (London, 1958), p. 187.

SIMILARITIES WITH STAGES-OF-GROWTH ANALYSIS

Now let us identify the broad similarities between Marx's historical sequence and the stages-of-growth analysis.

First, they are both views of how whole societies evolve, seen from an economic perspective; both are explorations of the problems and consequences for whole societies of building compound interest into their habits and institutions.

Second, both accept the fact that economic change has social, political, and cultural consequences; although the stages-of-growth rejects the notion that the economy as a sector of society—and economic advantage as a human motive—are necessarily dominant.

Third, both would accept the reality of group and class interests in the political and social process, linked to interests of economic advantage; although the stages-of-growth would deny that they have been the unique determining force in the progression from traditional societies to the stage of high mass-consumption.

Fourth, both would accept the reality of economic interests in helping determine the setting out of which certain wars arose; although the stages-of-growth would deny the primacy of economic interests and motives as an ultimate cause of war-making; and it would relate economic factors and war in ways quite different from those of Marx and Lenin.

Fifth, both would pose, in the end, the goal or the problem of true affluence—of the time when, in Marx's good phrase—labour 'has of itself become the prime necessity of life'; although the stages-of-growth has something more to say about the nature of the choices available.

Sixth, in terms of economic technique, both are based on sectoral analyses of the growth process; although Marx confined himself to consumption goods and capital goods sectors, while the stages-of-growth are rooted in a more disaggregated analysis of leading sectors which flows from a dynamic theory of production.

Marxism, Communism, and the stages-of-growth

With these two catalogues as background we can now isolate more precisely and more positively how the stages-of-growth analysis attempts, stage by stage, to deal with and to solve the problems with which Marx wrestled, and to avoid what appear to be Marx's basic errors.

The first and most fundamental difference between the two analyses lies in the view taken of human motivation. Marx's system is, like classical economics, a set of more or less sophisticated logical deductions from the notion of profit maximization, if profit maximization is extended to cover, loosely, economic advantage. The most important analytic assertion in Marx's writings is the assertion in the Communist Manifesto that capitalism 'left no other nexus between man and man than naked self-interest, than callous "cash payment"'.

In the stages-of-growth sequence man is viewed as a more complex unit. He seeks, not merely economic advantage, but also power, leisure, adventure, continuity of experience and security; he is concerned with his family, the familiar values of his regional and national culture, and a bit of fun down at the local. And beyond these diverse homely attachments, man is also capable of being moved by a sense of connexion with human beings everywhere, who, he recognizes, share his essentially paradoxical condition. In short, net human behaviour is seen not as an act of maximization, but as an act of balancing alternative and often conflicting human objectives in the face of the range of choices men perceive to be open to them.

This notion of balance among alternatives perceived to be open is, of course, more complex and difficult than a simple maximization proposition; and it does not lead to a series of rigid, inevitable stages of history. It leads to patterns of choice made within the framework permitted by the changing setting of society: a setting itself the product both of objective real conditions and of the prior choices made by men which help determine the current setting which men confront.*

* In the stages-of-growth some of the characteristics which have a persistent effect on the whole sequence of growth are rooted in the traditional society and its culture. They constitute an initial condition for the growth process with consequences for a time-period which transcends the sweep from the preconditions forward. See the author's *British Economy of the Nineteenth Century* (Oxford, 1948), chapter VI, especially pp. 128 n. and 140.

We shall not explore here the formal properties of such a dynamic system; but it follows directly from this view of how individuals act that the behaviour of societies is not uniquely determined by economic considerations. The sectors of a society interact: cultural, social, and political forces, reflecting different facets of human beings, have their own authentic, independent impact on the performance of societies, including their economic performance. Thus, the policy of nations and the total performance of societies—like the behaviour of individuals—represent acts of balance rather than a simple maximization procedure.

On this view it matters greatly how societies go about making their choices and balances. Specifically, it follows that the central phenomenon of the world of post-traditional societies is not the economy—and whether it is capitalist or not—it is the total procedure by which choices are made. The stages-of-growth would reject as inaccurate Marx's powerful but over-simplified assumption that a society's decisions are simply a function of who owns property. For example, what Marx regards as capitalist societies at no stage, even in their purest form, ever made all their major decisions simply in terms of the free-market mechanism and private advantage. In Britain, for example, even at the height of the drive to maturity—in let us say the 1815–50 period, when the power of the industrial capitalist was least dilute—in these years factory legislation was set in motion; and after the vote was extended in the Second and Third Reform Bills, the policy of the society was determined by a balance between interests of profit and relative utility maximization on the one hand, and, on the other, interests of welfare as made effective on a 'one man one vote' basis through the political process. Capitalism, which is the centre of Marx's account of the post-feudal phase, is thus an inadequate analytic basis to account for the performance of Western societies. One must look directly at the full mechanism of choice among alternative policies, including the political process— and, indeed, the social and religious processes—as independent arenas for making decisions and choices.

To be more concrete, nothing in Marx's analysis can explain how and why the landed interests in the end accepted the Reform Bill of 1832, or why the capitalists accepted the progressive income tax, or the welfare state; for it is absolutely essential to Marxism that it is over property that men fight and die. In fact one must explain such phenomena with reference to a sense of commitment to the national community and to the principles of the individualist-utilitarian creed that transcended mere profit advantage. Similarly, nothing in Marx's analysis explains the patient acceptance of the framework of private capitalism by the working class, when joined to the democratic political process, despite continued disparities in income.

Marx—and Hegel—were correct in asserting that history moves forward by the clash of conflicting interests and outlooks; but the outcome of conflict in a regularly growing society is likely to be governed by ultimate considerations of communal continuity which a Boston lawyer, Charles Curtis—old in the ways of advocacy and compromise—recently put as follows:

I suggest [he said] that things get done gradually only between opposing forces. There is no such thing as self-restraint in people. What looks like it is indecision....It may be that truth is best sought in the market of free speech, but the best decisions are neither bought nor sold. They are the result of disagreement, where the last word is not 'I admit you're right', but 'I've got to live with the son of a bitch, haven't I'.*

This ultimate human solvent, Karl Marx—a lonely man, profoundly isolated from his fellows—never understood. He regarded it, in fact, as cowardice and betrayal, not the minimum condition for organized social life, any time, anywhere.

And, as developed in chapter 8, a simple analysis of war, in terms of economic advantage, breaks down in the face of a consideration of the different types of armed conflict and how they actually came about. Nationalism—and all that goes with it in terms of human sentiment and public policy—is a hangover from the world of traditional societies.†

* C. Curtis, *A Commonplace Book* (New York, 1957), pp. 112–13.

† This theme is developed by Schumpeter in his writings about Marx and in his essay on Imperialism (J. Schumpeter, *Imperialism* (ed. B. Hoselitz, Meridian Books, New York, 1955), especially pp. 64 ff.; and *Ten Great Economists* (London, 1952), especially pp. 20 and 61 ff.). Whereas Schumpeter emphasized the persistence of irrational and romantic nationalist attitudes, the present analysis would underline two other factors. First, the role of certain groups and attitudes derived from the traditional society, in the growth process itself. Second, the structural fact that, once national sovereignty was accepted as a rule of the world arena, nations found themselves gripped in an almost inescapable oligopolistic struggle for power which did have elements of rationality.

One need look no farther than the primacy colonial peoples give to independence over economic development, or the hot emotions Arab politicians can generate in the street crowds, to know that economic advantage is an insufficient basis for explaining political behaviour; and all of modern history sustains the view that what we now see about us in Asia, the Middle East, and Africa is typical of human experience, when confronted with the choices faced in transitional societies.

Thus, the account of the break-up of traditional societies offered here is based on the convergence of motives of private profit in the modern sectors with a new sense of affronted nationhood. And other forces play their part as well, for example the simple perception that children need not die so young or live their lives in illiteracy: a sense of enlarged human horizons, independent of both profit and national dignity. And when independence or modern nationhood are at last attained, there is no simple, automatic switch to a dominance of the profit motive and economic and social progress. On the contrary there is a searching choice and problem of balance among the three directions policy might go: external assertion; the further concentration of power in the centre as opposed to the regions; and economic growth.

Then, indeed, when these choices are at last sorted out, and progress has gripped the society, history has decreed generally a long phase when economic growth is the dominant but not exclusive activity: the take-off and the sixty years or so of extending modern techniques. It is in the drive to maturity that societies have behaved in the most Marxist way, but each in terms of its own culture, social structure and political process; for growing societies, even growing capitalist societies, have differed radically in these respects. There has been no uniform 'superstructure' in growing societies. On the contrary, the differing nature of the 'superstructures' has strongly affected the patterns which economic growth assumed. And even in the drive to maturity we must be careful not to identify what was done—the energetic extension of modern technique— with a too-simple hypothesis about human motivation. We know that during take-offs and during the drive to maturity societies did, in fact, tend substantially to set aside other objectives and clear the way for activities which would, within human and resource and other societal restraints, maximize the rate of growth. But this is not to say that the profit motive itself was dominant. It certainly played a part. But in the United States after the Civil War, for example (perhaps the most materialist phase of any capitalist society, superficially examined), men did the things necessary to industrialize a great, rich continent, not merely to make money, but because power, adventure, challenge, and social prestige were all to be found in the market-place of a society where Church and State were relatively unimportant. The game of expansion and money-making was rewarding at this stage, not merely in terms of money, but in terms of the full range of human motives and aspirations. How, otherwise, can one explain the ardent striving of men long after they made more money than they or their children could conceivably use? And similar modifications in the Marxist view of human motivation would be required in an accurate account of the German, Japanese, Swedish, French, British, and—indeed—the Russian drives to maturity.

At this stage we come, of course, to Marx's familiar technical errors: his implicit Malthusian theory of population, and his theory of stagnant real wages.

It is an old game to point out that, in fact, population did not so move as to maintain a reserve army of unemployed, and that the workings of competitive capitalism yielded not stagnant real wages but rising real wages. Robinson and Kaldor have recently, for example, emphasized these deep flaws in Marx's economics.* And indeed they are, in formal terms, quite technical errors in judging how the economic process would operate. But they are more. They directly reflect Marx's basic proposition about societies; for neither political power, social power, nor, even, economic power neatly followed the fact that property was privately owned. Competition did not give way to monopoly; and competition, even imperfect, permitted wages to approximate net marginal value product; and this technical aspect of the market mechanism was buttressed by an acceptance of trade unions by the society and by a growing set

* Joan Robinson, *Marx, Marshall, and Keynes* (Delhi, 1955); and N. Kaldor, 'A Model of Economic Growth', *Economic Journal*, December 1957, especially pp. 618–21.

of political interventions allowed and encouraged by the democratic political process. Moreover, the fact of mass progress itself, ruled out in Marx's analysis, made men rethink the calculus of having children; and it yielded a non-Malthusian check on the birth-rate: a check based not on poverty and disease but on progress itself. Think here not only of the older cases of declining birth-rates in history but of the radical fall in the birth-rate in resurgent Japan and Italy of the 1950's.

And so, when compound interest took hold, progress was shared between capital and labour; the struggle between classes was softened; and when maturity was reached they did not face a cataclysmic impasse. They faced, merely, a new set of choices; that is, the balance between the welfare state; high mass-consumption; and a surge of assertiveness on the world scene.

Thus, compound interest and the choices it progressively opened up by raising the average level of real income becomes a major independent variable in the stages-of-growth; whereas, in Marx's theory, compound interest appears in the perverse form of mounting profits, capable only of being distributed in high capitalist living, unusable capacity, and war. Put another way, the income-elasticity of demand is a living force in the stages-of-growth analysis; whereas it is virtually ruled out in Marx's powerful simplifications.

Now the Leninist question: whether capitalism, having an alleged built-in tendency for profits to decline, causes monopolies to rise, and crises to become progressively more severe, and leads to a desperate competitive international struggle for markets, and to wars.

First, the question of industrial concentration. Here we would merely assert that the evidence in the United States, at least, in no way suggests that the degree of concentration has increased significantly in, say, the last fifty years. And where it has increased it has done so more on the basis of the economies of large-scale research and development than because the market environment has been too weak to sustain small firms. And I doubt that the story would be very different in other mature societies of the West. Moreover, where concentrations of economic power have persisted, they have been forced to operate increasingly on terms set by the political process rather than merely the maximization procedures of the market-place itself.

Second, the question of increasingly severe crises. Down to 1914 there is no evidence whatsoever that the amplitude of cycles in unemployment increased. On the contrary, the evidence is of a remarkable uniformity in the cycles of the nineteenth century, whether viewed in terms of such statistics of unemployment as we have, or in terms of years of increasing and decreasing economic activity. There was, of course, the unique depression of the 1930's. But, if the view developed in chapter 6 is correct, the relative inter-war stagnation in Western Europe was due not to long-run diminishing returns but to the failure of Western Europe to create a setting in which its national societies moved promptly into the age of high mass-consumption, yielding new leading sectors. And this failure, in turn, was due mainly to a failure to create initial full employment in the post-1920 setting of the terms of trade. Similarly the protracted depression of the United States in the 1930's was due not to long-run diminishing returns, but to a failure to create an initial renewed setting of full employment, through public policy, which would have permitted the new leading sectors of suburban housing, the diffusion of automobiles, durable consumers' goods and services to roll forward beyond 1929.

There is every reason to believe, looking at the sensitivity of the political process to even small pockets of unemployment in modern democratic societies, that the sluggish and timid policies of the 1920's and 1930's with respect to the level of employment will no longer be tolerated in Western societies. And now the technical tricks of that trade—due to the Keynesian revolution—are widely understood. It should not be forgotten that Keynes set himself the task of defeating Marx's prognosis about the course of unemployment under capitalism; and he largely succeeded.

As for that old classical devil 'diminishing returns'—which Marx took over in the form of his assumption of the declining level of profits—we cannot be dogmatic over the very long run; but the scale and pace of scientific enterprise in the modern world (which, as a sector, is at a rapid growth-stage) make it unlikely that we will lack things to do productively if people prefer productive activity to leisure. Besides, societies have it open to them, if they wish to continue the strenuous life, to follow the American lead and re-impose a Malthusian surge of population, when they get bored with gadgets.

Finally, the question of mature capitalism's dependence on colonies. Here we need only note that, while colonialism is virtually dead, capitalism in the Western Hemisphere, Western Europe and Japan is enjoying an extraordinary surge of growth. It is perfectly evident that, whatever the economic troubles of the capitalist societies, they do not stem primarily from a dependence on imperialism. If anything, their vulnerability now derives from an unwillingness to concern themselves sufficiently with—and to allocate adequate resources to—the world of underdeveloped nations. Domestic demand is not so inadequate as to force attention outward: it is too strong to make it possible for governments to mobilize adequate resources for external affairs. The current hope of Communism lies not in the exploitation of confusion and crises brought on by a compulsive struggle to unload exports, but from an excessive absorption of the capitalist world with the attractions of domestic markets.

This brings us to a comparison between Marx's view of Communism and the stage beyond mass consumption in the stages-of-growth. On this issue Marx was a nineteenth-century romantic. He looked to men, having overcome scarcity, permitting their better natures to flower; to work for the joy of personal expression in a setting where affluence had removed the need and temptation for avarice. This is indeed a decent and legitimate hope; an aspiration; and, even, a possibility. But, as suggested towards the end of chapter 6, it is not the only alternative. There are babies and boredom, the development of new inner human frontiers, outer space and trivial pleasures—or, maybe, destruction, if the devil makes work for idle hands. But while this is man's ultimate economic problem, if all goes well, it is a problem that we of this generation can set aside, to a degree, given the agenda that faces us in a world of nuclear weapons and in the face of the task of making a peaceful world community that will embrace the older and newer nations which have learned the tricks of growth.

MARX IN PERSPECTIVE

What can we say about Marx, then, in the light of the stages-of-growth analysis? Where does he fit?

Intellectually he brought together two sets of tools: an Hegelian view of the dynamics of history, and a generalized version of profit maximization (as well as various substantive propositions) from the world of the classical economists.

He applied this kit-bag to what he could perceive of one historical case: the case of the British take-off and drive to maturity; and he generalized and projected his result. His whole system was fully formed by 1848, when he and Engels wrote the *Communist Manifesto*; that is, it was formed before any other society except Britain had experienced the take-off. And although Marx commented *ad hoc* over the years on various short-run aspects of the French, German, and American cases—and was personally involved in the political events of France and Germany—it was the British Industrial Revolution and what followed the take-off in Britain that shaped his categories. Nothing really important in Marx post-dates 1848.

Now, as we have seen, the British case of transition was unique in the sense that it appeared to have been brought about by the internal dynamics of a single society, without external intervention; that is, there grew up within an agricultural and trading society an industrial middle class, which progressively transformed the politics, social structure, and values of the society, notably in the three decades after Waterloo. The French, German and American cases were not distinctive enough, at least in Marx's time, and within his understanding, to force him to revise his categories; Japan he did not study or incorporate in his system; Russia made him shudder, at least until late in life, when the Russian intellectuals began to take him seriously; and, like the parochial intellectual of Western Europe he was, the prospects in Asia and Africa were mainly beyond his ken, dealt with almost wholly in the context of British policy rather than in terms of their own problems of modernization.*

* I. Berlin, *Karl Marx* (London, 1956 edition), pp. 254–8. Marx did, however, make some interesting *ad hoc* observations on India and China, in writing as a journalist about British policy in the Opium Wars and the Indian Mutiny.

A concentration on the British case permitted a much simpler concept of the transition period and of the take-off than our contemporary range of historical knowledge would allow. Marx, generalizing his insights about Britain, could stick with the middle class and the profit motive. The role of reactive nationalism in transforming a traditional society and the problem of choice faced when a modern independent state was created could be ignored.

In short, Marx belongs among the whole range of men of the West, who, in different ways, reacted against the social and human costs of the drive to maturity and sought a better and more humane balance in society. Driven on—in his father's phrase—by a 'demonic egoism',* by an identification with the underdog and a hatred of those who were top-dog, but also disciplined to a degree by a passion to be 'scientific' rather than sentimental, Marx created his remarkable system: a system full of flaws but full also of legitimate partial insights, a great formal contribution to social science, a monstrous guide to public policy.

One failure of Marx's system began to be revealed before he died; and he did not know how to cope with it. Some believe that his inner recognition of this failure is responsible for the fact that *Das Kapital* is an unfinished book. The failure took the form of the rise in industrial real wages in Western Europe and the perfectly apparent fact that the British and Western European working classes were inclined to accept ameliorative improvements; accept the terms of democratic capitalism rather than concentrate their efforts on the ultimate bloody show-down, the seizure of property and its turn-over to a State which somehow, in Marx's view, the workers might then control. The First International which he formed and led disintegrated in the early 1870's, the union leaders turning their backs on Marx and seeking gradual reform within their own societies.

And so Marx—and Engels too—ended with a somewhat disabused view of the industrial worker on whom they counted so much to make their dialectic come true: the worker was content with a bit of fairly regular progress; a sense that things were getting better for himself and his children; a sense that, by and large, he was getting a fair share from the lay-out of society as a whole; a willingness

* C. J. S. Sprigge, *Karl Marx* (London, 1938), p. 27.

to fight for what he wanted within the rules of political democracy, under a regime of private property ownership; a tendency to identify himself with his national society rather than with the abstract world of allegedly down-trodden industrial workers everywhere; a willingness, despite conflict and inequity, to live with his fellow-men rather than to conspire to kill them. And that is where the story of Lenin and modern Communism begins.

THE EVOLUTION OF MODERN COMMUNISM

For modern Communism has been built directly on an effort to deal with the problems which Marx did not solve or solved incorrectly, both as a theorist and as a practising revolutionary politician. Modern Communism is shaped, in a quite concrete way, by Marx's errors and failures. Lenin had to deal with a world of workers as they were; and of peasants, whom Marx regarded as cloddish, and set aside in a few perfunctory phrases; a world where competitive nationalism was a powerful force; and a world at war. Marx disbanded the First International rather than wrestle with reality; Lenin stayed in the game of politics and power as he found it.

How did Lenin proceed? His first and most fundamental decision was to pursue political power despite the fact that the majority of the Russian industrial working class was unwilling to support a revolutionary attempt to seize power. Lenin's pamphlet, *What is to be Done?* published in 1902, is the true origin of modern Communism. He asserted there that if the Russian workers were unprepared to fulfil their historic Marxist destiny—as they evidently were—the Communist Party would make them fulfil that destiny. The Communist Party would not work as a fraction of the Socialist movement, as the Communist Manifesto counselled. It would form itself as a separate party, a conspiratorial élite, and seek power on a minority basis, in the name of the proletariat, 'swimming against the stream of history'.

Lenin decided, in short, to fulfil Marx's prophecy despite the failure of Marx's prediction. From the beginning to the present— from the pre-1914 split of the Socialist movement in Russia to the stand in 1956 of the Budapest workers and Moscow's continued unwillingness to contemplate free elections even in societies where the capitalist and large landowner are fully liquidated—this is the dead rat at the bottom of Communist thought and practice: the industrial worker has not thought and behaved as, in theory, he should.

Lenin's second decision followed directly from the first; and that was to seize power in Russia, in the confusion following the March 1917 revolution, even though by Marxist standards backward Russia was historically 'unripe' for Socialism. For a little while, the truer Marxists in Lenin's camp comforted themselves with the hope that Germany—an historically 'ripe' society—would also go Communist, after the First World War, and thus create a whole Communist area within which Russian historical backwardness could be subsumed. But that hope was lost; and Lenin proceeded on the basis of Communism in one country well before Stalin created the phrase.

Third, in the Kronstadt Revolt of March 1921, Lenin confirmed the pattern of 1902 and November 1917 by using force to repress the revolt of a probable majority within the Communist Party, a majority which opposed the rapid emergence of a dictatorial state apparatus. Lenin decided, after some soul-searching, to continue to rule on the basis of a police-state dictatorship.

Fourth, in the 1930's, Stalin, having cheerfully accepted the police-state dictatorship as the basis for rule, radically altered the tone of the society by introducing powerful material incentives for those willing to work effectively within the orbit of the Communist state and by supplementing Communist ideology with strong elements of Great Russian nationalism, yielding revisions in everything from soldier's uniform to the content of history books, primary education, and the approved pattern of family life.

Fifth, in the 19th Party Congress of October 1952, but more clearly after Stalin's death, the direction of Communist expansion was turned away from the advanced countries to the underdeveloped areas, following Lenin's prescription and, indeed, his practice. In effect, Marx's judgment about the sequence of history, and the inevitable passage of mature capitalist societies to Socialism, was abandoned in favour of the Leninist formula, which remains Khrushchev's guide in theory and in fact.

What has emerged, then, is a system of modern state organization based not on economic determinism, but on political or power determinism. It is not the ownership of the means of production that decides everything, it is the control of the army, the police, the courts, and the means of communication. Lenin and his successors have, in effect, turned Hegel back on his feet; and they have inverted Marx. Economic determinism did not work well for them; but power determinism has, quite well, filled the gap. They have operated on the perception that, under certain circumstances, a purposeful well-disciplined minority can seize political power in a confused ill-organized society; once power is seized, it can be held with economy of force, if the Communist élite maintains its unity; and with power held, the resources of a society may be organized in such a way as to make the economy grow along lines which consolidate and enlarge the power of the Communist élite.

The irony in this story even extends to the nature of political economy under Communism. In the history of modern Russia, and in post-1945 Eastern Europe and Communist China as well, one can find a quite good approximation to Marx's inaccurate description of how the capitalist economy would work: wages are held as near the iron minimum as the need for incentives permits; profits are ploughed back into investment and military outlays on a large scale; and the system is so structured that it would be fundamentally endangered if the vast capacity that results were to be turned wholeheartedly to the task of raising real wages. The difference between Marx's image of capitalism and Communist political economy is, of course, that the motive in the one case was to have been private profit; in the other it is the maintenance and extension of the élite's power.

Similarly, the political dictatorship of the élite over the majority, operating in terms of its own interests, is a fair approximation of what Marx believed to be the political conformation of capitalism, where those with property ruled; but Marx's automatic linking of property-ownership and political power left a certain gap in the mechanism of how power was exercised.* And this gap the Com-

* As Berlin points out (*op. cit.* p. 108), Bakunin perceived that, at bottom, Marx was 'a fanatical state-worshipper'; and his whole performance as a revolutionary politician, with its compulsion to exercise power personally or not at all, suggests that, in similar circumstances, he would have bridged this theoretical gap, much as Lenin did; although Marx clearly lacked Lenin's tactical gifts.

munists had to fill with the secret police, and the whole system of constraints and incentives which permit them to rule and to get the performance they want from those whom they control.

But this inversion of Marx in Marx's name also has its problems and dilemmas. While power can be held with economy of force, nationalism in Eastern Europe cannot be defeated; and, within Russia, Stalin's tactical evocation of nationalism in the 1930's and 1940's, steadily gathering force, has set up important cross-strains.

Similarly, while output can be increased by Communist techniques, the movement to technological maturity creates aspirations and levels of intellectual sophistication which also set up important cross-strains.

Moreover, the Buddenbrooks' dynamics moves on, generation by generation; those who seized power and used it to build an industrial machine of great resource may be succeeded by men who, if that machine cannot produce a decisive international result, decide that there are other and better objectives to be sought, both at home and abroad.

In short, while Lenin and Stalin—and now Mao—have succeeded in overcoming the weaknesses in Marx's analysis of the historical process, it does not follow that their techniques will prove to have long-run viability. Both Marxism and modern Communism are conceptions which set transcendent goals, independent of the techniques used to achieve them; but the long lesson of history is that the ends actually achieved are largely a function of the means used to pursue them.

COMMUNISM: A DISEASE OF THE TRANSITION

On the other hand, Communism as it is—a great fact of history—cannot be disposed of merely by revealing its nature, its deceptions, and its dilemmas. To identify the errors in Marxism and to demonstrate the un-Marxist character of Communism is not a very important achievement. The fact is that Communism as a technique of power is a formidable force. Although it was an un-Marxist insight, it was a correct insight of Lenin's that power could, under certain circumstances, be seized and held by a purposeful minority prepared to use a secret police. Although it was an un-Marxist insight, it was a correct insight that societies in the transition from traditional to modern status are peculiarly vulnerable to such a seizure of power.

It is here, in fact, that Communism is likely to find its place in history. Recall again the analysis of chapter 3, where the pre-conditions period is considered: a situation in which the society has acquired a considerable stock of social overhead capital and modern know-how, but is bedevilled not merely by the conflict between the residual traditional elements and those who would modernize its structure, but bedevilled as well by conflicts among those who would move forward, but who cannot decide which of the three roads to take, and who lack the coherence and organization to move decisively forward in any sustained direction.

It is in such a setting of political and social confusion, before the take-off is achieved and consolidated politically and socially as well as economically, that the seizure of power by Communist con-spiracy is easiest; and it is in such a setting that a centralized dictator-ship may supply an essential technical precondition for take-off and a sustained drive to maturity: an effective modern state organization.

Remember, for example, what it was in Communism that attracted the Chinese intellectuals after the First World War. It was not its Marxist strain; for the Chinese Communists were—and have re-mained—indifferent Marxists. It was not the Communist economic performance; for the Russian economy was in poor shape in the early 1920's. The Chinese intellectuals were drawn by Lenin's technique of organization as a means to unify and control a vast, deeply divided country. Both the Kuomintang and the Chinese Communists set themselves up on the Leninist model; and this was understandable in a transitional nation without an effective central government, dominated, in fact, by regional warlords. (Incidentally, if the First World War had not occurred—or had occurred a decade later—Russia would almost certainly have made a successful transition to moderni-zation and rendered itself invulnerable to Communism. Communism gripped Russia very nearly at the end of the phase when it was likely to be vulnerable to the kind of crisis which confronted it in 1917.)

Communism is by no means the only form of effective state organization that can consolidate the preconditions in the transition of a traditional society, launch a take-off, and drive a society to technological maturity. But it may be one way in which this difficult job can be done, if—and this still remains to be seen—if it can solve the problem of agricultural output in the take-off decades. Communism takes its place, then, beside the regime of the Meiji Restoration in Japan, and Ataturk's Turkey, for example, as one peculiarly inhuman form of political organization capable of launching and sustaining the growth process in societies where the preconditions period did not yield a substantial and enterprising commercial middle class and an adequate political consensus among the leaders of the society. It is a kind of disease which can befall a transitional society if it fails to organize effectively those elements within it which are prepared to get on with the job of modernization.

For those who would prefer to see the aspiring societies of the world not follow this particular road to modernization—in Asia, the Middle East, Africa, and Latin America—the Communist technique for mobilizing power and resources poses a formidable problem, almost certainly what historians will judge the central challenge of our time; that is, the challenge of creating, in association with the non-Communist politicians and peoples of the preconditions and early take-off areas, a partnership which will see them through into sustained growth on a political and social basis which keeps open the possibilities of progressive, democratic development.

A STATEMENT OF VALUES

Why is it that we want this result? What is it in our view of men and of life that reacts equally against Marx's economic determinism and Communism's Hegelian power determinism, its insistence that the correct judgment of history by the Communist élite justifies any use of power that élite judges necessary to fulfil history's laws or its own interests?

The answer lies in the nature of how we define good and evil. A colleague of mine, Professor Elting Morison of M.I.T., speaking in another context, recently said:*

My own view of evil is this: it consists of the effort to maintain a particular end—for reasons of order, logic, aesthetics, decency, for any reason at all —by means that deny men the opportunity to take into account the inevitable alternatives posed by the diversity and paradox in their own

* E. E. Morison (ed.), *The American Style*, New York, 1958, p. 321.

natures. The ends may be perverted—as to put Deutschland over all; or ideal—as to make men noble; the means may be base—as with rack, pinion, or castor oil; or benign—as to withhold from children the fact that gods got drunk and told ribald anecdotes on Olympus—it makes no difference.

This [Morison goes on] is no original view. For our civilization, we have agreed it was most memorably stated in the New Testament—with its intense concern for the relationship of a man to himself and the next man to him, with its distrust of logical system and uniform solutions, its parables radiating off their ambiguous meanings, its biting conflicting admonitions, and its insistence that wisdom is only wise if, as situations change, what is wise also changes. Such a view of things appears to have been in the minds of those who invented democracy—which is a method that in its looseness and disorder permits conflicting urges to work themselves out, and the ends of paradox to be held in tolerable but changing resolution. It does not prefigure the ends or final results. It awaits the arrival of the new occasions before supplying the new duties.

Something like Morison's statement of creed lies at the heart of all the Western societies. More than that, there is no major culture —including the Russian and Chinese—which does not, in its own way, make allowance for the uniqueness and diversity of men, and provide, in its structure and canons, for balance and for private areas of retreat and expression.

Morison's statement of the democratic creed can easily be translated into the terms of other cultures: it is, broadly speaking, what most human beings would choose, if the choice were theirs.

But societies must do more than have a creed. They must solve their problems. Democracy itself, when it works, is an extraordinary exercise in balance between imposed discipline, self-discipline, and private expression. If we and our children are to live in a setting where something like the democratic creed is the basis of organization for most societies, including our own, the problems of the transition from traditional to modern status in Asia, the Middle East, and Africa—the problems posed by the creation of the preconditions and the take-off—must be solved by means which leave open the possibility of such a humane, balanced evolution.

It is here, then, that in 1959, writing in the democratic north, the analysis of the stages-of-growth comes to an end: not with the age of affluence; not with the automobile and hire purchase; not with the problem of secular spiritual stagnation; not even with the United States and its vast baby crop; but with the dilemmas and worries of the men in Djakarta, Rangoon, New Delhi, and Karachi; the men in Tehran, Baghdad, and Cairo; the men south of the desert too, in Accra, Lagos, and Salisbury. For the fate of those of us who now live in the stage of high mass-consumption is going to be substantially determined by the nature of the preconditions process and the take-off in distant nations, processes which our societies experienced well over a century ago, in less searching and difficult forms.

It will take an act of creative imagination to understand what is going forward in these decisive parts of the world; and to decide what it is that we can and should do to play a useful part in those distant processes. We would hope that the stages-of-growth analysis, compressing and making a kind of loose order of modern historical experience, may contribute a degree of insight into matters which must of their nature be vicarious for us. We would hope, too, that a knowledge of the many diverse societies which have, in different ways, organized themselves for growth without suppressing the possibility of human freedom, will give us heart to go forward with confidence. For in the end the lesson of all this is that the tricks of growth are not all that difficult; they may seem so, at moments of frustration and confusion in transitional societies; and they seemed so when our own societies got stuck between maturity and high mass-consumption, as they did between the wars.

But on one point Marx was right—and we share his view: the end of all this is not compound interest for ever; it is the adventure of seeing what man can and will do when the pressure of scarcity is substantially lifted from him.

We should take economics seriously—but not too seriously—recalling always Keynes's toast before the Royal Economic Society in 1945: 'I give you', he said, 'the toast of the Royal Economic Society, of economics and economists, who are the trustees not of civilization, but of the possibility of civilization.' And we should bear this admonition in mind not only as an injunction to hasten the day when all can share the choices open in the stage of high mass-consumption and beyond; but in the process of moving to that stage. Billions of human beings must live in the world, if we preserve it, over the century or so until the age of high mass-consumption becomes universal. They have the right to live their time in civilized settings, marked by a degree of respect for their uniqueness and their dignity, marked by policies of balance in their societies, not merely a compulsive obsession with statistics of production, and with conformity to public goals defined by a co-optive élite. Man is a pluralistic being—a complex household, not a maximizing unit—and he has the right to live in a pluralistic society.

Moreover, as an hypothesis of social science and a statement of faith, the goals we achieve in history cannot be separated from the means we use to achieve them. There may not be much civilization left to save unless we of the democratic north face and deal with the challenge implicit in the stages-of-growth, as they now stand in the world, at the full stretch of our moral commitment, our energy, and our resources.

THE DIFFUSION OF THE
PRIVATE AUTOMOBILE

NOTES TO TABLE 8

The following sources are referred to below by abbreviated titles:

A.F. and F. = *Automobile Facts and Figures 1958*, Automobile Manufacturers Association (Detroit, 1958).
Handbuch = *Statistisches Handbuch der Weltwirtschaft* (Berlin, 1936).
Jahrbuch = *Statistisches Jahrbuch für die Bundesrepublik Deutschland*, 1953–8.
U.N.S.Y. = *United Nations Statistical Yearbook*.

UNITED STATES
Scope: The figures include taxis.
Sources: 1940–5, *Historical Statistics of the United States 1789–1945* (1949);
  1946–57, *Statistical Abstract of the United States*.
  1958, A.F. and F. (adjusted).

CANADA—including Newfoundland from 1949
Scope: The figures include commercial vehicles until 1921. The number of commercial vehicles then was 42,000. Taxis are included from 1931; there were 8,000 in 1930.
Sources: 1904–56, *Canada Yearbook*.
  1957, U.N.S.Y.

FRANCE (including Alsace-Lorraine from 1921)
Scope: The figures include commercial vans of under 1-ton capacity, except from 1951 to 1953.
Sources: 1904–10, 1914–33, *Annuaire Statistique de la France, 1936*.
  1913, Handbuch; 1934–36, Jahrbuch.
  1937–56, U.N.S.Y.
  1957, A.F. and F.

GREAT BRITAIN
Scope: The figures for 1904–20 include Ireland. In 1921 there were 4,000 private automobiles in Northern Ireland.
Dates: 1904–20, 31 March; 1921, highest Quarter; 1922–34, 1939–45, 31 August; 1935–8, 1946–58, September Quarter.
Sources: 1904–21, *Motor Industry of Great Britain, 1947* (Society of Motor Manufacturers, 1947).
  1922–34, *Statistical Abstract for the United Kingdom*.
  1935–57, *Annual Abstract of Statistics*.
  1958, *Monthly Digest of Statistics*.

GERMANY
Scope: 1913–38, figures are for Germany within its various frontiers, but excluding Austria in 1938. The figures include buses (28,000 in 1938).
  1939–57, figures are for the area of the Bundesrepublik, excluding the Saar and West Berlin.
Before 1954, dual-purpose vehicles were not separately distinguished. From 1954, when there were 33,000 dual-purpose vehicles, they are included with private cars.

GERMANY *(cont.)*

Sources: 1913–36, Handbuch.
    1937–8, *Statistisches Jahrbuch für das Deutsche Reich.*
    1939–58, Jahrbuch.

ITALY

Scope: The figures include taxis.
Sources: 1913, Handbuch.
    1911–12, 1914–57, *Annuario Statistico Italiano*, 1953–8.

JAPAN

Scope: The series are especially discontinuous because no single source was available, and because Japanese motor vehicles are not easy to classify. Motor-rickshaws are excluded until 1929. Midget cars, of which there were over half a million in 1955, are excluded throughout. The major discontinuity is between 1935 and 1937. On the 1935 basis the 1937–8 figures of 60 and 59 thousand would perhaps have been 100–105 thousand.
Dates: 1913, 1920–25, 31 March; 1916–19, 1926–30, December; 1931–3, August; 1934–5, October; 1937–57, December.
Sources: 1913, 1920–25, Handbuch.
    1915–19, *Annuaire Statistique de la France, 1936.*
    1926–30, *League of Nations Statistical Yearbook.*
    1931–35, Mitsubishi Economic Research Unit: *Japanese Trade and Industry* (London, 1936).
    1937–56, U.N.S.Y.
    1957, A.F. and F. (adjusted).

RUSSIA

Scope: From 1946 the figures are guesses, apparently originating from *American Automobile.*
Dates: 1924–8, 1931–2, 1 January; 1929–30, October; 1933–41, December.
Sources: 1913–32, Handbuch.
    1933–6, *Motor Industry of Great Britain.*
    1937–42, *Automobile Facts and Figures*, American Automobile Manufacturers Association, Detroit.
    1946–57, Jahrbuch.

NOTES TO TABLE 9

1. For scope of the automobile licensing figures, see Notes to Table 8.

2. Where the dates to which the licensing figures relate have varied, the population figures used have been adjusted for this. Where the licensing dates used are consistent, mid-year populations have been used throughout.

3. The sources for the population figures are generally the same as for the licensing figures. The 1913–38 figures for Japan are from K. Ohkawa, *The Growth Rate of the Japanese Economy Since 1878* (Tokyo, 1957). Figures for post-war years are generally from *United Nations Demographic Yearbook.*

4. Wartime population figures are seldom comparable with those for normal periods, which are usually *de facto* or approximately *de facto*; and ratios of automobiles to population signify very little in wartime. Thus ratios are, in general, not indicated for the years in which a country was involved in one of the World Wars.

5. Some of the figures used for France, Germany, Japan and Russia in recent years, and for Italy and Japan before 1920, have been added or revised since the charts were drawn.

TABLE 8. *Private automobiles in use in certain countries, 1900–58*

(Thousands)

Year	United States	Canada	France	Great Britain	Germany	Italy	Japan	Russia
1900	8	.	3	.	.	.	.	.
1901	15	.	.	.	.	.	.	.
1902	23	.	.	.	.	.	.	.
1903	33	.	.	.	.	.	.	.
1904	55	1	.	8	.	.	.	.
1905	77	1	22	16	.	.	.	.
1906	106	1	.	23	.	.	.	.
1907	140	2	.	32	.	.	.	.
1908	194	3	.	41	.	.	.	.
1909	306	5	.	48	.	.	.	.
1910	458	9	54	53	.	.	.	.
1911	619	22	.	72	.	14	.	.
1912	902	36	.	88	.	17	.	.
1913	1,190	54	91	106	50	20	1	7
1914	1,664	74	108	132	.	22	.	.
1915	2,332	95	.	139	.	23	1	.
1916	3,368	128	.	142	.	21	1	.
1917	4,727	204	.	110	.	17	1	.
1918	5,555	277	.	78	.	7	3	.
1919	6,679	342	.	110	.	24	4	.
1920	8,132	409	135	187	.	31	6	.
1921	9,212	423†	173	246*	61	34	8	.
1922	10,704	462	217	315*	83	41	10	.
1923	13,253	515	266	384	100	54	12	.
1924	15,436	574	352	474	132	57	15	7
1925	17,440	640	453	580	175	85	21	7
1926	19,221	736	541	676	207	105	28*	8
1927	20,142	821	643	778	268	119	35	8
1928	21,308	921	758	877	351	144	47	9
1929	23,060	1,014	930	970	433	170	52	11*
1930	22,973	1,047	1,109	1,042	501	183	56*	10
1931	22,330	1,024*	1,252	1,076	523	186	64	11*
1932	20,832	945	1,279	1,119	497	188	67	15
1933	20,586	917	1,397	1,196	522	219	68	26*
1934	21,472	952	1,432	1,298	675	236	76*	34
1935	22,495	990	.	1,477*	810	244	83	44
1936	24,108	1,042	1,687	1,643	960	222	.	45
1937	25,391	1,103	1,721	1,798	1,126	271	60†	65*
1938	25,167	1,160	1,818	1,944	1,300	289	59	85
1939	26,140	1,190	2,020	2,034*	713†	290	.	.
1940	27,372	1,235	.	1,423	.	270	.	.
1941	29,524	1,280	.	1,503	.	97	.	170
1942	27,869	1,217	.	858	.	74	.	.
1943	25,913	1,194	.	718	.	.	.	.
1944	25,466	.	.	755	.	.	.	.
1945	25,691	1,160	.	1,487	.	.	.	.
1946	28,100	1,234	1,550	1,770*	.	150	20	150†
1947	30,719	1,370	.	1,944	187	184	28	.
1948	33,214	1,497	1,519	1,961	215*	219	30	.
1949	36,312	1,672*	1,520	2,131	352	267	36	.
1950	40,185	1,907	.	2,258	516	342	43	.
1951	42,525	2,098	1,600*	2,380	682	425	58	180
1952	43,654	2,296	1,800	2,508	900*	510	88	180
1953	46,289	2,514	2,020	2,762	1,126	613	115	225
1954	48,324	2,688	2,677*	3,100	1,393*	744	139	225
1955	51,989	2,935	3,016	3,526	1,663	879	153	350
1956	54,004	3,187	3,477	3,888	2,030	1,051	181	400
1957	55,693	3,375	3,972	4,187	2,436	1,237	219	415
1958	56,645	.	.	4,549	2,936	.	.	.

* Change in series.　　　　† Major change in series.

TABLE 9. *Private automobiles in use per million population, in certain countries, 1900–58*

Year	United States	Canada	France	Great Britain	Germany	Italy	Japan	Russia
1900	100	.	80	.	.	.	.	.
1901	190	.	.	.	.	.	.	.
1902	290	.	.	.	.	.	.	.
1903	410	.	.	.	.	.	.	.
1904	670	86	.	220	.	.	.	.
1905	920	100	560	410	.	.	.	.
1906	1,240	230	.	600	.	.	.	.
1907	1,610	330	.	830	.	.	.	.
1908	2,190	470	.	1,030	.	.	.	.
1909	3,380	710	.	1,200	.	.	.	.
1910	4,960	1,320	1,370	1,310	.	.	.	.
1911	6,590	3,020	.	1,760	.	400	.	.
1912	9,460	4,930	.	2,150	.	480	.	.
1913	12,200	7,130	2,290	2,560	740	580	20	52
1914	16,800	9,420	2,710	3,160	.	610	.	.
1915	23,200	.	.	.	.	.	.	.
1916	33,000	.	.	.	.	.	.	.
1917	45,800	.	.	.	.	.	.	.
1918	53,800	.	.	.	.	.	.	.
1919	63,900	41,200	.	.	.	670	70	.
1920	76,400	47,800	3,460	4,440	.	870	100	.
1921	84,900	48,100†	4,410	5,660*	970	900	140	.
1922	97,300	51,800	5,500	7,320*	1,340	1,070	170	.
1923	118,000	57,200	6,670	8,870	1,610	1,390	210	.
1924	135,000	62,800	8,730	10,900	2,110	1,460	250	47
1925	151,000	68,800	11,200	13,300	2,770	2,160	350	53
1926	161,000	77,900	13,200	15,400	3,250	2,650	460*	54
1927	169,000	85,200	15,700	17,600	4,180	2,980	580	56
1928	177,000	93,700	18,500	19,800	5,460	3,570	760	57
1929	189,000	101,000	22,600	21,800	6,690	4,170	820	69*
1930	186,000	103,000	26,700	23,300	7,700	4,460	880*	61
1931	180,000	98,700*	29,900	24,000	7,990	4,490	980	68*
1932	167,000	90,000	30,600	24,800	7,570	4,510	1,010	92
1933	164,000	86,200	33,300	26,400	7,910	5,200	1,020	157*
1934	170,000	90,900	34,100	28,600	10,200	5,560	1,120*	201
1935	177,000	91,300	.	32,400*	12,100	5,700	1,200	260
1936	188,000	95,100	40,300	35,900	14,300	5,160	.	270
1937	197,000	99,900	41,900	39,100	16,600	6,250	850†	380*
1938	194,000	104,000	44,100	42,100	19,000	6,610	830	500
1939	200,000	106,000	49,000	43,600*	17,800†	6,710	.	.
1940	207,000	.	.	.	.	.	.	.
1941	222,000	.	.	.	.	.	.	930
1942	.	.	.	.	.	.	.	.
1943	.	.	.	.	.	.	.	.
1944	.	.	.	.	.	.	.	.
1945	.	.	.	.	.	.	.	.
1946	201,000	100,000	38,300	37,300*	.	3,240	.	1,100†
1947	214,000	109,000	.	40,600	4,160	4,020	360	.
1948	227,000	117,000	36,700	40,500	4,650*	4,730	380	.
1949	244,000	124,000*	36,500	43,800	7,480	5,750	390	.
1950	266,000	139,000	.	46,100	10,700	7,310	520	.
1951	277,000	150,000	37,900*	48,600	14,100	9,010	680	1,000
1952	280,000	159,000	41,300	51,100	18,500*	10,800	1,020	.
1953	292,000	169,000	47,200	56,100	23,000	12,900	1,320	1,200
1954	300,000	175,000	62,100*	62,800	28,000*	15,500	1,560	.
1955	316,000	186,000	69,300	71,100	33,100	18,200	1,710	1,800
1956	323,000	197,000	79,300	78,100	40,000	21,700	2,000	2,000
1957	327,000	203,000	89,700	83,600	47,300	25,500	2,410	2,000
1958	327,000			90,300	56,300			

* Change in series. † Major change in series.

THE CRITICS AND THE EVIDENCE

I. AN APPROACH TO THE DEBATE

A good many economists and historians have commented on *The Stages of Economic Growth.* In replying to the debate, I have grouped the questions raised analytically rather than *ad hominem.**
One or another critic is sometimes strongly associated with a particular line of argument; and this will naturally emerge, where necessary. But my purpose here is to get at certain issues of substance in as constructive a way as I can rather than to perpetuate the title of Henry Rosovsky's engaging review article, 'The Take-off into Sustained Controversy' (*Journal of Economic History*, June 1965, pp. 271–5). I believe that we are at a point in the study of economic growth where a good many of the issues under debate can be resolved or lucidly narrowed in ways which would permit us to get on with the common job from a reasonably common perspective.

I have, therefore, organized this exposition around the following questions of substance:

Is the stages of growth a teleological argument, as Myrdal claims, 'in which a purpose, which is not explicitly intended by anyone, is fulfilled while the process of fulfillment is presented as an inevitable sequence of events'? (G. Myrdal, *Asian Drama*, New York, 1968, p. 1851.) Or, in more familiar terms, how self-sustained (or automatic) is self-sustained growth?

Does the stages of growth violate the uniqueness of the historical

* Some of the issues dealt with here were debated at length at the Conference of the International Economic Association held at Konstanz, Germany, in the summer of 1960. The papers prepared for that conference, a summary of the debate, and a reply by the author to the debate, are incorporated in *The Economics of Take-off into Sustained Growth*, W. W. Rostow (ed.), New York, 1963. At a few points in this Appendix I have drawn on passages from that book, but, essentially, I have dealt with the matter afresh. The interested reader can pursue at greater length in that volume some of the issues discussed here.

cases? If the legitimacy of some form of generalization about growth is admitted, what legitimacy can be claimed for the stages of growth?

Do the leading sector complexes provide a reasonable working basis for dating the stages of economic growth? How do they relate to movements in such aggregates as GNP, the rate of investment, and the productivity of investment?

Where, in the light of the evidence, does the analysis of the debated British, French, and United States take-offs stand?

Does the evidence available on the unfolding of the growth process in the contemporary developing world support or deny the concept of stages of economic growth?

The Appendix closes with some observations on the Marxist critics.

II. GROWTH AND AUTOMATICITY

First, then, Myrdal and teleology.

On my view there is a good deal that is automatic about the process of growth after take-off, and a good deal that is not.

One must start with the British take-off and what it is that has spread the modern process of growth out from the British base where it first took firm roots.

Behind the British take-off was the process discussed on pages 31–5, which I shall not recount here. At its core was acceptance of the view that the physical world was understandable in terms of a few stable principles and, therefore, capable of systematic manipulation to man's advantage. This attitude, which I have called the Newtonian perception, provides an element of automaticity to growth because it drives men, in the face of problems, to search for solutions rather than passively to accept the burdens and frustrations the problems impose. It also leads men to perceive and exploit possibilities for profit. It thus helps induce invention and innovation as a more or less regular flow; and it is this which distinguishes the modern world from all previous history.

The Newtonian perception was given a special thrust and direction because those who acted on it early gained power (economic, political, and military) relative to those who acted on it late. The strongest force that has operated to induce and diffuse the impulse to growth has been the intrusion of the more advanced nations on the less advanced. Between *Le Défi Brittanique* after 1815 and *Le Défi Americain* after 1945 many parts of the world experienced a series of intrusions much less benign. Colonialism filled the vacuums left in Africa and Asia. Mexico, Russia, China, Japan, Turkey, and others, were shocked by military pressure on to the long, slow road to modernization. The profit motive played its part in the spread of modern growth; but it was Alexander Hamilton's insight that was critical in one nation after another down to the present day: 'not only the wealth but the independence and security of a country appear to be materially connected with the prosperity of manufactures'.

The process of political and social as well as economic modernization that was induced by such external pressures, reflections on them, and reactions to them, created the human and institutional basis not merely for take-off but for the stages of growth beyond.

There *is* an element of teleology here: the nations intruded upon intended to retain or recover their dignity. It usually took some time before the Hamiltonian insight was sufficiently accepted—and the political, social, and institutional life of the society sufficiently reorganized—to get on with growth as a way of defending or re-achieving that dignity. In a sense, economic growth has been a derived demand.

I take growth to be one manifestation of a much wider process of modernization forced upon more backward nations by the consequences of failing to modernize in an inherently competitive and contentious arena of world power. *The Stages* asserts that a theory of economic growth must be part of a larger theory of modernization. I would hold that the theory of modernization embedded in this book is not tautological, once the first case of take-off is accounted for.

Out of economic modernization, however, came a technical economic factor that contributed an element of automaticity to the growth process; that is, a rise in the investment rate. Such an increase before and during take-off—and even at later stages—did not guarantee uninterrupted growth; but the savings habits of individuals, the plough-back policies of firms, and the public investment patterns set within government tended to make growth an ongoing—if not a continuous—process.

We have arrayed, then, psychological, political, institutional, and technical factors which, taken together, tended to make growth, once begun, automatic.

On the other hand, the sectoral view of growth incorporated in *The Stages* immediately suggests that growth is not continuous and automatic; for any given sectoral complex is subject to retardation. It follows directly from sectoral retardation that growth is not mechanically assured.

If, on this view, a society is to sustain a high average rate of growth, it must engage in an endless struggle against deceleration; for while the flow of modern science and technology may offer the potentiality of fending off Ricardian diminishing returns indefinitely, a society which wishes to exploit this potentiality must repeat the creative pain of actually introducing new production functions as the old leading sectors decelerate; and it must demonstrate the capacity to exploit with vigour their potential spreading effects. In this sense sustained growth requires the repetition of the take-off process. It requires the organization around new technology of new and vigorous management; new types of workers; new types of financing and marketing arrangements. It requires struggle against constraints created in the previous generation or two around the peculiar imperatives of an older set of leading sectors now no longer capable of carrying the economy forward at its old pace.

These transitions from one set of leading sectors to another are neither trivial nor abstruse phenomena. We can identify their consequence in the sweep of modern economic history and on the contemporary scene. I am inclined to think, for example, that when we have fully examined the 1880's in Western Europe and the United States, we shall find the widespread deceleration in that decade related in part to the process of disengagement from the railroad era and to the process of catching hold fully of the potentialities implicit in the new leading sectors: steel, electricity, and chemicals, and all their secondary consequences. I believe we shall increasingly interpret a significant element in the interwar sluggishness of Western Europe as due to the process of disengagement from the old leading sectors of the pre-1914 and wartime years and to the rather slow preparation for the age of high mass-consumption which, in the 1950's, at last fully seized Western Europe, as the lessons of income analysis were learned and the old men of steel and electricity and heavy chemicals were superseded by the bright young men of automobiles and plastics, electronics, and aeronautics. It is true that the level of per capita income in Western Europe was less than in the United States in the 1920's; but, as the European experience during the recovery in the 1930's indicates, it was sufficiently high so that policies of full employment could have brought the automobile sectoral complex into play, if such policies had been pursued. The Soviet Union in the 1960's has experienced the discomfiture of deceleration for reasons not unlike those that shaped interwar Western Europe. It is, however, not the level of income per capita but a refusal of public policy to permit the economy to respond to the income elasticity of demand which has delayed for so long the high mass-consumption Soviet citizens so palpably desire. And it may not be unhelpful to view the sluggishness of the American economy in the late 1950's as an interval between the time when the automobile and all its works had lost the capacity to serve as a leading sector and the time when new leading sectors— mainly private and public services—take hold in the search for quality.

In addition to the discontinuities in growth built into the process of moving from one leading sector complex to another, there have been business cycles and trend periods, revolutions and wars, and self-inflicted distortions like those which flowed from Chinese and Indian agricultural policy in the 1950's and 1960's—distortions noted in the text (p. 45) which subsequently had major consequences in both countries.

There is, moreover, nothing in theory that decrees a society might not, after a certain degree of modernization, decide to pull back from the effort as a matter of political and social policy. Burma has done something like this in recent years, just as some American Indians, having taken a look around, have returned to their reservations. In the contemporary world, however, three factors are likely to make such a policy of withdrawal untenable for a nation state over a substantial period of time:

(1) Intrusion or threatened intrusion by more powerful neighbours who accept the burdens and disciplines of growth.

(2) Pressures arising from a continued rise in population, since it is extremely difficult to deny the people public health and, therefore, difficult to maintain a stable equilibrium without a purposeful growth policy.

(3) The real or believed attractions of modern living standards to the people, as projected by modern communications.

In short, on present evidence it appears fair to say that the larger psychological, social, political, technological, economic, and institutional changes required for a take-off are such—and the international environment is such—as to make it unlikely that we shall see a true lapsing back. Men in societies must continue to struggle to keep growth moving forward; and one of the purposes of this mode of analysis, rooted in leading sectors, is to specify one substantial part of that struggle. But the deeper fundamentals required for an effective take-off appear, on present evidence, sufficiently powerful to make growth an ongoing process, on long term.

In this context perhaps the oddest of the criticisms made of *The Stages* was Myrdal's notion that it encouraged the view that it was 'futile and "unhistorical" for the state or any other group to intervene with the intention of promoting freely chosen objectives' (p. 1855). As an old advocate of development planning (and of foreign assistance geared to national development planning), I found this incongruous. But the charge could still be valid if the theoretical structure of *The Stages* encouraged an inevitability beyond the capacity of men and governments to shape. In fact, the theory leaves place at every stage for societies to intervene politically—and otherwise—to shape the manner in which they absorb the stock and flow of technologies (for example, pp. 14–16). It sought to underline—not limit or render inevitable—the choices men must make as they decide how to deploy their enlarged resources; although the range of choices available at any particular time is, as always, framed and limited by the resources a society can mobilize and the imperatives of the technologies it desires to absorb.

I would assert, then, that there is uniformity in the technologies available at a given period of time; and the absorption of these technologies does carry with it some significant economic, social, and political imperatives which set a range on the choices open to a society at a given stage of growth, at a given period of time. But within those constraints *The Stages* argues that there is and will be great variety in the patterns of public policy, political systems, and social structures which have accompanied their absorptions. (In writing *The Stages*—and examining the evidence accumulated since—I found the income elasticity of demand more uniform internationally than I would have guessed, although it is by no means identical.)

I conclude that there are elements of automaticity built into the nature of the growth process; but there are also a succession of challenges which must be overcome as growth unfolds, whose solutions are not automatic, as the irregularities of growth—in the past and present—attest. Assessing these forces, it was my judgment —and remains my judgment—that the contemporary developing nations will persist in their efforts and, on balance, move ahead; although the lion of excessive population increase will have to be removed from their path if tragic Malthusian crises are to be avoided along the way. But that is an assessment of how conflicting forces will net out, not a statement of theoretical inevitability, automaticity, or mechanical continuity.

III. UNIQUENESS AND GENERALITY

Some of the criticisms of *The Stages* asserted that the concept did violence to the uniqueness and variety of national experiences, past and present; for example, A. K. Cairncross: 'in the present volume he seems to me to have made the Muse of History lie on the bed of Procrustes' (*Economic History Review*, April 1961, p. 458). Underlying this criticism is a basic problem of social science.

We all start, I assume, with two propositions about economic growth since the late eighteenth century:

(1) in a meaningful sense, each story of national development is unique;

(2) there are some meaningful generalizations to be made about them.

These propositions hold because we are dealing with phenomena where the results emerge from interactions too complex to trace in full detail; where no two cases will be identical; but where certain common forces and principles are at work which yield sufficient similarities to permit classification, orderly analysis, and, at least, a degree of predictability. (In *The Stages* I ventured a number of predictions; for example, a statement of the issues American society would confront as it moved beyond high mass-consumption; the slowdown in the Soviet economy and rising pressures for high mass-consumption; the diffusion of power away from Moscow and Washington; the possible vicissitudes of Indian and Chinese take-offs due to inadequate allocations to agriculture; the likely acceleration in Spanish growth, etc.)

In economic growth, as in any form of analytic history, we are dealing, then, with a biological science.

In approaching a body of evidence of this kind, a variety of perspectives can be fruitful. I do not regard it as a criticism of my critics to say that the bulk of their comments (for example, at the International Economic Association meeting at Konstanz in 1960) were, in fact, justifications for their ways of making some order of the evidence rather than mine.

I greatly respect the work of, say, Kuznets, Gerschenkron, and Solow, to take three who have sought to classify substantial bodies of evidence on growth at different levels of generality with different tools. But something more than mutual tolerance is needed for progress in science. Therefore, I shall try to state here precisely why I believe the approach used in *The Stages* is not only legitimate but fundamental to making the analysis of growth a useful biological science.

The first question to be answered is this: What is basic about economic growth? Here, I believe, we all agree: growth is the consequence of the progressive, efficient absorption into the economy of new technologies. Or, as Kuznets put it: 'Behind all this is the increasing stock of useful knowledge derived from modern science, and the capacity of society, under the spur of modern ideology, to evolve institutions which permit a greater exploitation of the growth potential provided by that increasing stock of knowledge.' (*The Economics of Take-off*, p. 22.)

The second question to be answered is: What is universal about the process of growth? The answer is: Technologies are, essentially, uniform at particular times in modern history. (I shall deal with the changing content of technologies later.)

In focusing on the coming in of new technologies, we are isolating, then, a factor both basic and relatively uniform. We have, therefore, a good initial scientific platform to proceed to classification.

The societies which have experienced take-off, or gone beyond, represent wide variations in culture, social structure, and politics. They have been of various sizes, endowed with various resources and resource/population balances, and have had different trade and capital flow relations to the international economy. They have had a variety of experiences of military or other intrusion from more advanced external powers; and their allocations of resources to military purposes have varied over a considerable range. And they have been drawn into the process of modernization at different times, with a different mix of technologies available to them.

Since all these economic and non-economic factors bear on the path of a society's economic development, we must expect wide variation in patterns of growth; and we find them.

But if we choose to proceed towards generalization, I would hold that the most fundamental approach is to identify the extent to which particular technologies have been absorbed efficiently into the economy, and the sequence in which they are absorbed. This means we must look at the sectors and sub-sectors, not merely the aggregates. Technology is not absorbed in GNP. Movements in GNP reflect the process of absorption, as well as other variables. Technologies are absorbed in particular industries and sub-sectors of industry or in branches of agriculture, mining, services, etc.

To be concrete, I believe that the approach of Simon Kuznets and Walther Hoffmann in the 1930's (*Secular Movements in Production and Prices*, 1930, and *Stadien und Typen der Industrialisierung*, 1931) had the root of the matter in it; as does the shift towards disaggregation to be noted in the latter part of Hollis Chenery and Lance Taylor's statistical analysis of growth patterns ('Development Patterns: Among Countries and Over Time', *The Review of Economics and Statistics*, November 1968, pp. 405–15.)

Every historian who embeds himself in the evidence on a particular economy knows, in fact, that the story of its growth must be told by sectors and sub-sectors, as well as by using the large aggregates. That is why the debate over *The Stages* is intellectually much narrower with the historians of particular countries than it is with, say, Kuznets.

Every development planner knows he must make his investment plans by sectors, sub-sectors, and, even, major particular installations, not merely in terms of GNP, levels of investment, and such broad but ambiguous categories as agriculture, industry, and services. That is why development planners have, by and large, found *The Stages* a congenial construct.

I shall have more to say about aggregation and disaggregation when we consider the question of continuity and discontinuity in the next section.

The argument here is that the sectoral approach used in *The Stages* does get directly at what is most basic and universal in growth; that the leading sector complexes on which stages of growth analysis is based are, relatively, uniform and that by breaking into the evidence on growth through the leading sector complexes, we have a correct initial base for the task of classification which growth as a biological science demands.

Now, what about the changing pool of international technology as it has evolved over the past two centuries?

In *The Stages* I noted that the most profound current advantage of the contemporary developing nations lies in the enormous backlog of technology available to them, although this backlog is also the proximate source of their very high rates of population increase which is their greatest relative disadvantage (pp. 140–1). It is undeniable that the changing pool of technology has caused differences in patterns of growth at different periods: in the late eighteenth century one could only build turnpikes and canals, not railways; the first railway had to be built with iron, not steel; the automobile and the airplane were not available in the nineteenth century, nor satellite communications, IR–8 rice, and antibiotics. And all this must be taken into account. On the other hand, when the sectoral pattern of growth is examined over, say, the past twenty-five years, what is striking is the broad degree of continuity with the past in the sectoral tasks of growth at different stages in the contemporary world.

Appendix B

(I make this point in 'The Past Quarter-Century as Economic History and the Tasks of International Economic Organization', *Journal of Economic History*, March 1970; and evidence bearing on it is presented below, pp. 230–3 and 235–7.)

The tasks of the preconditions period (e.g., in Black Africa) remain as they have long been: the buildup of infrastructure, the education of a generation of modern men, the creation of institutions which can absorb technology and mobilize capital; the expansion of agriculture to permit the growing cities to be fed; and the generation of increased export earning capacity. The first range of industries tends to remain light-consumers' goods, including the most classic of all— factory-manufactured textiles. Beyond take-off there are, evidently, sub-sectors of the engineering, chemical, and electricity industries not known before, say, 1914. But the capital deepening that goes with the drive to technological maturity in, say, contemporary Mexico, Iran, Taiwan, and Turkey bears an unforced family resemblance to that which occurred in, say, post-Civil War America, post-1870 Germany, post-1905 Japan and Russia.

The automobile–durable consumers' complex, in its widest sense, is, of course, distinctly a product of the twentieth century. Only in this century has the level of income per capita in certain countries, in conjunction with existing technologies, permitted the way of life for substantial proportions of national populations that goes with the automobile age. And in Latin America (and elsewhere) the automobile sectoral complex is proving a route into heavy engineering and fabricating industries not unlike the nineteenth-century railways in Western Europe and the United States.

In short, the alteration of technologies with the passage of time must be taken into account. It does change the sectoral content of the stages of growth for the latecomers (as, indeed, it did to a lesser extent for the pre-1914 latecomers). But it does not make the approach to growth via stages—rooted in a sequence of sectoral complexes—less germane; nor does it repeal the relevance of economic history to the contemporary world.

What about Gerschenkron and degrees of backwardness? As a student of European economic history, Gerschenkron has chosen to focus his attention on the differences he perceives among those who absorbed modern technologies late rather than early in that region. This is, of course, a wholly legitimate as well as interesting problem to explore. He has made it clear that he is not sure—and I am not sure—how his general propositions, based essentially on a comparison of Britain, France, Germany, and Russia, relate to all the other parts of Europe, let alone the rest of the world; although he has significant things to say, also, about Italy, Bulgaria, and the Austro–Hungarian empire. (Steven L. Barsby has conducted a general test of Gerschenkron's hypothesis, 'Economic Backwardness and the Characteristics of Development', *Journal of Economic History*, September 1969.) But generalizations about regional similarities and differences clearly have their place along with many other types of generalization in the study of growth.

Since Gerschenkron focused so sharply on what distinguishes, in particular, the pre-1914 pattern of Russian growth from the earlier European cases, I find no difficulty understanding that he would resist the argument in chapter 7 on the parallelisms between Russian and American growth.

But chapter 7 is, in my view, also a legitimate way to get at a significant question. It begins by recognizing that: 'There are, of course, profound special elements in the story of the evolution of modern Russian society and its economy...' It then explored certain parallelisms in two major continental economies—starting from such different points, as Tocqueville pointed out so long ago—whose take-offs came some half century apart. It examined in the late 1950's the prospects for Soviet growth in the 1960's, and it tried to define the sense in which relative United States–Soviet growth rates did and did not constitute a challenge to the United States. With the benefit of an additional decade's evidence, I would not alter substantively what is said in chapter 7.

In short, a biological science has place within it for studies of both similarities and differences of pattern.

The major alternative to the sectoral approach used in *The Stages* is, of course, that carried forward by Simon Kuznets and those whom he has led and inspired. Moving beyond the pioneering work of Colin Clark, Kuznets, in one of the major modern efforts in social science, has organized and arrayed in a systematic way certain statistical data on growth, historical and contemporary. We are all in his debt.

The problem posed by his work in relation to *The Stages* is, simply, that the kinds of data available for systematic international comparison over considerable periods of time force his studies to a level of aggregation which does not permit the sequence of leading sector complexes to be clearly identified. Therefore, the actual coming in of new technologies is by-passed or masked. Given his early pioneering work in the field of leading sectors, he is, of course, sensitive to the problem. In his *Modern Economic Growth* Kuznets has this to say (pp. 24–6):

With all these problems in defining and measuring comprehensive aggregates like national product, it may be thought that more circumscribed measures, whose meaning can be more easily specified, might be taken as indexes of economic growth. For example, if certain production sectors are typically modern, in the sense that they are using the science-based technology of modern times, the increase in *their* output—either total or per capita—might seem a less equivocal measure of economic growth than an increase in the more diverse congeries of goods entering total national product. One might then try to measure the economic growth of a country by the increase in per capita output of one or several modern sectors, setting aside for the moment any difficulties that might arise in identifying these for a given country and for a long period.

It can hardly be denied that the growth of modern sectors is of primary interest in the study of the mechanism of economic growth, particularly if one adheres to the view that at any given time in the history of a country's economy some dynamic 'leading' sectors are the loci of rapid growth which, through various linkages, induce growth elsewhere in the economy. But unless the relation between changes in these modern, 'leading' sectors and the rest of the economy is significant, stable, and general, a marked rise in these modern sectors may have little effect on the persistently stagnating remainder of the economy of some countries and thus on their overall growth; whereas in other countries a smaller rise in the output of the modern sectors may have a far greater effect on the growth of the economy. Presumably a variety of factors determine and affect this relation between the modern or 'leading' sectors and the rest of the economy, but insofar as one of these factors is the relative magnitudes of the individual sectors, we must again face the problem of defining and measuring the aggregate of which a leading sector is a part.

In defining and measuring the economic growth of a country, there is at present no escape from the obligation to be comprehensive. Our knowledge of the structure is still not firm enough to permit us to use a part as representative of the whole. Indeed, there is danger in making premature claims that we can do so; in assuming, for example, that a few blast furnaces and electric power stations in and of themselves—not for what they represent (under certain conditions *but not always*), and not for what they may induce elsewhere (under certain conditions *but not always*)—are reliable evidence of significant growth of a country's economy. And this comment applies even to an index of manufacturing production or of mechanical energy consumption.

This does not mean that a whole battery of such partial indexes could not be constructed—one that would provide a sound basis for diagnosing growth of a country's economy. But it would be a sizable research task to identify an adequate number of such partial indexes; and even then, they would remain nonadditive unless we could assign the proper weights to them, which we cannot do now. Particularly, they would not now yield an easily additive aggregate like national product, of which so many significant sub-divisions can be measured as components.

Kuznets offers, then, a variety of related reasons for not proceeding in his study of *Modern Growth* on the basis of his insights in *Secular Movements in Prices and Production*: the difficulty of measuring the extent of the impact of leading sectors on the economy as a whole; the inherent variability of that relationship (depending on whether the institutions of the society respond to potential spreading effects); the problem of sub-sectoral data collection; the problem of weighting sub-indexes in relation to the aggregates.

In short, Kuznets made a strategic decision to proceed at a high level of aggregation, knowing its intellectual and conceptual cost. He knew he could not establish the linkage between the coming in of new technologies and the growth process, a linkage he recognized as fundamental. The comparable data for a full and systematic statistical analysis on an international basis were simply not there; and there was the extremely difficult conceptual and technical problem of the spreading effects. As a statistician, he chose to exploit the data he had. In so doing, he cut his analysis of growth down to the level of reputable formal statistical techniques he could apply with the data available.

Conscious of precisely these problems, I made a different strategic decision. For a decade (in some cases, for much more than a decade) I had pored with my students over the stories of national growth, country by country, on a sectoral basis. The reality of leading sector complexes—and the sequences of them which constitute the bone structure of national economic development—became quite clear. I also studied, of course, the aggregative data available. I decided to build *The Stages* around these leading sector complexes even though I was not in a position to present in a formal statistical way the role of the leading sectors in relation to the aggregates. I did not believe that what I regard as a correct approach to growth analysis should await the day when all the statistical data could be arrayed in a formally correct statistical manner. I was satisfied by my examination of the data that the phenomena identified were real; and their quantitative importance could be confirmed as our common knowledge expanded.

Behind this decision of strategy in *The Stages* was an experience and a judgment.

The experience was the work I did within the project of Arthur D. Gayer on the British economy from 1790–1850 (A. D. Gayer *et al.*, *The Growth and Fluctuation of the British Economy, 1790–1850*, Oxford, 1953). In that book a group of us came closer, I believe, than in any other study of a whole national economy, to fulfilling Wesley Mitchell's dream of uniting formal statistical analysis with history, institutional analysis, and theory. Working closely together, Anna Jacobson Schwartz, Isaiah Frank, Gayer and I were able, using National Bureau of Economic Research measures of cyclical and trend analysis, to identify average patterns of behaviour and average deviations from them. Perhaps most important, we were able to understand the analytic meaning of average behaviour because we had a full, case-by-case factual grasp on the deviations. But I emerged from that exercise with the judgment that when the body of statistical data had been examined carefully in the light of all the known statistical and qualitative evidence that bore upon it, the formal statistical analysis added little that we did not already know.

Other experiences also brought me to this conclusion: while it is always preferable to have complete data—capable of formal statistical measurement and comparison—I am not intimidated by data which fall short of such high standards, but which are sufficiently full to illuminate the key questions at issue.

There would, in fact, not be much economic history written—or economic policy made—if intellectual judgment were suspended until data were available capable of manipulation at the highest level of statistical correctness and sophistication. And none of the classics in economic theory—from *Wealth of Nations* to *The General Theory* —would have been published if their authors had waited until their quantitative conceptions could be rigorously presented in the form of statistics.

This relates to my second reason for the strategy adopted in *The Stages*: how data come to be available.

The data we have are not the product of immaculate conception: they are usually the product of bureaucracies. Bureaucracies come to collect data because they are evidently needed for policy purposes or because the intellectual climate of the time suggests that they are relevant to public policy. The data we have are, with a considerable time lag, the product of policy or intellectual questions posed in the past—sometimes the distant past.

In formulating and writing *The Stages*, I wished to encourage the collection and organization of data in new ways that would, for example, disaggregate the arbitrary and sometimes misleading categories of agriculture, industry, and services; which would break down the typical nine-fold classification of manufacturing: food, beverages, tobacco; textile products; leather and rubber; forest products; paper and printing; stone, clay, and glass; chemical and petroleum; metal products; miscellaneous. I also wished to encourage the collection of data that would group industries by leading sector complexes; that is, the leading sector itself (e.g., automobiles) plus those parts of other industries linked to it (e.g., strip steel, rubber tires, petroleum refining, etc.).

The work of Fabricant and others has told us a great deal about the divergent movements within the conventional industrial categories—divergencies which cast a shadow over the question of how such data are to be interpreted. In textiles, at least, there is some meaning on the side of price and income elasticity of demand. But the chemical and metal industries are not, in fact, significantly homogeneous, except in the broad sense that their rapid expansion usually signals a period of capital deepening. They are a collection of different industries with different technological histories and different relations to the expansion of income. In some ways services is the worst hodgepodge of all.

Although bound like the rest of us to try to use the data we have, I felt at the time *The Stages* was written, and I feel now, that progress in the analysis of growth requires that we struggle to disaggregate so that we can actually link the coming in of new technologies to the sub-sectors where they enter and to the sectors which are linked to them and produce the spreading effects which justify the concept of leading sector complexes.

A good deal is said about these leading sector complexes in chapters 3–7. And the basic concept was defined and illustrated in *The Process of Economic Growth* (including Appendix I) and other earlier published work. Footnote references in *The Stages* carry the reader back to some of the key sources for disaggregated national data; for example, Ashton, Lockwood, Ohkawa, Lindahl, Nutter. But *The Stages* was not taken as the occasion to assemble all the data which led to its formulation. It presented briefly the fruits of considerable study, teaching, and reflection in the form of a some-what new mapping of the terrain—a method with ample precedent in the social sciences.

Kuznets and I proceeded, then, from the same basic definition of what growth is about. In the face of certain statistical problems, of which we were equally aware, he took one route, I took another, both understanding the limitations our respective decisions would impose on our results. He accepted a flawed conceptual basis for the statistical calculations which he related to the concept of modern growth. I accepted a lack of internationally comparable statistical data, capable of formal linkage to the aggregates, in presenting the notion of stages of growth. I would guess that Professor Kuznets does not regret his decision any more than I regret mine.

We agree, however—and I presume this agreement is shared—that a conceptually correct growth analysis requires the linking of leading sectors to the aggregates. Without the leading sectors the fundamental connection between growth and new technologies disappears into the mists of the Harrod–Domar equation and statistical aggregates of highly ambiguous meaning. If we can all proceed on that agreement, I believe our common commitment to the study of growth can usefully be carried forward.

IV. CONTINUITY VERSUS DISCONTINUITY

The problem of the aggregates and the sectors lies also at the basis of the most contentious issue raised by *The Stages*: Is the take-off a definable discontinuity in the process of growth? A good many historians recognize the acceleration of growth involved in the take-off and have no difficulty with the sectoral concept as applied to the countries they have studied. I do not regard the debate as serious on this point, for example, with respect to Belgium, Germany, Russia, Sweden, Japan, Canada, Mexico, and a good many of the more recent entrants into take-off; although all historians of those countries would not necessarily accept my vocabulary (e.g., David Landes) or even the usefulness of stage analysis (e.g., Alexander Gerschenkron).

The controversy over continuity and discontinuity is best pursued, in fact, in terms of specific countries and concrete data, rather than abstractly. And this is done in the sections that follow.

But since there is some intellectual content to the question, as well as an argument about numbers, a brief summary of the debate may be in order.

The take-off is defined, of course, in essentially sectoral terms (*The Stages*, pp. 57–8):

as an industrial revolution, tied directly to radical changes in methods of production, having their decisive consequence over a relatively short period of time.

This view would not deny the role of longer, slower changes in the whole process of economic growth. On the contrary, take-off requires the massive set of preconditions, going to the heart of a society's economic organization, its politics, and its effective scale of values, considered in chapter 3.

What this argument does assert is that the rapid growth of one or more new manufacturing sectors is a powerful and essential engine of economic transformation. Its power derives from the multiplicity of its forms of impact, when a society is prepared to respond positively to this impact. Growth in such sectors, with new production functions of high productivity, in itself tends to raise output per head; it places incomes in the

hands of men who will not merely save a high proportion of an expanding
income but who will plough it into highly productive investment; it sets
up a chain of effective demand for other manufactured products; it sets
up a requirement for enlarged urban areas, whose capital costs may be
high, but whose population and market organizations help to make
industrialization an on-going process; and, finally, it opens up a range of
external economy effects which, in the end, help to produce new leading
sectors when the initial impulse of the take-off's leading sectors begins to
wane.

I then sought to link this way of looking at the take-off—in
sectoral terms—to the approach to economic growth of Arthur
Lewis and others who defined the critical transition to sustained
growth in aggregate terms. Keynesian income analysis had been
tilted upward via the Harrod–Domar model within which population was permitted to increase and certain highly formal assumptions
were made about the productivity of investment in a world of changing technology. In terms of income analysis, the transition to
sustained growth could be viewed as a rise in national income per
capita resulting from a sufficient rise in net investment, given the
capital/output ratio. I found the formal hypothesis of an increase
in the net investment rate from approximately 5 to 10 per cent as one
way of defining the transition to sustained growth *prima facie*
interesting. As Arthur Lewis would be the first to assert, it doesn't
take you very far forward in understanding what economic growth is
about and how it happened; but it does provide an aggregative
theoretical and statistical framework to which the essentially sectoral
process of absorbing new technologies can, ultimately, be related.

In using this construct, I knew from the beginning two things
about it. First, it was only a rough approximation, as the historical
and contemporary data cited in chapter 4 indicate. Therefore, like
damn-yankee, I never separated the figure from '(say)' or some other
symbol of approximation. Second, I was clear that the rise of the
investment rate and income per capita were not central to my
essentially sectoral analysis of growth. Therefore, when I settled
down to analyse the inner structure of the take-off (p. 46), I began
as follows:

Whatever the importance and virtue of viewing the take-off in aggregative
terms—embracing national output, the proportion of output invested,

and an aggregate marginal capital/output ratio—that approach tells us relatively little of what actually happens and of the causal processes at work in a take-off; nor is the investment-rate criterion conclusive.

I still regard the Arthur Lewis perception, properly interpreted, as useful, and data on the contemporary world roughly confirm it (see below, pp. 233–5). But its linkage in *The Stages* to sectoral analysis gave the proponents of aggregative analysis a convenient locale for an irrelevant pitched battle. At Konstanz a major line of criticism of the take-off bore on the allegation that there was not, in a number of historical cases, evidence of a doubling of the net investment rate during the take-off years (although pre-take-off investment rate data were then—and remain—hard to come by).*

A focusing on investment rates took the argument off sectoral grounds and got it back to the aggregates, where some participants were more comfortable, given the nature of easily accessible data and the variant on Keynesian income analysis incorporated in the highly aggregated Harrod–Domar growth model. Thus, Kuznets concluded (*The Economics of Take-off*, p. xvi):

All that is claimed here is that aggregative data for a number of countries do not support Professor Rostow's distinction and characterization of the 'take-off' stage. On the other hand, the fact that the evidence is confined to aggregative data does not limit their bearing. Economic growth is an aggregative process; sectoral changes are interrelated with aggregative changes, and can be properly weighted only after they have been incorporated into the aggregative framework; and the absence of required aggregative changes severely limits the likelihood of the implicit strategic sectoral changes.

To which I replied (*The Economics of Take-off*, pp. xvi and xiv):

With this I disagree. Modern economic growth is essentially a sectoral process. It is rooted in the progressive diffusion of the production functions modern technology can provide. These changes in technique and organization can only be studied sectorally. The sectors are, of course, intimately interrelated; and changes in income flows play a role; but the aggregates—like any other index number—merely sum up the performance of the sectors. Put another way—of course growth is, in one sense and on one definition, an aggregative concept; that is, it consists in a regular

* A. Fishlow ('Empty Economic Stages', *Economic Journal*, March 1965, p. 15) notes certain factual weaknesses in Kuznets' summing up of the evidence on this point in his paper in the Konstanz volume (pp. 31–5).

expansion of output per head. But without sectoral analysis we cannot explain why growth occurs...

In fact, a rise in the rate of investment need not yield an equivalent acceleration in national product. The magnitudes are not rigorously related in the short period; and even over the long period capital-output ratios may vary. Moreover, forces may be operating during the take-off which yield stagnation or even decline in certain massive sectors of the economy (for example, within agriculture, in agricultural surplus areas); and these could damp or even overwhelm the effects on real product of the rise in the rate of investment in social overhead capital and industry.

In the general case, I am confident that the data—if we had them— would exhibit an acceleration in national product during the take-off years; but I shall confine my observations here to the movement of the investment rate during take-off.

In presenting the notion of the take-off, I pointed out the following factors which might alter what we might call 'pure Arthur Lewis' (or 5–10 per cent) behaviour of the investment rate during the take-off.

(1) Variations as among nations in the rate of population increase.
(2) Variations in the level of investment required for social overhead capital (mainly transport) in the pre-take-off and take-off decades.
(3) Variations in the capital/output ratio.
(4) The enclave case; that is, a high rate of investment in a narrow region or export sector, with very damped effect—if any—on the economy as whole.

In addition, I noted a difficulty which has evidently not been remedied and may prove beyond remedy; that is, we do not have reliable investment data for the pre-take-off decades in most societies.

The reader may also recall that I referred to the rise in the investment rate during take-off as a 'necessary but not sufficient condition for the take-off'; and in the summary of the stages of economic growth (*Economic History Review*), I referred to the achievement of a sustained rate of net investment of the order of 10 per cent as an 'essentially tautological' way of defining take-off.

What is the point here? The point is that within normal ranges of population increase and of the capital/output ratio, a regular and substantial increase in national product per head requires, by definition, a net investment rate of something like 10 per cent. We can find cases where such rates persisted in pre-take-off decades, usually because of heavy outlays for long-distance transport or because of limited enclaves of modern economic activity. There is nothing in the take-off analysis as a whole to make a shift in the investment rate itself a crucial test of the take-off.

On the other hand, I am confident that a rise in the investment rate will prove to be a normal take-off phenomenon, when more evidence is available. Of its nature, the take-off process is likely to bring about a rise in the investment rate for three reasons. The rise will come about in part through the plough-back of profits in the rapidly industrializing sectors; that is, in the leading sectors themselves and those directly linked to them, where a high marginal rate of saving is likely to prevail.

It will come about also from the more widespread expansion of investment in modern sectors that the acceleration of urbanization (and the probable rise in *per capita* income) during take-off are likely to bring about.

And the usually substantial role of governments during the take-off—notably in mobilizing social overhead capital—is likely to reinforce the other two tendencies.

In short, I held—and hold—that:

the essence of the take-off lies in sectoral expansion and its spreading effects;

the take-off is likely to produce a rise in the investment rate in the usual case;

the extent of the rise as opposed to the level of investment in the late preconditions period can vary with a number of factors;

a rise in the investment rate is not a sufficient criterion for take-off.

If the investment rate data are not, in themselves, conclusive, how, then, are take-off dates set?

Working with historical data, I have used the full range of statistical and qualitative data available to form an approximate judgment as to when the rate and scale of a leading sector's growth has been such as to induce substantial further expansion in the economy, also of high momentum, via its backward and lateral linkages. The take-off dates I offered in *The Stages* are the product of such investigations of the total impact of the initial group of leading sectors on the industrialization process of particular economies.

It cannot be too strongly emphasized that the secondary effects of rapid growth in a sector suffused with new technology are not automatic. They are potential effects which require active exploitation by a society's men and institutions. In fact, one measure of a society's ability to move into sustained economic growth is its ability to seize upon and to exploit with vigour all three types of potentiality which flow from a leading sector.

Growth is only an automatic process if one can assume that a society will respond actively and effectively to the potentials for growth available to it. To assess that likelihood one must move into political, social, and institutional analysis of its history over the relevant period of time.

The take-off must, therefore, be defined in two steps. First, it is the period in the life of an economy when, for the first time, one or more modern industrial sectors exhibit high rates of growth, bringing in not merely new production functions but inducing backward and lateral spreading effects on a substantial scale. Second, the economy must demonstrate the capacity to exploit the forward linkages as well, so that new leading sectors emerge as the older ones decelerate. It is the demonstration of a capacity to shift from one set of leading sectors to another which distinguishes a true take-off from some abortive industrial surges of the preconditions period. This functional requirement has determined that the take-off be defined as embracing, say, a twenty-year interval. Some such substantial period is necessary to demonstrate that a society is capable of overcoming the structural crisis which the initial surge of growth is likely to bring and is capable of introducing the changing flow of technology upon which sustained growth depends.

I would be gratified—and I am sure others would be easier in mind—if I could offer a straightforward statistical test; for example, the period of maximum rate of growth in a designated leading sector. But the problem is not that easy. First, the maximum rate of growth for a new industry is likely to come at a time when its scale is not significant enough to induce the spreading effects which are key to the take-off analysis. Second, the spreading effects themselves are difficult to trace with statistical precision, notably what I call the lateral and forward effects.

Nevertheless, the spreading effects are key to the notion of leading sectors. The fact that the leading sectors in take-off may constitute a small proportion of the industrial production index misses this point. The industrial growth directly and indirectly induced by the surge in British cotton production in the last two decades of the eighteenth century or induced by the railway surge in the United States in the two decades before the Civil War cannot be estimated by looking at cotton or railway statistics alone.

In the present state of knowledge, then, the estimate of when a take-off occurs cannot be a simple statistical exercise, although it requires the use of all the statistical data available. One must examine the whole performance of an economy to satisfy oneself that it is responding actively to the potential spreading effects which derive from the leading sectors. It follows from this fact that there is a margin of legitimate debate about when a take-off should be dated.

There are two particular problems in dating take-off.

One is the case of an abortive industrial surge which does not lead to self-sustained growth. Many nations have experienced such surges: the United States during the Napoleonic Wars, for example; India in the last decade of the nineteenth and the early twentieth century; Brazil in the period 1901–12; Argentina and China during the First World War. The subsequent periods of stagnation or relapse are so clear in such cases that they do not present great difficulty.

The more difficult problem is what one might call the problem of the decade preceding take-off. The surges of industrial growth which marked the take-off did not, of course, arise out of the blue. The take-off, in my view, is a recognizable discontinuity in the stream of history; but it is not a process without a history.

The pre-take-off decades are, generally, dominated by changes in the economy and in the society as a whole which are essential for later growth. These changes are likely to involve the training of new men; alterations in agricultural institutions and techniques; an expansion of trade at home and abroad, and expansion of cities; and in many cases there are important political changes as well in the pre-take-off decades which are necessary before take-off can begin. But, of course, there is likely also to be some expansion in industrial output.

In Britain the years of war with the United States ease the problem; that is, there is, despite much industrial ferment, not much basis for including the 1770's in the take-off. But what about the 1830's for the United States; the 1840's for Germany; the 1860's for Sweden; the 1880's for Russia?

These are all, in my view, debatable cases on a sectoral definition of take-off. I have examined the evidence and weighed it. I have concluded that, on balance, the scale of the leading sectors and the extent of their spreading effects in these preceding decades do not justify their inclusion in the take-off; and that the activities dominating the economy in these intervals were primarily non-industrial, typical of the preconditioning process rather than the take-off. But I do not regard my assessment of each case as final or beyond challenge.

Of its nature, this is a problem that can only be dealt with case by case. But the quite tractable problem of 'the preceding decade' is the only problem I perceive in distinguishing, in particular cases, the preconditions from the take-off, if the analyst is prepared to immerse himself in all the statistical and qualitative evidence available.

Although a good deal of the debate about *The Stages* concentrated on the take-off, there were comments also on how leading sector complexes did (or did not) relate to the drive to technological maturity and high mass-consumption; for example, those of Goran Ohlin ('Reflections on the Rostow Doctrine', *Economic Development and Cultural Change*, July 1961, especially pp. 650–3).

First, technological maturity. At any given time there are a finite number of major technologies available in the international economy. In what might be called the first round of industrialization (say, 1783 to 1873) Britain led the way with the textile leading sector complex; but in the period from about 1830 to 1873 (New England starting a little earlier) the United States, Belgium, France, and Germany absorbed that complex; and all these nations, plus Britain, absorbed the new technologies that went with the railway complex: railways themselves, iron, engineering, modern coal mining, etc. In this second phase Britain was again ahead, although with a lesser lead; and by the end of the boom in 1873 the four major industrial nations were more nearly together in technology. (They were not together in income per capita nor in rate of growth, which were affected by other variables.)

Since that first round, the process of absorbing the technologies available has proceeded in definable stages for other nations as well: a first stage, confined to a narrow range of manufacturing sectors, usually (but not always) linked to light consumers' goods: then a longer stage in which the other technologies then available are absorbed efficiently within the economy in relation to their natural resources, levels of income per capita, foreign trade patterns, etc.

What have been those other technologies? In broad terms they have consisted of various (unfolding) branches of metals and metal-working, chemicals, electricity and electronics. As suggested in chapter 5 (and in my March 1970 article in the *Journal of Economic History*), it is not difficult to establish the approximate time when the shift occurred from the first leading sector complex to these differentiated and capital-deepening sectors and sub-sectors. Gerschenkron, for example, agrees that it began for Russia in the years between 1906 and 1914; Ohkawa and Rosovsky agree that it began for Japan about 1906; Ohlin agrees that it began for Sweden in the 1890's. The movement of the major Latin American economies into these sectors since the 1950's is well documented; and it can be observed beginning in the late 1960's in, say, Turkey, Iran, and Taiwan.

It would have made my task much easier in *The Stages* if I could have accepted GNP per capita as a legitimate measure of stages of growth and proceeded to associate that measure with changing structures and leading sectors as Colin Clark, Kuznets, and Chenery (see below, pp. 230–4) have done. There are statistical associations to be made on this basis; but the averages that emerge with such statistical elegance are conceptually flawed.

They are flawed because GNP per capita is determined by a number of variables which do not link to the degree to which technologies are absorbed in the economy. The structure of the economy is affected by the degree to which technologies are absorbed, by GNP per capita, and by other factors. As noted above (p. 180), economies come in various sizes, with various population/resource balances, and they have had various trade and capital-flow relations to the international economy. Moreover, societies and their governments have made a wide variety of decisions about how much of their resources to allocate to military purposes. These variations affect both GNP per capita and the industrial structures that go with a given level of GNP per capita.

This fundamental point (made on p. 69) was not generally appreciated by reviewers of *The Stages*:

Appendix B

The process of growth, by definition, raises income per head, but it does not necessarily lead to uniformity of *per capita* income among nations or, even, among regions within nations; and, in Canada and certain other cases, we even have societies which have entered into the stage of high mass-consumption before technological maturity was attained.

There are—and there are likely to be—technologically mature societies that are, so to speak, both rich and poor. When historical data on national income are developed to permit systematic comparison, we are likely to find that incomes per head, at maturity, vary over a considerable range.

India and China, for example, may well have absorbed all the then existing technologies, with some efficiency, round about the year 2000; but their GNP per capita may only be something like one half that of contemporary Argentina, which is still short of technological maturity.

This brings us to the sectoral complex that accompanies high mass-consumption. The entrance into high mass-consumption is primarily a matter of consumers' income per capita and its distribution—if the income elasticity of demand is not frustrated by public policy, as in the Soviet Union of the 1960's. An economy with a good population/resource balance, like Canada or Australia, can, therefore, move into high mass-consumption before it has applied the full range of existing technologies to its natural resources.

Now what about high mass-consumption as a sectoral complex? (Ohlin, for example, in 'Reflections on the Rostow Doctrine', p. 651, says: 'It appears that "high consumption" is not a statistical concept at all. It is defined as the consumption of durables: automobiles, refrigerators, washing machines, TV sets, and all the gadgetry of modern life.')

The Stages was somewhat more precise on this point than Ohlin makes out; *vide*, the argument and charts of chapter 6 as well as the references to Fabricant (p. 77) and Svennilson (p. 83). Fabricant clearly delineated the automobile sectoral complex, on a limited basis, embracing the automobile industry itself plus petroleum refining, lubricants, tires, tubes, and other rubber products; and he showed its dramatic rise within United States total manufacturing from 1899 to 1929, from 1 per cent to 10 per cent of value added (*The Output of Manufacturing Industries, 1899–1937*, New York, 1940, p. 102). Fabricant's definition of the complex does not include anything like its full range; for example, in 1938 the American automobile industry consumed 51 per cent of strip steel production; 34 per cent of steel bars; 41 per cent of steel sheets; 53 per cent of malleable iron; 54 per cent of alloy steel; 69 per cent of plate glass; 29 per cent of nickel; 25 per cent of lead; 40 per cent of mohair— quite aside from 90 per cent of gasoline and 80 per cent of rubber (*Automobile Facts and Figures*, New York, 1939, p. 39). And this wider array does not include the outlays for roads, the buildup of suburbia and its infrastructure.

The sectoral complex that goes with high mass-consumption is, in my view, a statistical concept; although it has not been fully and precisely measured. Moreover, as I argue in an article in the March 1970 *Journal of Economic History*, it is a sectoral complex whose expansion lies at the heart of growth in Western Europe and Japan of the 1960's and whose deceleration (as foreshadowed in *The Stages*, pp. 79–81) is essential for an understanding of the stage of growth into which the United States has now entered.

To sum up: the issue of continuity versus discontinuity hinges on whether growth is seen in terms of leading sector complexes plus the aggregates, or in terms of the aggregates alone. The data we have— and the data statisticians have thus far developed—do not make it easy to present with elegance the leading sector complexes. Nevertheless, I believe they constitute an essential component in growth analysis; and I was not—and am not—prepared to let my analysis of growth be determined by the kind of data that happen to be available and can be organized conveniently for purposes of formal comparisons of international growth patterns.

Fortunately, the issue becomes more manageable if we turn from the world of theoretical and statistical abstraction on an international basis to stories of national growth, where disaggregated data can and are regularly used by economic historians.

V. SOME ARGUMENTS ABOUT ECONOMIC HISTORY

The 1960's was a remarkably lively and productive decade in economic history; and to summarize all the materials generated that bear on the argument in *The Stages* would require a volume, not an appendix. I shall restrict what follows, therefore, to three important cases which have been the subject of debate: the English, French, and American take-offs.

Some of the language used in the discussion of the British take-off at Konstanz suggested a wide difference between the view taken by H. J. Habakkuk and Phyllis Deane, on the one hand, and myself, on the other. The central issue was whether the discontinuity in growth in the period 1783–1802 was sufficient to justify designating those years as the period of British take-off. Both at the time (*Economics of Take-off*, p. 338) and in retrospect, I regard the issues between us as narrow and dependent on what J. T. Dunlop once called, in another context, the 'propensity to be surprised' (*Wage Determination Under Trade Unions*, New York, 1950, p. 151). We all agree that the British economy accelerated in the twenty years after 1783; we all agree that there was a remarkable expansion in cotton textiles, coal and iron, the former linked to a surge in foreign trade; we all agree that there was a rise in output per capita and a rise in the investment rate. The question is whether the acceleration is 'surprising' enough to be called a take-off.

I might add that the analysis of this period by Deane and Cole in their valuable book *British Economic Growth, 1688–1959* (Cambridge, 1969) provides even less basis for contention than the paper prepared for the Konstanz conference.

It may, nevertheless, be worth recalling some of the evidence which has led virtually all historians—and contemporaries—to note the two decades after 1783 as a remarkable passage in British economic growth and led me to designate the period as the take-off, despite distortions caused by war in its second half.

First, the major leading sector, cotton textiles. Three factors interacted to produce the surge in cotton textile production reflected in the following import and export data: the coming in of new machinery, including Watt's more efficient steam engine; the cotton gin, after 1793; normalization of foreign trade after 1783, combined with the American export boom of the 1790's (and its consequently enlarged import capacity) and with Britain's ability to keep continental trade routes open during the first decade of the French wars.*

* Phyllis Deane and W. A. Cole, *British Economic Growth, 1688–1959* (second edition),

Appendix B

TABLE 10

	Retained imports of raw cotton (m. lb)		Cotton exports (£000)
1695–1704	1·14	1697–1704	16
1700–9	1·15	1700–9	13
1705–14	1·00	1706–15	8
1710–19	1·35	1710–19	8
1715–24	1·68	1715–24	15
1720–9	1·55	1720–9	16
1725–34	1·44	1725–34	12
1730–9	1·72	1730–9	15
1735–44	1·79	1735–44	15
1740–9	2·06	1740–9	11
1745–54	2·83	1745–54	38
1750–9	2·81	1750–9	86
1755–64	2·57	1755–64	162
1760–9	3·53	1760–9	227
1765–74	4·03	1765–74	236
1770–9	4·80	1770–9	247
1775–84	7·36	1775–84	388
1780–9	15·51	1780–9	756
1785–94	24·45	Great Britain	
1790–9	28·64	1792–9	2,896
1795–1804	42·92	1795–1804	5,371

These overlapping annual average rates of growth in domestic exports plus retained imports suggest, in a damped and understated way, the overall surge in foreign trade in the period 1783–1800.*

TABLE 11

England and Wales	%
1700–30	1·2
1710–40	1·0
1720–50	1·1
1730–60	1·5
1740–70	1·9
1750–80	1·1
Great Britain	
1760–90	1·8
1770–1800	2·3

As for ferrous metals, Deane and Cole conclude:†

Cambridge, 1969, pp. 51 and 59, where sources are indicated. See, also, Arthur D. Gayer *et al.*, *Growth and Fluctuation of the British Economy, 1790–1850*, vol. I, pp. 11–21 and 31–43.
* Deane and Cole, *British Economic Growth*, p. 29, where sources are indicated.
† *Ibid.* p. 55, where footnote references to sources are given.

If we focus on the fortunes of the iron and steel producers, we must conclude that the rapid growth of Britain's capital goods industries dates from the 1780's. There are no reliable statistics of iron output in the early part of the century, but the traditional view is that about 1720 the production of pig-iron in England was not more than 25,000 tons, and that for the next twenty or thirty years it was stationary or declining. More recently, however, it has been argued that the contemporary estimates of output on which this view was largely based may be misleading. Judging by the erection of new blast furnaces, there seems to have been no protracted period of inactivity, and it is possible that in the century before 1760 output may have increased by upwards of 10,000 tons. Nevertheless, it remains true that the growth of the industry must have been comparatively slow before 1760, and even between 1757 and 1788 the rate of increase can hardly have reached as much as 40 per cent per decade. Between 1788 and 1806, on the other hand, the decennial rate of growth was over 100 per cent.

Overall reflectors of economic activity, not directly linked to the coming in of major new production functions, show substantial expansion on a lesser scale.*

TABLE 12

	Woollen exports (£000)	Wood imports (£000)	Glass production (000 cwt)	Cornish copper ore production (000 tons)	London coal imports (000 London chaldrons)	Strong beer production (000 barrels)
1775–84	3,363	249	121	30	666	4,220
1795–1804	6,323	558	167	53	875	5,407

The whole process reflected in these figures was accompanied by large investments in roads and canals, docks and ships plus a rapid acceleration of urbanization.†

In an heroic effort, Deane and Cole produced the following estimates for total and average per capita real output for four twenty-year periods in the eighteenth century. These sum up vividly the acceleration at the end of the eighteenth century caused by these key sectoral movements, spreading effects, and generalized expansion.‡

* *Ibid*. p. 51 and (for woollen exports) p. 59.

† See, for example, A. D. Gayer, *Growth and Fluctuation*, vol. 1, pp. 14–16 and pp. 35–7. For accelerated urbanization, notably in cotton textile towns, see Deane and Cole, *British Economic Growth*, pp. 7–8.

‡ *Ibid*. p. 80.

TABLE 13

	Total real output			Average real output		
	(i)	(ii)	(iii)	(i)	(ii)	(iii)
1695/1715–1725/45	0·3	0·4	0·2	0·3	0·4	0·1
1725/45–1745/65	1·0	1·1	0·8	0·6	0·8	0·5
1745/65–1765/85	0·7	0·8	0·6	0·0	0·1	0·0
1765/85–1785/1805	1·8	2·1	1·5	0·9	1·1	0·6

(i) 1700 base, *including* home industries; (ii) 1700 base, *excluding* home industries; (iii) 1800 base, *including* home industries.

Deane and Cole conclude:*

Before 1745, when total output grew very slowly, the population also changed very little, with the result that average real output rose, slowly but fairly steadily at the rate of about 2½ per cent per decade. After 1745, on the other hand, the sharp increase in the rate of growth of total output soon appears to have been swallowed up by the population increase which began at the same time. It is true that for twenty years per capita output seems to have grown more than twice as fast as it had done before. But with the continued expansion of numbers and the somewhat slower growth of total output in the sixties and seventies, the advance was halted, and over the four decades ending in 1785 the average rate of increase was almost exactly the same as it had been in earlier decades. At the end of the century, however, there was a crucial change. After 1785, both total output and population were growing much faster than before, but the former now began to draw decisively ahead of the latter. For the first time, per capita output started to increase by nearly nine per cent per decade— or at more than three times the average rate for the rest of the period under review.

This 'crucial change' is, essentially, the story on which we have all been brought up, for example, in the work of Paul Mantoux and T. S. Ashton; although Deane and Cole have introduced the findings of later investigators and added their valuable efforts at aggregation.

What remains in contention?

First, Deane and Cole give considerable emphasis to the rise in absolute levels of production in the 1740's:†

In a chapter on 'The Eighteenth-century Origins of Economic

* *Idem.* See, also, pp. 280–1 for a summary which concludes: 'The acceleration in the rate of growth found for the last two decades of the century is in accordance with what now seems to be the generally accepted view among economic historians.'

† *Ibid.* pp. 80–2.

Growth' they discuss the fortunes of various industrial sectors in the whole sweep of the eighteenth century, isolating particular elements that contributed to the 'many-sided wave of expansion that began in the 1740's'.*

There is nothing in *The Stages* which would deny the importance of technical, economic, and commercial progress before the take-off. On the contrary, that is what the concept of the preconditions is all about.

But we cannot quite leave it there. The question remains in terms of stage analysis: why was the surge in production at the end of the century so critical, not only for Britain but for the world? Why were these years (accepting the importance of their antecedents, from at least 1688) the beginnings of modern economic history in an important sense? The answer is that:

the convergence of developments in spinning machinery, steam engines, and the efficient cleaning of cotton produced a radical decline in the cost of manufacturing articles with a high price and income elasticity of demand, and, therefore, yielded extraordinary rates of increase in output:

the modern system of factory production emerged in England on a relatively massive scale due to its leadership in the process and command over foreign trade;

the improvements in steam-power and machinery manufacture generated laid the basis for the technology that was to lead on to the railway, as well as creating an incentive to lower transport costs from the manufacturing centres, on the one hand, and the ports and domestic markets, on the other, thus helping encourage such early railway lines as the Manchester–Liverpool and Boston–Lowell;

the precocious British advantage in manufactures put economic, psychological, and political pressure on the United States and Western Europe to follow suit.

This is what distinguishes what happened in the 1780's and 1790's from what happened in the 1740's.

We can, therefore, all rally round Ashton's summing up:†

* *Ibid.* p. 61.

† T. S. Ashton, *An Economic History of England: The 18th Century* (London, 1955), p. 125.

When Arnold Toynbee gave currency to the term 'industrial revolution' he set the beginnings of the movement at 1760; and the tendency of later scholars has been to seek an earlier *terminus a quo*. The roots of modern industrial society can be traced back indefinitely into the past, and each historian is at liberty to select his own starting point. If, however, what is meant by the industrial revolution is a sudden quickening of the pace of output we must move the date forward, and not backward, from 1760. After 1782 almost every statistical series of production shows a sharp upward turn. More than half the growth in the shipments of coal and the mining of copper, more than three-quarters of the increase of broad-cloths, four-fifths of that of printed cloth, and nine-tenths of the exports of cotton goods were concentrated in the last eighteen years of the century.

The other residual question is the movement of investment rates in relation to national income. We start, as usual, in preconditions and take-off periods with extremely wobbly statistics. Deane and Cole, nevertheless, courageously struggle with the data. They conclude that:*

1. It is impossible to say whether capital accumulation grew faster than the national income in Britain in the immediately pre-industrial period, i.e. between, say, 1688 when King's calculations suggest a long-term rate of capital formation of under 5 per cent of national income, and 1783 which marks the beginning of Professor Rostow's 'take-off' period.

2. There seems no doubt that there was an increase in the relative level of capital formation in the last two decades of the eighteenth century, but it is unlikely that it amounted to an increase of more than about $1\frac{1}{2}$ per cent of the national income. Thus, if the rate of capital formation amounted to between 5 and 6 per cent of national income by the early 1780's it may have reached about 7 per cent by the beginning of the nineteenth century.

As I made clear above (pp. 190–3), there is nothing in *The Stages* which requires me to argue for 'pure Arthur Lewis' (5–10 per cent) behaviour of the net investment rate during take-off. In the case of eighteenth-century Britain, blessed (like Japan) with short transport distances and the possibilities of coastal shipping, one would not expect high infrastructure investment in the late preconditions and take-off periods.

I would, however, offer two observations on Deane and Cole's conclusions.

* *Ibid.* p. 263. The figure of 5–6 per cent is 'an impression' of the level of investment 'before the American War depressed the economy' (p. 261).

First, they calculate the increase in the investment level after 1783 by estimating capital construction in cotton, iron, and transport sectors alone (although, apparently, ships are not included). This, in my view, is too restricted a view of the spreading effects stemming from the leading sectors. The tripling of population in Manchester and Glasgow, for example, in the latter part of the eighteenth century undoubtedly required expanded investment, as did accelerated urbanization in general.*

Accelerated urbanization helped induce some part of the increase in agricultural investment, as Britain began to shift to a grain-importing posture; although bad harvest conditions and wartime supply restrictions yielded disproportionate agricultural investment in the 1790's.

Finally, the general expansion in income per capita that took place in these years, stemming, ultimately, from the leading sectors (plus the radical increase in government outlays after 1793) must have yielded an expansion in investment in other sectors; e.g., wool, beer, etc.

I am not, therefore, prepared to accept the Deane and Cole calculation of the increment in investment after 1783 as definitive

Second, unless there is evidence of a fall in the capital/output ratio between the mid-century expansion and the expansion in the generation after 1783, either the mid-century investment rate of 5–6 per cent is too high or the estimate of its relatively modest increase by Deane and Cole is too low. It will be recalled (see above, p. 203) that real output in the mid-century period (1725/45–1745/65) is taken to be increasing at the rate of about 1 per cent; at something like twice that rate during take-off (1765/85–1785/1805). Except for some highly generalized propositions (pp. 276–7 and 304), Deane and Cole provide no analysis of how this doubling in the rate of growth in real product could be brought about by so limited an increase in the proportion of resources invested.

These are only questions, not conclusions. It is doubtful that any of us will ever be able to be dogmatic with conviction about the aggregates for this period of British history. Having lived with the

---

* *Ibid.* p. 8. I count accelerated urbanization as a 'lateral' linkage to the leading sectors.

sectoral evidence (none of which is new) and studied this story from various angles for some thirty-five years, it is my impression that the rise in British investment after 1783 is a somewhat more massive phenomenon than the Deane and Cole analysis makes out. But—to repeat—that is not what the take-off is all about. I do not find the Deane and Cole conclusions in fundamental conflict with the view I take in *The Stages*.

France

There are parallels between my debate on Britain with Phyllis Deane and my debate on France with Jan Marczewski. Both have made major creative efforts in organizing continuous statistical data over a span of two and a half centuries: both have resisted, to a degree, the notion of a discontinuity in the period I designate as the take-off. In the British case, the remarkable goings-on after 1783 come through clearly enough. In the less melodramatic French take-off, I regard, also, Marczewski's data as confirmatory.*

The debate on France centres on this question: Do the sectoral developments in the French economy in the years 1830–60 constitute a critical transition of France into modern industrialization?

These are, I believe, matters that would be agreed:

The substantial French expansion of the eighteenth century was based primarily on a lateral extension of existing methods rather than on the new technologies and capital-deepening which marked Britain in the latter years of the eighteenth century.†

France fell grossly behind Britain in relative industrial development by 1815 as compared to 1793.

---

* Marczewski's results are presented in the volume on the Konstanz conference, chapter 7, discussed pp. 354–66; and in 'Some Aspects of Economic Growth of France, 1660–1958', *Economic Development and Cultural Change*, April 1961 ('Essays in the Quantitative Study of Economic Growth, Presented to Simon Kuznets on the Occasion of His Sixtieth Birthday'). I might note, parenthetically, that the Konstanz debate often seemed to centre on my article on the take-off published in the *Economic Journal*, March 1956, rather than on *The Stages*. Some commentators appeared to miss the importance I would attach to the complex process of the preconditions for take-off as set out in chapter 3. In combating the view (which I do not hold) that the take-off was a sudden breakthrough, unrooted in past events and developments, I had considerable sympathy with what was said.

† On this point, see, especially, F. Crouzet, 'England and France in the Eighteenth Century: A Comparative Analysis of Two Economic Growths', chapter 7 in R. M. Hartwell, *The Causes of the Industrial Revolution* (London, 1967).

Between 1815 and 1830 there was considerable textile (and other) industrial development in France, embracing the silk as well as cotton textile industry.

The French economy was fundamentally transformed by the massive railway boom of the 1850's and 1860's.

The key questions debated at Konstanz were, therefore, quite narrow and lucid:

Was the pre-1830 expansion of textiles a substantial enough phenomenon, given the limitation on French export markets, to bring France into sustained modern growth?

TABLE 14. *French industries whose growth exceeds by more than 20% the general growth of industrial product and whose share in this product exceeds 2%*

Dates and length	General rate of growth of industrial product	Selected industries		
		Designation	Percentage share	Rate of growth
1701–10 to 1781–90 (80 years)	1·91	Cotton spinning and weaving	3·5	3·81
		Cotton fabrics	5·4	3·81
From 1781–90 to 1803–12 (22 years)	1·98	Cotton fabrics	8·21	5·15
		Cotton spinning and weaving	6·37	5·14
		Residual industries*	3·61	2·96
From 1803–12 to 1825–34 (22 years)	2·86	Cotton spinning and weaving	7·72	4·73
		Cotton fabrics	6·57	4·14
		Silk spinning and weaving	2·37	3·47
		Residual industries*	7·92	7·1
From 1825–34 to 1835–44 (10 years)	3·52	Silk fabrics	3·12	9·00
		Iron and steel	2·19	5·5
		Cotton spinning and weaving	8·50	5·1
		Silk spinning and weaving	3·35	5·0
		Cotton fabrics	4·43	4·8
		Iron and steel products	5·43	4·4
		Residual industries*	11·84	6·3
From 1835–44 to 1845–55 (10 years)	2·45	Silk spinning and weaving	5·01	5·0
		Silk fabrics	4·75	4·3
		Iron and steel	2·20	3·0
		Residual industries*	16·84	4·6
From 1845–54 to 1855–64 (10 years)	2·76	Iron and steel products	5·40	5·9
		Worked skins	2·10	3·7
		Leather	5·12	3·7
		Residual industries*	17·47	4·0

* Industries for which we still do not dispose of direct quantitative data; the rates of growth and relative shares of these industries have been estimated globally and may undergo considerable revision.

TABLE 15. *Railway construction in France*

Period	Initial investment expenditure Annual average (in million francs)	Trunk lines			Local lines		
		Network (km)	Loco-motives	Other rolling stock no.	Network (km)	Loco-motives no.	Other rolling stock no.
1825/34	4	52	—	—	—	—	—
1835/44	34	560	—	—	—	—	—
1845/54	175	1987	1222	26,660	—	—	—
1855/64	437	6191	2358	62,084	—	—	—
1865/74	263	7206	1346	51,070	432	—	—
1875/84	398	7198	2206	69,280	1770	185	3348
1885/94	280	6553	2408	67,969	517	119	1527
1894/1904	210	8033	977	36,442	2067	245	3466
1905/13	312–15*	2502	2033	60,225	3432	385	5089

* Annual average 1905/12.

Were the heavy industry, engineering, and (rather modest) railroad development of 1830–50 sufficient to justify bringing the take-off back to 1830 from 1850?

The sectoral data on the French economy had led me to answer the first question in the negative, the second, affirmatively.

Tables 14 and 15 show Marczewski's sectoral calculations which bear upon the matter.*

In his paper at Konstanz Marczewski commented on earlier calculations of similar import as follows:†

The ten-year period 1825/34 to 1835/44 has similar characteristics as the preceding one. The general rate of industrial growth is 3·5 per cent. Silk ...and cotton...still head the list of rapidly growing industries. The iron and steel industry...is strengthening its position, and iron and steel products...are newcomers in the leading sector. Among the residual industries, the gas industry is noteworthy for especially rapid progress.

All in all, the first forty years of the nineteenth century constitute a fairly homogeneous period of fast growth...largely dominated by the cotton and silk industries. Engineering, the iron and steel industry, and coal assume importance only towards the end of the period.

The next decade, 1835/44 to 1845/54, is marked by a slackening of

* 'Some Aspects of the Economic Growth of France, 1660–1958', p. 380; and *The Economics of Take-off into Sustained Growth*, p. 130.
† *The Economics of Take-off*, p. 128.

growth. The weighted average rate of growth of industrial product falls to 2·45 per cent. Cotton disappears from the leading sector; silk still forms part of it, but with growth rates not above 5 per cent. Jute and the chemical industry make great strides forward, without as yet giving any significant impulse to other activities. Iron and steel, as well as coal continue to expand at moderate rates. We may say that the period is one of transition between the rapid expansion of the cotton and silk industries, the edge of which is already blunted, and the upsurge of the railways, the full effect of which is not seen until the 1850's.

The three decades from 1845/54 to 1875/84 show an almost uniform rate of growth a little over 2·7 per cent. Iron and steel, metal products, and coal are the leaders, with rates of growth generally ranging from 3 to 6 per cent.

My reply at Konstanz was summarized by the rapporteur in these terms:*

On the main point of substance in the analysis of growth, the difference between Professor Marczewski and himself was a simple one. In assessing French evolution, Professor Rostow said that he had decided, as with Germany and some other countries, that the development of a modern textile industry for the home market alone did not have a sufficient scale effect to act as a base for sustained growth. For textiles to serve that function, the lift which foreign trade gave was also necessary. This was an arbitrary judgment which led him to deny that the early nineteenth-century cotton industries in France and Germany would have acted as leading sectors in take-off. This had been reinforced by later experience. China and India had both had cotton textile industries supplying the home market but this market had not been sufficiently large to allow take-off to occur.

In short, I held—and would still hold—that only with the emergence on a substantial scale of the French heavy industry base, in the 1830's, and then the railroads, were the sectoral foundations laid for the modern French economy. Textiles were, in my view, simply not sufficient.

The data in Table 16 suggest why, on a sectoral basis, I am inclined to include the 1830's in the French take-off.†

The 1840's are not accorded in French economic history the dramatic role of the previous or following decades because of the

* *Ibid.* p. 359.

† *Annuaire Statistique de la France, 1966, Résumé Rétrospectif*, Paris, pp. 229 (coal) and 340 (pig iron).

Appendix B

TABLE 16. *France: Coal and pig iron*

	Coal production (in million tons)	Coal consumption (in million tons)	Pig iron production (in tons)
1820	1·1	—	140,000
1830	1·8	2·5	266,000
1840	3·0	4·3	348,000
1847 (decade peak)	5·2	7·6	592,000
1850	4·4	7·2	406,000
1860	8·3	14·3	898,000

traumatic economic and political events at the decade's end. But these data on the expansion of steam-power are not unimpressive. They also suggest how limited the use of steam-power must have been before the 1830's.*

TABLE 17. *France: Steam-power installed*

	Engines, number			Horse-power			
Year	Fixed	Loco-motives	Steam-boats	Fixed	Loco-motives	Steam-boats	Fixed
1835	—	—	—	—	—	—	19,000
1840	2,591	142	263	34,000	42,000	11,000	87,000
1850	5,322	973	537	67,000	291,000	22,000	380,000
1860	14,936	3,101	681	181,000	930,000	37,000	1,148,000
1870	27,958	4,835	973	341,000	1,452,000	60,000	1,853,000
1878	38,880	6,669	1,183	492,000	2,363,000	169,000	3,024,000
1885	50,980	9,155	4,290	695,000	3,290,000	530,000	4,515,000

Marczewski's aggregative data tend to reinforce this view. His estimate of annual average growth for industry and handicrafts exhibits a marked lift in the 1830's.†

TABLE 18

1701/10–1781/90	1·91%
1781/90–1803/12	1·98
1803/12–1825/34	2·86
1825/34–1835/44	3·52
1835/44–1845/54	2·45
1845/54–1855/64	2·76

Marczewski's estimate of the annual average growth rate for

* Michael Mulhall, *The Dictionary of Statistics*, London, 1892, p. 547.
† 'Some Aspects of the Economic Growth of France, 1660–1958', p. 375.

physical product at constant prices also exhibits a clearly marked acceleration in these years.*

TABLE 19

1781/90–1803/12	0·82%
1803/12–1825/34	1·22
1825/34–1835/44	1·95
1835/44–1845/54	1·41
1845/54–1855/64	1·69

Marczewski's calculations of the gross and net investment rates in the critical years come remarkably close to 'pure Arthur Lewis' behaviour.†

TABLE 20

	Gross private capital formation per cent of gross domestic product	Net capital formation per cent of net domestic product
1788–1839	5·8%	3·0%
1839–1852	11·2	8·0
1852–1880	17·0	12·1

These figures led Marczewski to observe:‡

These figures would seem to fit in with Rostow's condition of a doubling of the rate of net capital formation to net product during the take-off. However, we must bear in mind that neither product nor capital developed in a linear fashion. This is particularly true of the period 1788–1839. From rather high initial levels before the Revolution, both product and capital declined during the years of the Revolution, probably reaching their lowest level around 1796. From 1797 onwards, and especially after the establishment of the Consulate in 1799, industrial production recovered rapidly. Thus the increase in the rate of capital formation to product may well have begun—and in my opinion probably did begin—not around 1840, but at the beginning of the nineteenth century.

I rather doubt this observation. The experience of Britain and others is that the coming of the age of the railway and heavy industry requires an enlarged proportion of income invested than the lighter industries which characterized the pre-1830 period in France.

---

* *The Economics of Take-off*, p. 135. See, also, Marczewski's estimates under alternative assumptions about relative agricultural and industrial prices, 'Some Aspects of the Economic Growth of France, 1660–1958', p. 376.

† *The Economics of Take-off*, p. 121.   ‡ *Ibid.* pp. 122–3.

Appendix B

Without solid evidence to the contrary, the behaviour of coal, iron, and steam-power data incline me to the view that the pre-1830 expansion of French industry belongs, on balance, rather more with French eighteenth-century lateral expansion than with modern growth; although the modern steam-powered factory did make its début.

Marczewski, in the end, makes his peace with what historians of France have long known—or, at least, sensed with confidence:* 'the spurts observed [in physical product] took place during periods which, by common consent, have always been regarded as periods of especially rapid growth: the first years of the July Monarchy and of the Second Empire, and the "Belle Epoque" of the 1900's'.

It is because I believe that the capital-deepening heavy industry and engineering developments of the 1830's belong with the massive railway building that came only after the passage of the 1842 railway law that I dated the French take-off as 1830–60; and I excluded the 1815–30 period because I did not believe the textile and light industry development of those years was likely to be on a scale sufficient to move France into a progressive absorption of the emerging technologies and self-sustained growth. Marczewski's sectoral and aggregative data I find wholly consistent with that assessment.

But the essential difference with Marczewski may be similar to that with Deane and Cole. Surveying as they do long periods, including the whole sweep of the eighteenth century, it is natural that they should be impressed by industrial expansion that took place before the modern technologies were efficiently introduced. Surely, eighteenth-century Britain before 1783 and pre-1830 France were not stagnant—as a matter of trend. (Neither is contemporary Black Africa, in the period of the preconditions for take-off.) But I would hold that the coming in of the cotton textile leading sector complex—on the scale that British foreign trade permitted in the period 1783–1802—and the coming of the heavy industry-railroad leading sector complex to France in the period 1830–60 were authentic watersheds. They are reflected in both sectoral and

* *Ibid.* p. 135.

213

aggregative data. They justify the concept of take-off without in any way rendering irrelevant all that preceded and made possible these surges.

Subsequent to the debate between Marczewski and myself, Crouzet has published a series of sector indexes of industrial production on an annual basis and combined them in two indexes for French industrial production as a whole, covering the period 1815–1914.* So far as the issues discussed here are concerned, Crouzet's work:

confirms the rather steady textile expansion from 1815;

reflects the high rate of increase in mining production in the 1820's and beyond;

demonstrates the surge in metals, metalworking, and chemicals, starting in the 1830's;

identifies, in aggregate terms, that the period 1840–60 was the interval of maximum industrial growth (in excess of trend) for the nineteenth century.

By developing annual indexes, rather than using overlapping or decadal averages, Crouzet portrays the 1840's as a period of remarkable acceleration, despite the severe setback of 1848, when cyclical depression and a highly disruptive revolution converge.

On the basis of Crouzet's clarifying effort, the French take-off might be dated 1840–60, and we are left with a quite familiar take-off problem; that is, the question of 'the preceding decade', in this case, the 1830's. I am content to leave it there.

The United States

The debate about the American take-off is less sharply drawn—and more diffuse—than that on the British and French take-offs. At Konstanz, Douglass North's paper on 'Industrialization in the United States (1815–60)'† tersely summarized some of the

* François Crouzet, 'Essai de construction d'un indice annuel de la production industrielle française au XIXᵉ siècle', *Annales Économies, Sociétés, Civilisations*, No. 1, January–February 1970.

† *The Economics of Take-off*, chapter 3. North did raise earlier a number of points in criticism of my account of the American take-off in 'A Note on Professor Rostow's "Take-off" into Self-sustained Economic Growth', *Manchester School*, January 1958, to which I shall later allude.

findings in his subsequently published book, *The Economic Growth of the United States, 1790 to 1860* (Englewood Cliffs, N.J., 1961). Quite properly, he chose to do so in his own terms; but the story as he presented it there did not clash with my own view, concluding as it did:* 'The surge of expansion that began in 1843 was clearly an era in which the North-east had ceased being a marginal manufacturing area and could successfully expand into a vast array of industrial goods. By 1860 the "problems" of industrialization were behind in the development of the United States.'

In his thoughtful review of the Konstanz volume ('Empty Economic Stages?') and his *American Railroads and the Transformation of the Ante-Bellum Economy* (Cambridge, Mass., 1965), Albert Fishlow by no means accepts wholly my analysis of the American take-off; although, as in the case of North, I regard our differences as of second order. I take this view because Fishlow leans strongly to sectoral rather than merely aggregative analysis and his detailed findings on the role of the American railroads in the period 1840–60 leave them, still, a central phenomenon, despite his real or believed differences with my assessment.

Paul David ('The Growth of Real Product in the United States Before 1840: New Evidence, Controlled Conjectures', *Journal of Economic History*, June 1967) does come roaring down to the wire with quite a peroration, after his imaginative and sophisticated recalculation of the aggregates from 1790 to 1860:†

it was during the thirty years before 1850, and not in the thirty years after, that the relative transfer of labor into nonfarm pursuits (including factory employment) had brought about an impressive change in the structure of the U.S. economy.

Are we then to conclude there was no true 'take-off' in the antebellum era, and plunge immediately into the diverse histories of the American colonial economies in the hope of locating some prior fundamental 'break in the trend' of aggregated per capita production? Or will we attempt to refurbish with cast-off Rostovian garb the now very unfashionable idea of the Industrial Rèvolution 'taking hold' in the United States only after the northern victory in the Civil War? At present, it seems, a far more sensible solution would be to abandon the whole idea

* *Ibid.* p. 62.

† P. 195. As pp. 203–5, above, indicate, the British aggregate data do indicate a rather sharp rise in per capita real income in the last two decades of the eighteenth century.

that significant, portentous stirrings of urban-industrial development within the predominantly agrarian ante-bellum economy must have been immediately reflected in a discontinuous and permanent alteration of the per capita real product growth rate, or in a parallel upward shift of the aggregate capital formation ratio.

British economic historians now freely entertain the hypothesis that some time elapsed before the structural transformations associated with rapid industrialization made their impact felt throughout the entire British economy; and that while a discontinuity can be seen in the long-term rate of *industrial output* growth late in the eighteenth century, the ensuing acceleration of per capita real income growth to a higher secular rate was a much more gradual affair. Is it not fit that in this, as in other things, we might fruitfully follow a British lead?

The literature on the problem also includes a. rather systematic check-out of the take-off hypothesis by Charles H. Hession and Hyman Sardy—mainly confirmatory.*

I shall proceed by first stating my general understanding of how the American economy evolved in the period 1790–1860 and then dealing with certain specific points that have been raised with respect to the references to the United States in *The Stages*.

Industrialization came to the United States against a background of territorial and agricultural expansion, interwoven with price and other impulses from the international economy. These gave the first seven decades of national life a particular cast. In the end—with the expanded international demand for American wheat—and the related attractiveness of throwing the railway lines to the West, the impulses for agricultural and industrial expansion fully converged.

But before the 1850's there is a kind of alternating rhythm between extensive agricultural expansion and industrialization, both contributing to increases in output, both requiring relatively high levels of investment.

The key phases of industrialization have for long been familiar:

the mainly abortive efforts during the years of war (say, 1806–15);

the sturdy expansion centred around textiles in New England launched substantially in the 1820's carried forward vigorously thereafter;

the wider-based industrialization of the 1840's and 1850's,

---

* *Ascent to Affluence* (Boston, 1969), Part 4, pp. 221–306.

centred in the 1840's on the railroadization of the East, in the 1850's on the railroadization of the Middle West, accompanied by heavy industry expansion.

Because I view the essence of economic modernization as the bringing in of new technologies, it is to these three phases that I mainly referred in my rather brief references to pre-1860 American growth in *The Stages*.

In a kind of counterpoint, however, there were phases where the expansion of agricultural production, acreage, and exports were more nearly at the centre of American enterprise.* Thus:

the export boom of the 1790's (which survived the vicissitudes of the Peace of Amiens and continued to 1806), frustrating Hamilton's desire to launch America promptly into industrialization;

the brief postwar export boom (to 1817), accompanied by a surge of movement into new land beyond the Appalachians and in the south;

the massive expansion of cotton land and production of the 1830's, accompanied also by the expansion of land and infrastructure in the mid-west, supported by heavy capital imports;

the great agricultural (as well as industrial) expansion of the 1850's.

I recall these rough but familiar phases, shaped by wartime disturbances and cycles of considerable amplitude, because a good deal of the debate on the application of *The Stages* to the American take-off relates to them.

David, for example, appears to believe that if he can demonstrate a relatively continuous rate of expansion in real output per capita of 1·3 per cent for the entire interval between 1790 and 1860 plus a considerable expansion of the non-farm labour force before 1840, one cannot, in good conscience, 'withhold the *coup de grace*' to 'Rostow's explanation of the U.S. "take-off"'.†

I shall not enter into the fine-grained debates between David and some of his colleagues who have also done creative analyses of the rather unpromising pre-1860 statistical data. I shall, for these limited

---

* W. B. Smith and Arthur H. Cole caught this counterpoint well in their classic *Fluctuations in American Business, 1790–1860* (Cambridge, Mass., 1935).

† 'The Growth of Real Product', p. 157.

purposes, accept his calculations and pose the question: How, if at all, do they alter my conception of what transpired in the American economy before 1860?

David relates his aggregative findings to the erratic course of early American economic history in a lucid and broadly acceptable way:*

The first surge of growth extended from the early 1790's into the opening decade of the nineteenth century. In all likelihood, the boom had already begun to slacken before it was brought to an abrupt halt by the disruption of the United States' opportunities for large-scale participation in international commerce and shipping, followed by the War of 1812, and the transitional economic dislocations ensuing upon the restoration of international order which returned Britain's commercial policy to its *status quo ante bellum*. The next burst of accelerated growth, getting under way in the early 1820's, thus came after a prolonged period which may well have seen no permanent advance in per capita real product beyond the level attained when the century was new. This second surge seems to have run on for more than a decade, sustaining an average per capita product growth rate close to 2·5 per cent per annum, before it gave way to marked retardation; direct estimates indicate the average annual rate of growth of per capita real GDP had slowed down to roughly 0·6 per cent during the decade from 1834/35 to 1844/45. The third acceleration, commencing in the latter half of the 1840's, had, in turn, already lost considerable momentum before the outbreak of civil conflict—like the disturbed international conditions of 1807–1815—brought in its wake an attenuated period of slower per capita real product growth.

As far as the chronological sequence and the broad features of these movements are concerned, there is little that is new in the foregoing line of conjecture. If an element of novelty is to be found, it lies in the proposition that this unsteady course of development was reflected in accelerations and retardations of *near-term* rates of per capita product growth, but not in any significant alteration of the secular, or long-term pace of economic advance between the ratification of the Constitution and the rupture of the Union. A highly speculative estimate suggests a 1·31 per cent per annum rate of growth of per capita real GDP over the whole period 1790–1860; corresponding average growth rates for the 1800–1835 and 1835–1855 'trend-intervals' are virtually identical, 1·22 to 1·35 per annum, and 1·30 per cent per annum, respectively.

The heart of David's argument, as it bears on *The Stages*, concerns a narrower period, 1820–40; since his conjectural rate of growth for the period 1800–20 is low.† In effect, he argues that the

---

* *Ibid.* pp. 187–8. † *Ibid.* p. 155.

rate of growth for the period 1820–40 is at least as high as that for the period 1840–60. He attributes this phenomenon to two major factors:

(1) the rapid shift of labour to non-agricultural pursuits after 1820;*

(2) a substantial rise in labour productivity in agriculture as new cotton, wheat, and corn lands were opened up to the west and the iron plow, grain cradle and other measures to increase productivity were introduced.†

As for the first point, I have always held that serious industrialization began in the United States with the regional take-off of New England, with cotton textiles as a leading sector (*The Stages*, p. 55 n). This phenomenon had substantial spreading effects in the region; and one would expect overall U.S. statistics to show a relative shift of labour out of agriculture from the 1820's. I chose to designate the take-off years for the United States in the generation before 1860 because from earliest days distance and geography were a fundamental problem in American growth. Only with railroad technology was the problem effectively solved, making the United States an efficient continental market. Whether it could have been solved by canals, horses, and wagons is another matter. Railroads were evoked in America as in Western Europe to do the job. The process of diffusing the railroad took time; but the railroad networks created by 1860, plus their backward and lateral spreading effects, plus their forward linkages (including steel), provided the transport and heavy industry foundations for the post-Civil War drive to technological maturity on a truly continental basis. The technologies of precocious New England in the 1820's did not suffice, and canals, horses, and wagons would not have had such powerful spreading effects.

As for American growth in the 1830's, I noted (*The Stages*, p. 38 n.) 'the extensive agricultural expansion' of that decade, accompanied by massive capital imports.‡ In *The Stages* I did not address

* *Ibid.* p. 166.

† David argues this—his critical point—*ibid.* pp. 174–86.

‡ I had, of course, written extensively about the rhythm of American expansion, as it interwove with British economic history, in the Gayer study; for example, vol. I, chapter 5 (1833–42).

myself to the question of when American income per capita began to rise; and I explicitly exempted the United States (p. 17) from the general case of the modernization of a traditional society.

In presenting the concept of the take-off in the *Economic Journal*, March 1956, I pursued this question at greater length in a passage and footnote (pp. 28–9) which bears on David's thesis:

In the second case, of naturally wealthy nations, with a highly favorable balance between population and natural resources and with a population deriving by emigration from reasonably acquisitive cultures, the story of establishing the preconditions differs mainly in that there is no major problem of overcoming traditional values inappropriate to economic growth and the inert or resistant institutions which incorporate them; there is less difficulty in developing an *élite* effective in the investment process; and there is no population problem. Technically, much the same slow-moving process of change occurs at high (and, perhaps, even expanding) levels of *per capita* output, and with an extensive growth of population and output still based on rich land and other natural resources. Take-off fails to occur mainly because the comparative advantage of exploiting productive land and other natural resources delays the time when self-reinforcing industrial growth can profitably get under way...

Theoretically, such fortunate societies could continue to grow in *per capita* output until diminishing returns damped down their progress. Theoretically, they might even go on as growing non-industrial societies, absorbing agricultural innovations which successfully countered diminishing returns. Something like this process might describe, for example, the rich agricultural regions of the United States. But, in general, it seems to be the case that the conditions required to sustain a progressive increase in agricultural productivity will also lead on to self-reinforcing industrial growth. This result emerges not merely from the fact that many agricultural improvements are labor-saving, and that industrial employment can be stimulated by the availability of surplus labor and is required to draw it off; it also derives from the fact that the production and use of materials and devices which raise agricultural productivity in themselves stimulate the growth of a self-sustaining industrial sector.

It, therefore, seems to me wholly possible that agricultural productivity per worker rose in the period 1820–40, as the new cotton, wheat, and corn lands were opened up. After all, we have been teaching our students for many generations that the availability of cheap good land in America yielded that result and set up, as well, incentives to introduce labour-saving agricultural and industrial gadgetry.

David's basic misconception is, then, about the relation of *The Stages* to aggregative analysis. As I hope this Appendix makes clear once and for all, growth as conceived in *The Stages* is rooted in the progressive introduction of new technologies under conditions of reasonable efficiency. This process does set up forces which have an impact on the aggregates. But stages of growth can be distinguished and dated under a wide range of population/resource balance and other factors that can affect income levels and their movements. There is nothing in my consideration of the American take-off in *The Stages* that would deny the lively activities in New England that occurred starting in the 1820's, or deny that the United States expanded into good lands to the West as industrialization proceeded. David's highly aggregated model is simply not an instrument capable of denying or confirming my view of the American take-off.

The exact course of agricultural productivity before 1860—and the other interesting aggregative questions posed by David—I shall leave for others to debate.

North's review of the 1956 *Economic Journal* take-off article (*Manchester School*, January 1958) raises two minor points and one major point, worth brief comment.

To clear the ground:

I do not regard the American capital imports of the 1850's as having initiated American railroadization; but I would not quite characterize them as 'very modest' (p. 70). Railroad investment rose from $37 million in 1849 to a peak of $111 million in 1854, by Fishlow's calculations. North's balance of trade and specie figures (p. 70) show an overall deficit (presumably covered by foreign loans) of $37 million and $26 million for 1853 and 1854, respectively. These numbers suggest that a significant proportion of railroad investment was financed from abroad. Turning to direct railway investment evidence, it seems inescapable that the $83 million in railway bonds held abroad by 1856 plus the substantial holdings of state and local bonds floated primarily to subsidize the railroads helped substantially to make possible railroad expansion on the scale on which it actually occurred in the 1850's (A. Fishlow,

American Railroads, pp. 112–13 and 117). I would still regard foreign capital as having played 'a major role' in the American take-off (p. 49); but I would wholly agree with North that it was expanded foreign demand for wheat in the 1840's and increase in the wheat price which created the 'newly favourable international environment' (*The Stages*, p. 37) for the railroad boom of the 1850's.

On American tariffs, I rate the textile duties of 1828 and the iron duties of 1841–2 as 'important' on the basis of the conventional literature on the subject. North says they were not 'critical' and invokes the magisterial conclusions of Taussig. I add, in the *Economic Journal* article (p. 29): 'Although these actions [tariffs] undoubtedly served to assist take-off in leading sectors, they usually reflected an energy and purpose among key entrepreneurial groups which would, in any case, probably have done the trick.' The complexities of sorting out the impact of tariffs from all the other factors at work are great. (With respect to the increase and relaxation of iron duties in the 1840's, R. W. Fogel and Stanley L. Engerman have illustrated the complexities well in 'A Model for the Explanation of Industrial Expansion During the Nineteenth Century: With an Application to the American Iron Industry', *Journal of Political Economy*, May/June 1969.) I am not prepared to give my impression of 'importance' a quantitative form for tariffs on cotton textiles; although the role of the iron duties does not emerge as trivial from the Fogel and Engerman analyses. We can, perhaps, conclude that we need more work on the subject before differences in impression can be put to a mutually satisfactory quantitative test.

The major point raised by North reflects a misapprehension about the relation between leading sectors and the forces which may induce their coming into being. He says (p. 74):

it was the rich land and primary production of the west which made the railroad boom of the 1850's feasible. In short, one could advance a hypothesis which is the reverse of Rostow's, namely, that the opening up and development of new areas capable of producing primary goods in demand in existing markets induced the growth of industrialization.

I would underline that I have no quarrel with this proposition, as indicated in 'Trends in the Allocation of Resources in Secular

Growth' (Leon H. Dupriez, editor, *Economic Progress*, Louvain, 1955, pp. 370, 373, 374). *The Stages* asserts (pp. 36–7):

The beginning of take-off can usually be traced to a particular sharp stimulus...It may come about through a technological (including transport) innovation, which sets in motion a chain of secondary expansion in modern sectors and has powerful potential external economy effects which the society exploits. It may take the form of a newly favourable international environment, such as the opening of British and French markets to Swedish timber in the 1860's or a sharp relative rise in export prices and/or large new capital imports, as in the case of the United States from the late 1840's, Canada and Russia from the mid-1890's; but it may also come as a challenge posed by an unfavourable shift in the international environment, such as a sharp fall in the terms of trade (or a wartime blockage of foreign trade) requiring the rapid development of manufactured import substitutes, as with the Argentine and Australia from 1930 to 1945.

In short, the critical element in the take-off is the effective introduction of the new technologies in an environment where the spreading effects occur. The attractiveness of opening up of new areas in the West could serve in the 1850's as well as the attractiveness of cutting transport costs between existing commercial and industrial centres in the East in the 1840's.

Finally, the question of railroads and the take-off.

Here is the passage in *The Stages* that began the debate (pp. 55–6):

The introduction of the railroad has been historically the most powerful single initiator of take-offs. It was decisive in the United States, France, Germany, Canada, and Russia; it has played an extremely important part in the Swedish, Japanese and other cases.

The railroad has had three major kinds of impact on economic growth during the take-off period. First, it has lowered internal transport costs, brought new areas and products into commercial markets and, in general, performed the Smithian function of widening the market. Second, it has been a prerequisite in many cases to the development of a major new and rapidly enlarging export sector which, in turn, has served to generate capital for internal development, as, for example, the American railroads before 1914. Third, and perhaps most important for the take-off itself, the development of railways has led on to the development of modern coal, iron and engineering industries. In many countries the growth of modern basic industrial sectors can be traced in the most direct way to the requirements for building and, especially, for maintaining substantial railway systems. When a society has developed deeper institutional, social and political prerequisites for take-off, the rapid growth of a railway system, with these powerful triple effects, has often served to lift it into self-sustained growth. Where the prerequisities have not existed, however, very substantial railway building has failed to initiate a take-off, as for example in India, China, pre-1895 Canada, pre-1914 Argentina, etc.

I enlarged somewhat on this proposition in the paper on 'Leading Sectors and the Take-off' prepared for the Konstanz conference, notably in the course of discussing spreading effects from the leading sectors (*Economics of Take-off*, pp. 3–7).

In both efforts I sought to generalize certain conclusions, embracing a number of national experiences, rather than to present an analysis of the American case. Nevertheless, it was wholly proper for experts on a national economy to set about criticizing and testing the general hypothesis advanced. Indeed, it was—and remains—one purpose of *The Stages* to stimulate and encourage such efforts.

The two central figures in the debate are, of course, Robert Fogel (*Railroads and American Economic Growth: Essays in Econometric History*, Baltimore, 1964) and Albert Fishlow, to whose study of American railroads I have already referred.

I shall deal with Fishlow's work here because he deals more extensively with the issues raised by Fogel as well as with some Fogel did not address.

What Fishlow (and Fogel, too) has done is to define sharply and then seek to measure the direct and indirect effects on American growth of pre-1860 railroadization.

Fishlow distinguishes the following routes of impact:

(1) reduced transport costs;

(2) an enlarged market leading to increased incentives to specialization, capital formation, and technological progress;

(3) resource demands generated by railroad construction and operation, including both consequences for the general level of demand and resource utilization and for the demand for particular inputs, notably from the capital goods industries.

His conclusions can be set out as follows:

(1) Reduced transport costs provided direct benefits to the Ameri-

can economy of the order of \$175 million, about 4 per cent of 1859 gross national product.

(2) Railroad gross investment over the period 1849–58 accounted for more than 15 per cent of gross capital formation, reaching almost a fourth at the peak in 1844. (The role of the railroad in inducing capital imports in the 1850's was noted above, p. 221–2.)

(3) As for sectoral inputs, railroad requirements for pig iron rose through the period, amounting to the order of 20 per cent of net consumption for the 1850's; railroad demands 'contributed heavily' to the critical transition of the pig iron industry to anthracite and, then, coke as a source of fuel; they 'achieved still greater pre-eminence' in stimulating rolling mills; and (post-Civil War) rail requirements introduced the Bessemer process to the United States. As for machinery, the locomotive industry and repair shops (domestic from the beginning) had greater spreading effects in engineering than the textile and steamboat engine shops from which they initially stemmed. The initial inputs of coal and lumber to railroads were modest.

(4) The railroads had a massive effect on agricultural output, population expansion (including immigration) and the growth of agricultural processing industries in the West in the 1850's.

(5) With respect to the 1840's, Fishlow concludes (p. 261): 'One could write an independent history of manufactures and railroads in the 1840's; one could not do the same for western expansion and railroads in the 1850's. This contrast is the important point.'

Wherein does this view of the process differ from mine?

I would make two points.

The first concerns what I call the lateral effects spreading out from the leading sectors. I defined them as follows in *The Economics of Take-off* (pp. 5–6):

the leading sector will induce around it a whole set of changes which tend to reinforce the industrialization process on a wider front. Modern industrial activity surrounded itself with urban men, services, and institutions whose existence strengthened the foundations for industrialization as an ongoing process: a disciplined working force organized around the hierarchies decreed by technique; professional men to handle the problems of law and relations to the various markets for input and products; urban overhead capital; institutions of banking and commerce; and the construction and service industries required to meet the needs of those who manned the new industrial structure. The coming in of a new leading sector thus often transformed the whole region where it took hold; as, for example, the cotton textile revolution transformed Manchester and Boston and the automobile industry transformed Detroit. Wherever they went, the railroads induced the transformation of old urban centres or the creation of new ones, not merely for railroad maintenance but also to handle the marketing and commercial traffic that the railroads made possible and profitable. These lateral effects—symbolized by the acceleration in urbanization during take-off—expanded the proportion of modern folk in the total population and strengthened modern attitudes towards the production process far beyond the narrow impact of the new activity itself and the inputs it directly induced.

On this concept Fishlow has the following to say (p. 16 n.): 'The "lateral" effects of Rostow, by which he means the induced "set of changes which tend to reinforce the industrialization process on a wider front," might seem to be another possibility. But these are so general as to constitute the very process of industrialization and are a *consequence* of the other effects rather than an additional route of influence.'

I do not believe this comment quite disposes of the matter. The proportion of urban to total population moved as in Table 21 from 1790 to 1860:*

TABLE 21

1790	5·1%	1830	8·8%
1800	6·1	1840	10·8
1810	7·3	1850	15·3
1820	7·2	1860	19·8

This table clearly reflects the beginning of industrialization in New England in the 1820's and (in my view) its acceleration in the period 1840–60. In all conscience, the lateral effects symbolized by these movements are extremely difficult to quantify as distinct from other forces at work; and the direct and indirect role of the railroads in this acceleration (which I would guess is substantial) may be impossible to isolate statistically. But difficulties of measure-

---

* Data for 1790–1810 from W. S. Woytinsky and E. S. Woytinsky, *World Population and Production: Trends and Outlook* (New York, 1953), p. 124; for 1820–60 from Abram Bergson and Simon Kuznets (eds.), *Economic Trends in the Soviet Union* (Cambridge, Mass., 1963), p. 72.

ment do not justify dropping factors from the equation. The acceleration of urbanization in the period 1840–60 was, evidently, the result of other factors; but growth is an interacting process, and rapidly enlarging cities, in turn, played back on the economy, reinforcing the industrialization of the economy in many directions. In short, I do not believe lateral spreading effects can be dealt with in quite the cavalier way Fishlow's footnote suggests.

Second, the 1840's. There is a possible misunderstanding here; and it may stem from the language I used in *The Stages* (p. 55): 'perhaps most important for the take-off itself, the development of railways has led on to the development of modern coal, iron, and engineering industries.' The phrase 'led on' was meant to suggest a process taking place over time. I was, of course, quite aware that it was not until the 1850's that American rail production began to reduce reliance on imports. But I do not regard the railroad construction of the 1840's as irrelevant to events in the following decade. The take-off is defined as a dynamic process taking place, say, over a generation. It does not require that the inputs generated by the leading sector emerge instantly. For my purposes, it suffices to relate the railroad expansion of the period 1840–60 to the structure of the economy that evolved by the end of the period; and, awkward as it may be for statisticians, the forward linkages generated by take-off (e.g., the post-Civil War coming in of the Bessemer process) are one consideration I have taken into account in setting take-off dates (see above, pp. 193–4).

Fishlow's interpretation of the 1840's in general leaves me uneasy and feeling we all have more work to do. He is correct in observing that, after the boom and bust of the 1830's (based on the expansion of cotton and other acreage, plus infrastructure expansion in the mid-West), capital in London and the eastern United States was inclined to stay closer to home in the 1840's. The British domestic railroad boom and the intensive railroadization of the American northeast were concurrent phenomena. But neither the availability of capital for eastern investment nor his observations on the limited role of transport development in relation to textiles, boots and shoes, coal and iron, quite support his conclusion:*

* Fishlow, *American Railroads*, p. 261.

I do not overlook the existence of interactions and dynamic sequences. The expenditure effect of railroad construction, for example, did aid eastern prosperity somewhat. And cost reductions even of a limited sort might have set in motion a chain of cumulative response far beyond its initial importance. But there is no evidence that such was the case, while there are abundant indications that it was improbable. One could write an independent history of manufactures and railroads in the 1840's; one could not do the same for western expansion and railroads in the 1850's. This contrast is the important point.

There is no doubt that the economics of linking up new agricultural lands with railroads differs from the economics of linking up existing commercial and industrial centres. But an increase of railway mileage of 211 per cent in a decade for the nation (a quadrupling in the major industrial region, New England) is both too massive and too interwoven with the whole life of the economy to be separated from all the rest that happened in the 1840's, which Fishlow summarizes well:*

At the same time that New England's rail connections were being forged, the tempo of regional industrial expansion quickened. Whether the criterion be the 175 per cent increase in domestic cotton consumption over the course of the decade, the dividends of New England industrial firms, or the statistics of Massachusetts industry, the impression is all of one piece. Within the Middle Atlantic area the forces of manufacturing were making themselves felt as well. Philadelphia, its dreams of commercial and financial pre-eminence finally buried by the undeniable ascendance of New York, concentrated upon manufactures instead, and emerged with the highest rate of population increase between 1840 and 1850 among America's large cities. This performance was symptomatic of the rising prosperity of the iron and coal industries with which the economy of the Quaker City had become so intimately entwined: capacity of anthracite blast furnaces in eastern Pennsylvania increased more than 5 times between 1840 and 1849, while anthracite production almost quadrupled over the same period.

I suspect that the heart of his argument is that industrial growth of the 1840's would not have been 'stymied'† if the railroad boom had not occurred. I would guess that this is true; but that is not the same thing as arguing that the industrial and railroad development, which actually did occur, were substantially 'independent'.

* *Ibid.* pp. 237–8. † *Ibid.* p. 250.

The difficulty here for the analyst is real; and, understanding the labour that went into Fishlow's chapter VI, I am not inclined to be over-critical. The difficulty is that the effects of a railroad boom of the kind experienced in the 1840's is much more diffuse than, say, the throwing of railroads into new wheat lands. The expansion of investment and income is general, and hard to track out except in aggregative terms. The effects of transport cost reductions for freight and passengers are, again, diffuse; but they could be powerful even if they did not break a dramatic bottleneck in growth.

Reflecting on the problems of routing and measurement that Fogel and Fishlow addressed with such boldness, skill, and energy, I would offer a, hopefully, constructive suggestion. Perhaps what we need for the period 1790–1860 is an American equivalent of the Gayer study of Britain for the years 1790–1850 that would go beyond Smith and Cole's pioneering effort. The analytic tools might be different and more refined than those used in the Gayer study some thirty years ago. But some, at least, of the more elusive problems of interconnection might be illuminated if we were to march through these years cycle by cycle, year by year, bringing together all that statistical and qualitative data might provide. In considering American growth over this span, we are, after all, summing up the results of a series of cyclical expansions—surges of investment and technological absorption in changing directions; although the periods of cyclical recession were not wholly barren. Some of our present uncertainties might be reduced if we looked hard at these changing patterns of investment. We might be able to get at the interconnections among the parts of the economy—and the links between sectors and the aggregates—more sensitively by the intensive study of particular periods of time than we can by looking only at certain broad movements over decades, uncertainly linked to institutional and technical histories of sectors.

In any case, having, as it were, lived through the British railway boom of the 1840's (Gayer study, vol. I, chapter VI), I remain sceptical that the railway development of the American northeast of the 1840's was as divorced from industrial development in that decade as Fishlow suggests.

Taken altogether, I believe David, Fishlow, Fogel, North (and many others) have greatly deepened our knowledge of the years before 1860; but they have not, in my view, shaken the judgment in *The Stages* that the first surge of American industrialization began in New England in the 1820's; that this regional take-off was based on cotton textiles; that the railroad construction of the 1840's and 1850's had all three of the consequences I impute to railroads in other societies ready to respond to their spreading effects; and that these take-off decades laid the foundations for the American drive to technological maturity after 1865 on the basis of a continental market.

VI. SOME EVIDENCE ON THE CONTEMPORARY WORLD

The passionate concern with economic growth over the past generation—notably, in the developing world—combined with the data collection of governments and the United Nations—has yielded us some basis for testing two central hypotheses in *The Stages*:

(1) Are there distinctive sectoral complexes that go with stages of economic development, present as well as past?

(2) In the normal case, is there a rise in net investment in take-off?

The data we have are, for the most part, organized in terms of GNP per capita rather than stages of growth. My reservations on a simple linking of stages of growth and GNP per capita have already been fully explained (see above, pp. 197–8).

Moreover, conventional industrial classifications do not, in my view, match precisely the leading sector complexes (see above, pp. 187–8).

Nevertheless, the data are sufficient for a rough test.

In their important paper on 'Development Patterns: Among Countries and Over Time', Chenery and Taylor first examine the paths of primary and industrial sectors in relation to GNP per capita for a sampling of large and small countries; and, within the group of small nations, they examine those oriented to industry and primary sectors.

They then turn to analyze changes in industrial structure, using twelve industrial groups (*op. cit.* pp. 405 ff.).

They are led by their results to group the industrial sectors under three headings: 'early', 'middle', and 'late' industries. Following are their conclusions (pp. 409 and 412), summarized for the three types of countries examined in the accompanying charts:

Early Industries: The early industries are those which (1) supply essential demands of the poorest countries, (2) can be carried on with simple technology, and (3) increase their share of GNP relatively little above income levels of $200 or so. They consist of food, leather goods, and textiles... These industries have income elasticities of domestic demand of 1·0 or less and exhaust their potentials for import substitution and export growth at fairly low income levels. The group as a whole maintains a fairly constant share of GNP; it declines from 56 per cent to 23 per cent of manufacturing as per capita income rises from $100 to $1000...

Middle Industries: We define the middle industries as those which double their share of GNP in the lower income levels but show relatively little rise above income levels of $400–$500. These characteristics are shown... by nonmetallic minerals, rubber products, wood products, and chemicals and petroleum refining. This group of industries accounts for 40 per cent of the increase in the industrial share in large countries from $100 to $400 but contributes considerably less thereafter.

The finished goods produced by these industries (roughly half their output) typically have income elasticities of 1·2–1·5. The early rise of this group is due to a considerable extent to import substitution, which is exhausted at fairly low income levels.

The share of the middle group in total manufacturing does not vary much above the level of $200 per capita...

Late Industries: The late industries are those that continue to grow faster than GNP up to the highest income levels; they typically double their share of GNP in the later stages of industrialization (above $300). This group includes clothing, printing, basic metals, paper, and metal products. Taking an income of $300 as the half-way mark in the process of industrialization, the late industries account for 80 per cent of the subsequent increase in the share of industry in large countries.

This group includes consumer goods with high income elasticities—durables, clothing, printing—as well as investment goods and the principal intermediate products used to produce them.

Broadly speaking, Chenery and Taylor's 'early industries' are similar to the typical leading sectors of take-off—a point made earlier by Chenery in his 'Patterns of Industrial Growth', *American Economic Review*, September 1960, p. 651. Their 'middle industries' embrace capital-deepening sectors typical of the drive to technological maturity. Their 'late industries', including consumers'

Appendix B

TABLE 22. *Decomposition of patterns*

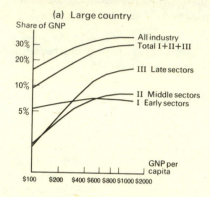

(a) Large country

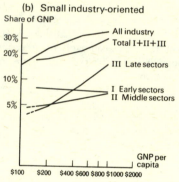

(b) Small industry-oriented

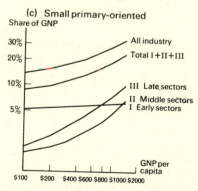

(c) Small primary-oriented

232

durables (automobiles are subsumed in 'metal products'), embrace the sectors whose rapid expansion characterizes high mass-consumption.

Given the industrial categories used, the linkage to my leading sector complexes can only be rough and suggestive. It would, therefore, be interesting to see if the technique developed by Chenery and Taylor could be more closely related to leading sector analysis when applied to the more disaggregated data available. But their work has already brought the statistical analysis of growth and stages analysis closer together.

Chenery has also arrayed investment rates in relation to GNP per capita for a sample of 100 countries over the period 1950–65, in 'Targets for Development' (Economic Development Report No. 153, March 1970, Project for Quantitative Research in Economic Development, Cambridge, Mass.).

Correcting his gross investment figures for a conventional 40 per cent estimate of capital consumption, they move as follows in relation to GNP per capita.

TABLE 23

GNP per capita ($ 1964)	Gross domestic investment, as % of GDP	Net investment proportion
50	11·7%	7·0%
100	15·1	9·1
200	18·2	10·9
300	19·7	11·8
400	20·8	12·5
600	22·2	13·3
800	23·0	13·8
1000	23·7	14·2
2000	25·4	15·2

The big jump comes between $50 and $200 per capita.

It would be convenient if we could, in good conscience, identify take-off as moving from, say, $50 to $200 per capita; the drive to technological maturity from, say, $200 to $500 per capita; high mass-consumption from $500 per capita onwards. But, as I have tried to emphasize, stages of growth and GNP per capita do not match up so neatly. For example, some of the poorest countries in the world (e.g., India and Pakistan)—at GNP per capita of under

$100—are already well into take-off, having lifted their investment rates off the minimum (say, 5%) level prevailing during the pre-conditions period. Bearing this fact in mind, Chenery's data do suggest a sharp lift in the net investment ratio during the first phase of industrialization, a slow rise thereafter.

Arthur Lewis' hypothesis fares rather well from Chenery's evidence on the contemporary world.

Irma Adelman and Cynthia Taft Morris (*Society, Politics and Economic Development*, Baltimore, 1967) have also examined and classified countries, on the basis of investment rates, as follows (pp. 95–6):

The classification scheme for the indicator of gross investment rates during the period 1957–62 follows below.

A. Countries in which gross investment rates were 23 per cent or more. Countries in which the overwhelming proportion of investment originated in a single foreign-financed extractive sector are excluded, however: Israel, Jamaica, Japan, Trinidad, Venezuela.

B. Countries in which gross investment rates were from 18·0 to 22·9 per cent. Countries in which the overwhelming proportion of investment originated in a single foreign-financed extractive sector are excluded: Argentina, Colombia, Costa Rica, Peru, Taiwan, Tunisia.

C. Countries in which gross investment rates were from 16·0 to 17·9 per cent. Also included in this category and classified C− are countries that had gross investment rates of 16 per cent or more in which the overwhelming proportion of investment originated in a single foreign-financed extractive sector: Algeria, Brazil, Burma, Ceylon, Cyprus, Ecuador, Ghana, Greece, Iran (−), Iraq (−), Lebanon, Liberia (−), Libya (−), Mexico, Nicaragua, Panama, Rhodesia, South Africa, Surinam, Syria, Zambia (−).

D. Countries in which gross investment rates were from 14·0 to 15·9 per cent: Afghanistan, Bolivia, Cambodia, India, Kenya, Nigeria, South Korea, Tanganyika, Thailand, Turkey, U.A.R., Uganda, Uruguay.

E. Countries in which gross investment rates were from 12·0 to 13·0 per cent: Chad, Chile, Dahomey, El Salvador, Gabon, Guatemala, Guinea, Honduras, Ivory Coast, Jordan, Niger, Pakistan, Paraguay, Philippines, Senegal.

F. Countries in which gross investment rates were 11 per cent or less: Cameroun, Dominican Republic, Ethiopia, Indonesia, Laos, Malagasy, Malawi, Morocco, Nepal, Sierra Leone, Somali Republic, South Vietnam, Sudan, Yemen.

This array dramatizes certain rough uniformities but also usefully

Appendix B

underlines (as does *The Stages*) some of the complexities in associating investment rates with stages of growth.

Again applying a conventional 40 per cent for capital consumption, we have, at the extremes, rather good Arthur Lewis behaviour; that is, I would estimate the countries in categories A and B as in or beyond take-off, on the basis of all the evidence available (net investment rates of 10·8 per cent and up); and I would estimate the countries in category F as still in the preconditions (net investment rates of 6·6 per cent or less). I would underline that these evaluations of the particular countries listed are *not* circular. They are *not* based on investment rates but on knowledge of their general state of economic modernization, patterns of investment, and leading sectors. The categories in between are a mixed bag (C, D, and E). They contain countries engaged in a vigorous process of preconditioning for take-off (e.g., Senegal, Ivory Coast, Ecuador, Afghanistan); some take-off countries (e.g., South Korea, Thailand, El Salvador, India, Pakistan) and some beyond (e.g., Brazil, Chile, and South Africa). They also include some where the investment rates cited are *prima facie* subject to some suspicion (e.g., Burma, Cambodia).

Given the range of forces that may affect the relation between investment rates and the degree of absorption of modern technology, this variety is not unexpected.

Adelman and Morris then turn to a criterion much closer to stages of growth analysis; that is, 'the level of modernization of industry'. They introduce an interesting additional benchmark—kilowatt-hours per capita of installed electrical capacity. As of 1961 they emerge with the following four broad categories:*

A. Countries with industrial sectors that, as of about 1961, were producing a wide variety of domestic consumer and/or export goods and at least some intermediate goods by means of power-driven factory production methods. In addition, these countries had several industries in which the most modern large-scale or otherwise relatively efficient production methods were applied. Finally, all countries had at least 80 kilowatt-hours per capita installed electrical capacity. While handicraft industry and domestic putting-out systems were still significant in the production

* *Society, Politics and Economic Development*, pp. 98–9. The authors inform me that a (−) indicates that one, at least, of the criteria for assignment to category A is judged weak.

of domestic consumer goods in many of these countries, they were less important than factory production for a considerable variety of consumer goods: Argentine (−), Brazil, Chile, Costa Rica (−), Cyprus (−), Greece (−), Israel, Jamaica (−), Japan (+), Mexico, Rhodesia (−), South Africa, Taiwan, Trinidad (−), Uruguay, Venezuela.

B. Countries with industrial sectors that, as of about 1961, were producing a fair variety of consumer and/or export goods by means of power-driven factory production methods and that had several industries in which the most modern large-scale or otherwise relatively efficient production methods were applied to some extent. These countries, however, are differentiated from those in category A by the fact that handicraft industry and/or the domestic putting-out system were relatively more important in the production of domestic consumer goods, taken as a whole, than were modern methods of production. Finally, almost all the countries in this category had from 25 to 80 kilowatt-hours per capita installed electrical capacity. Countries in which the majority but by no means all of the modern production units were in the foreign-financed and managed sector are classified B−: Algeria (−), Bolivia (−), Colombia, Iran (−), Iraq (−), Morocco (−), Peru, Philippines (+), South Korea (+), Syria, Tunisia (−), Turkey.

C. Countries with industrial sectors in which, as of about 1961, a limited number of domestic consumer and/or export goods were produced by means of small-scale, power-driven factory production methods and in which the most modern large-scale or otherwise relatively efficient production methods, if they existed, were generally confined to production that was foreign-financed and managed. Countries that had a very limited number of the most modern large-scale or otherwise relatively efficient domestically financed production units are classified C+. In addition, these countries were characterized by the overwhelming predominance in consumer goods production of handicraft industry and/or the domestic putting-out system. Finally, with only a few exceptions, countries in this category had less than 25 kilowatt-hours per capita of installed electrical capacity: Burma (−), Cambodia (−), Ceylon, Dominican Republic, Ecuador, El Salvador (+), Gabon, Ghana, Guatemala, Honduras, India (+), Indonesia (−), Ivory Coast (−), Jordan (+), Kenya (−), Lebanon, Liberia (+), Libya, Malawi (−), Nicaragua (+), Nigeria, Pakistan, Panama, Paraguay (−), Senegal (−), Sierra Leona (−), South Vietnam (−), Sudan (−), Surinam (−), Thailand (−), Uganda (−), U.A.R. (+), Zambia.

D. Countries in which industrial development as of about 1961 was very slight and was characterized by handicraft industry and/or the domestic putting-out system. Small-scale factory production was either non-existent or contributed a negligible proportion of the output of domestic consumer and export goods. The most modern large-scale or otherwise relatively efficient production methods in most instances did not exist; countries that had a single modern foreign-financed large-scale plant are classified D+. Finally, in almost all these countries there were less than 10 kilowatt-hours per capita installed electrical capacity: Afghanistan, Cameroun (+), Chad, Dohemy, Ethiopia, Guinea, Laos, Malagasy, Nepal, Niger, Somali Republic, Tanganyika, Yemen.

Here the results are clearer—and can be more closely linked to stages of growth analysis, as well as to the disaggregated portion of the Chenery–Taylor analysis cited above.

Broadly speaking, I would estimate that the category A countries are, as of 1961, towards the end of take-off or beyond; category B, in take-off, although the cases must be carefully corrected for the role of foreign-financed and managed industrial enclaves; category C are mainly fairly advanced preconditions countries, with a few cases at an early phase of take-off as of 1961 (e.g., India, Pakistan, U.A.R.); category D countries are all clearly pre-take-off.

Like the disaggregated Chenery–Taylor data, this part of the Adelman–Morris factor analysis of modernization moves stages of growth and other approaches to the analysis of economic development closer together.

In general, I conclude that the leading sector approach—with its links to industrial structure—does permit us to get at the degree to which modern technology has been absorbed in the economies of the contemporary developing world; that stages of growth analysis, and the larger theory of modernization of which it is a part, remain a useful tool in viewing the present as well as the past; and that, properly and flexibly interpreted, the Arthur Lewis hypothesis about net investment rates in relation to take-off is supported—not contravened—by evidence on the contemporary world.

VII. A NOTE ON THE MARXIST CRITICS

The Stages was the object of a good deal of attention in the press and periodicals of Communist countries; and it was the subject of a review by two Western Marxists, Paul A. Baran and E. J. Hobsbawm (*Kyklos*, vol. XIV, 1961, Fasc. 2).

In July five of its editors published articles in reply to *The Stages* in the Soviet journal *Mirovaya ekonomika i mezhdunarodniye otnoshenia*, No. 7, pp. 142–57 (condensed in *Current Digest of the Soviet Press*, 1961, vol. XIII, no. 39, 7–14).

These comments were marked by a mixture of quite fair paraphrase of the argument; routine polemical denunciation; and occasional points that could be made the basis for rational debate.

For example:

I. Osadchaya:

While doing his utmost to play up the importance of the sociological factors of growth, W. Rostow is completely silent on the role and significance of people's economic relations, determined by the prevailing form of property ownership. And this is no accident. His entire reasoning on the multiplicity of factors determining the distinctive features of a given stage of growth and the transition to the next one is aimed at playing down the principal factor characterizing the real stages of economic development—the economic base of society.

V. Kollontai:

W. Rostow does not consider it expedient to defend particular, specific aspects of capitalism. He is even prepared to forgo using the terms 'capitalism' and 'capitalist', and refers to enterprise and to people 'willing to take a risk'. It is important for him to defend the basic principles and features of private capitalist enterprise and to foist upon the underdeveloped countries the idea of the need to develop in the capitalist way.

V. Semenov:

What does W. Rostow's philosophy of the development of society really boil down to? While professing an 'economic' approach, he is actually using the following three stratagems: First, not only does he deny that the economic aspect of society's development is the determinative and decisive force, he denies that it is a force of greater importance in any way than the other aspects of social life...

Second, speaking of the balance, the equilibrium, of various aspects of both human motives and social development, W. Rostow gradually pushes the economic aspect back from a position of equality to one of secondary significance. Here is what he writes: 'the central phenomenon of the world of post-traditional societies is not the economy—and whether it is capitalist or not—it is the total procedure by which choices are made...' (p. 150).

And, third, to cap all of W. Rostow's arguments on the significance of 'choice', of the taking of 'decisions', etc., the factor in the development of society and in human behavior that is pushed to the forefront is a purely subjective one: 'freely' exercised choice in history, 'freely' taken decisions in the development of society, etc. Thus the development of productive forces, the development of technology and the change in the share of capital accumulation in the national income are seen by W. Rostow not as evidence of the objective economic laws of social development but as a result of a subjective factor—the spiritual life of people, their psychology. W. Rostow makes his whole so-called 'economic' and 'materialist' approach in the final analysis dependent upon the subjective factor.

In dealing with the role of foreign intrusion in relation to modernization, Baran and Hobsbawm first argue that the explanation of modernization in *The Stages* 'is crippled by Rostow's refusal to admit the profit motive into his analysis, a refusal not concealed by an occasional parenthetical remark granting its existence' (*op. cit.* p. 237). They then make their major point (*op. cit.* pp. 238–9):

Unlike other and wiser—we shall not say abler—scholars with similar objectives, he has chosen to abandon not merely Marx's conclusions and his arguments, but even the basic posing of the problem of economic development as Marx saw it. It was, as we have tried to show, an unwise decision, for the Marxian questions are fundamental to any attempt at an understanding of the process of economic development. What is required is at least an *understanding* of Marx's questions. To that level Professor Rostow has yet to rise...

What historical materialism does claim is to have discovered an indispensable *approach* to the understanding of historical constellations and to have focused attention on the nature of the principal energies responsible for their emergence, transformation, and disappearance. To put it in a nutshell: these energies are to be traced back to the always present tension between the degree of development of the forces of production on one side, and the prevailing relations of production on the other. To be sure, neither 'forces of production' nor 'relations of production' are simple notions...

Marx's historical materialism insists, however, that the development of the forces of production has thus far been *the* commanding aspect of the historical process.

Chapter 10 of *The Stages* speaks for itself in reply, notably pp. 148–9, where similarities and differences between the stages of growth and Marx's analysis are detailed.

I would only add observations on two points.

Baran and Hobsbawm were quite correct in sensing that the role assigned in *The Stages* to reactive nationalism in response to external intrusion (or its threat) was a major difference between Marx's analysis of the transition to modernization and mine. The Hamiltonian perception that industrialization and national independence were linked was—and remains—a critical force in a brutally competitive world where the tricks of manufacture were acquired by some earlier than others. But the large role played by reactive nationalism is not taken in *The Stages* to eliminate the role played by the profit motive in societies where private enterprise sectors developed, any more than it eliminates the role played by the consumers' price and income elasticities of demand, where they have been given scope to play upon the markets.

What Semenov appeared to understand better than Baran and Hobsbawm was that I would assign throughout the sweep of development an important role for the political process, where a variety of interests, economic and otherwise, could and did determine the scale (and incidence) of resources mobilized for public purposes and how those resources were allocated as among military, welfare, and growth objectives. In that process, non-material interests and values could—and do—play an important part, indeed.

Baran and Hobsbawm react strongly against my insistence that the heart of Marx's analysis lies in the assertion in the Communist Manifesto that capitalism 'left no other nexus between man and man than naked self-interest, than callous "cash payment"' (quoted, *The Stages*, p. 149). They argue that one can find more sophisticated formulations in Marxist literature. I agree. Indeed, I took pains to point this out in a substantial footnote (*The Stages*, pp. 145–6). But I did take the view in *The Stages* that in the end—when the chips are down—the Marxist argument brings you back to the 'cash nexus'. I believe a dispassionate reading of the Marxist criticisms of *The Stages*, including the passages quoted above, supports that judgment.

In *The Stages* I suggested—but only suggested—another way to look at how societies make decisions (pp. 149–50):

net human behaviour is seen not as an act of maximization, but as an act of balancing alternative and often conflicting human objectives in the face of the range of choices men perceive to be open to them.

This notion of balancing among alternatives perceived to be open is, of course, more complex and difficult than a simple maximization proposition; and it does not lead to a series of rigid, inevitable stages of history. It leads to patterns of choice made within the framework permitted by the changing setting of society: a setting itself the product both of objective real conditions and of the prior choices made by men which help determine the current setting which men confront.

We shall not explore here the formal properties of such a dynamic system; but it follows directly from this view of how individuals act that the behaviour of societies is not uniquely determined by economic considerations. The sectors of a society interact: cultural, social, and political forces, reflecting different facets of human beings, have their own authentic, independent impact on the performance of societies, including their economic performance. Thus, the policy of nations and the total performance of societies—like the behaviour of individuals—represent acts of balance rather than a simple maximization procedure.

But that is the subject of another book, called *Politics and the Stages of Growth*.

ACKNOWLEDGMENTS

Thanks are due to the following for permission to reproduce copyright material:

Simon Kuznets, *Modern Economic Growth*, pp. 24–6, Yale University Press; T. S. Ashton, *An Economic History of England: the Eighteenth Century*, p. 125, Methuen & Co. Ltd; Jan Marczewski, 'Some Aspects of the Economic Growth of France, 1660–1958', pp. 375, 376, 380, reprinted from *Economic Development and Cultural Change*, April 1961, by permission of The University of Chicago Press, © 1961 by The University of Chicago Press, all rights reserved; W. W. Rostow (ed.), *The Economics of Take-off into Sustained Growth*, pp. xiv, xvi, 5, 6, 121, 122, 123, 128, 130, 135, 359, International Economic Association; Paul David, 'The Growth of the Real Product in the United States before 1840: New Evidence, Controlled Conjectures', pp. 157, 187–8, 195, *Journal of Economic History*, June 1967, The Graduate School of Business Administration, New York University; W. W. Rostow, 'The Take-off into Self-sustained Growth', pp. 28, 29, *Economic Journal*, March 1956, Royal Economic Society; A. Fishlow, *The American Railroads and the Transformation of the Antebellum Economy*, pp. 261, 237, 238, Harvard University Press; H. Chenery and L. Taylor, 'Development Patterns among Countries and over Time', pp. 409, 412, *Review of Economics and Statistics*, November 1968, Harvard University Press; Irma Adelman and Cynthia Taft Morris, *Society, Politics and Economic Development*, pp. 95, 96, 98, 99, Johns Hopkins Press; Passages from *Mirovaya ekonomika i mezhdunarodniye otnoshenia*, No. 7, translated in the *Current Digest of the Soviet Press*, Vol. XIII, No. 39, pp. 7–14. Translation copyright 1961 by the *Current Digest of the Soviet Press*, published weekly at the Ohio State University, Columbus, Ohio, by the American Association for the Advancement of Slavic Studies, by permission.

INDEX

Index

Index

Communism (*cont.*)
  prospects of, 2, 128, 134, 135, 137, 138
  in Russia, 66, 93, 131–3, 159–62
Communist Manifesto, 149, 159
Communist Party, in Russia, 102n, 159, 160
'compound interest' in take-off and beyond, 2, 7, 10, 36, 123, 127, 148, 154
Conservative Party, British, 76, 87
consumer durable goods, *see under* high mass-consumption
consumer goods sector
  balance of production between capital goods sector and, 13, 148
  full employment and, 78, 88
  as leading sector in take-off, 23, 27, 56, 196
  in mass-consumption stage, 10, 53, 155, 199
  in Russia and U.S.A., 98, 99–100
consumption, *see* high mass-consumption
Cootner, P. H., 55n
copper industry, xi, 202
Corn Laws, repeal of, 61
cost of living, 82
Costa Rica, 234, 236
cotton
  British imports of, 53–4, 201
  production of, 21, 32
cotton gin, 55, 60
cotton textile industry
  in pre-take-off stage, 23, 53, (China and India) 210
  in take-off, (Britain) xi, 53–5, 114, 194, 200–1, 204, 213, (France) 208, 209, (Japan) 64, (New England) 216, 219, 230, (Russia) 66
Crimean War, 27, 115
Croce, B., 1
Crouzet, F., 207n, 214
Crystal Palace Exhibition (1857), 61, 68
Curtis, C., 151
Cyprus, 234, 236

Dahomey, 234, 237
David, P., 215–16, 217–18, 221, 229
Deane, P., 200–7 *passim*, 213
deceleration
  normal path of a sector, 13, 175
  in Russia, xv, 102, 176, 179
  in U.S.A., 79–80, 199
Dehn, P., 137
democracy, 104, 151, 158, 159, 165

de Madariaga on, 92
Democratic Party (U.S.A.), 119
Denmark, 113, 126
  take-off in, 39n, 41n–42n, 56
depreciation, 99
depression, *see* trade depression
determinism, economic, and political or power, 161, 164
Detroit, 206
devaluation, in Britain, 87
development planners, 181
differentiation, industrial
  in Britain, 62
  in Japan, 64–5
  in Russia, 66, 197
  in Sweden, 59, 63, 197
diminishing returns, 6, 155, 175, 220
Dominican Republic, 234, 236
drive to maturity, stage of, 4, 9–10, 12, 59–72, 150, 152–3
  Marx and, 157
  in Russia, 66–7, 71, 72, 99, 197
  in U.S.A., 75, 98, 219, 230
Dunlop, J. T., 200

Eaton, J., 147n
economic growth, 2, 14–16
  achievement of regular, 36–8; *see also* take-off
  choice of, 152
  choices offered in, 15
  differences in timing of, 116, 121, 130
  efficient absorption of technology as measure of, xiii, 179–80
  leading sectors in, *see* sectors
  preconditions for, 17–31
  in Russia and U.S.A. compared, 93–105
  uniqueness or generality of stages of, 178–89
  without take-off, 40
economic history, 13, 14, 40, 72n
  data for, 186–8, 199
education, 6, 28, 30, 182
Ecuador, 234, 235, 236
Egypt, 126, 234, 236, 237
Eisenhower, President, 131
El Salvador, 234, 235, 236
electric power, 63, 102
electrical industries, x, 9, 59, 63, 65, 67, 95, 175, 197
electronics, xi, 67, 176
Empire Preference, 87
enclave economies, 44–5, 192, 234

245

Index

Index

Newton, Isaac, symbol for watershed in history, 4, 173
Nicaragua, 234, 236
Niger, 234, 237
Nigeria, 45, 234, 236
Nonconformists, 17, 33, 34
North, Douglass, 214–15, 221, 222, 229
nuclear weapons, 121–2, 123–6, 129–37 *passim*
  non-proliferation treaty on, xv
Nutter, C. W., 94, 102, 103, 188

O.E.E.C. countries, 82
Office of Intelligence Research (U.S.A.), 44
Ohkawa, K., 88n, 188
Ohlin, G., 196, 198
'Organization Man', 87
Osadhaya, I., 238
outer space, exploration of, 91, 93, 156
output
  per capita, in Russia and U.S.A., 93, 94, 95
  per capita, in take-off, 37, 203, 204
  per capita, in traditional society, 4
  ratio of, to capital, 20, 37, 141, 190, 191, 192, 206
  see also gross national product

Pakistan, 44n, 126, 233–4, 235, 236, 237
Panama, 44, 234, 236
Paraguay, 234, 236
peace, relative stages of growth and problem of, 123–44
peasants, 47, 67, 88, 140
Peru, 234, 236
petroleum, 21, 66, 102
Philadelphia, 228
Philippines, 44, 75, 76, 111, 234, 236
plastics industry, 176
Poland, 126
police state, in Russia, 132, 136, 160, 162
politics, xvi, 177
  in transition to take-off, 26–7, 30, 36, 39
population
  balance of resources and, 61, 65, 68, 95, 98, 102, 197, 220, 221
  rate of growth of, and rate of investment, at take-off, 20, 21, 22, 140–1, 143, 192, 203
  ratio of urban to rural, 10, 12, 18, 22, 68, 71, 226
  structure of, in U.S.A., 80–1

post-maturity, choices in stage of, 11, 73–4, 114
poverty, 92, 154
Prest, A. R., 82
price elasticity of demand, 16, 133, 139, 240
production
  differentiation of, 59, 62, 63, 64–5, 66
  dynamic theory of, 12–16, 148
  forces of, in Marxist theory, 239
productivity
  in take-off, 46, 57, 58
  in traditional society, 4, 5
  see also under agriculture
profits
  maximization of, 50, 51, 157, 167
  motive of, 26, 239, 240
  plough-back of, before and during take-off, 8, 24, 25, 48, 50, 64, 139, 193
Prohibition, in U.S.A., 88
proletariat, dictatorship of, in Marxist theory, 145, 147
Protestant ethic, 26, 51
public health, 30, 91, 140, 177
Puerto Rico, 44

Quebec, 18, 67

railways, xi, 49, 59, 62, 223–4
  in Britain, 61
  in Canada, 43, 55
  disengagement from era of, 175
  in France, 55, 61, 208, 209, 210, 213
  in Germany, 55, 61
  in Japan, 55, 64
  in Russia, 55, 66, 95
  as social overhead capital, 17, 25
  in Sweden, 55, 62, 63
  in U.S.A., 38, 55, 61, 194, 215, 216, 219, 221, 222, 224–30 *passim*
raw materials, 7, 18, 31
  lack of, 10, 33
  as leading sector in take-off, 56
  prices of, 89
Reform Bills (Britain), 69n, 150
Republican Party (U.S.A.), 75, 119
revolution
  industrial, 33, 57, 61, 215
  political, social, and religious, 33, 36
Rhodesia, Southern, 45, 234, 236
roads, 18, 78, 84, 90, 99
Robbins, L., 73
Robinson, Joan, 153
Roosevelt, President Franklin, 79
Roosevelt, President Theodore, 75

Index

Rosovsky, H., 172
Rostow, W. W., xvi, 13n, 47n, 143, 149n,
    172n, 182, 191–3, 199, 200, 219, 220,
    222–3, 224
Royal Economic Society, 166
Ruhr coal and iron complex, 66
Russia
    automobiles in, xv, 84, 86, 103, 169,
        170–1
    Communism in, 66, 93, 131–3, 159–62
    compared with U.S.A., 93–105, 183
    date of maturity in, 59
    drive to maturity in, 66–7, 71, 72, 99, 197
    pre-take-off stage in, 22, 40, 47, 65, 174,
        195
    and problem of peace, 100–2, 124–5,
        126, 129–37
    prospects for mass-consumption in,
        xv, 10, 11, 103, 132, 133, 136, 176, 179
    take-off in, xiii, 37, 38, 40, 65–8, 115
    traditional society in, 98
Russo-Japanese War, 27, 113, 115

Sardy, H., 216
Scandinavia, 18, 92
    see also Denmark, Sweden
scarcity, 81
    in Marxist theory, 146
    prospect of lifting of burden of, 16,
        145, 156, 166
science
    changing stocks of, 13n
    in pre-take-off stage, 6, 20, 32
Schumpeter, J., 151n
sectors, leading, in economic growth, x,
    xii, xiii, 13, 14–15, 148, 181–2
    applying new technology, xii, xiii, 180,
        188, 193–4
    data for, 186–7
    differing growth rates in, 52
    interaction of, 150, 231
    in Marxist theory, 148
    in mass-consumption stage, 10, 53, 78,
        155, 199, 233
    non-industrial (agriculture, foreign-
        exchange-earning, social overhead
        capital), 26, 139
    in take-off, 52–7, 231
    take-off as surge of output in relatively
        few, 62
    transitions to new groups of, 63, 175,
        194
    see also individual sectors

Semenov, V., 238, 240
Senegal, 234, 235, 236
services
    data for, 188
    in U.S.A., 155, 176
shipbuilding, in Japan, 64
Sierra Leone, 234, 236
silk industry
    in England, 32
    in France, 208, 209, 210
    in Japan, 21, 56, 64
Smith, Adam, 24, 32, 47n, 55
Smith, W. B., 217n
Social Democrats, 72
social overhead capital, 2, 24–6
    in colonies, 112
    government and, 25, 30, 51
    population growth and, 104
    as requirement for take-off, 8, 17–18,
        22, 65, 139, 142, 182, 192
    U.S.A. deficit in, 12, 81
socialism
    in Marxist theory, 145, 160
    in Western Europe, 82
societies
    decision-making by, 149–50, 240–1
    as interacting organisms, 2
    stages of growth of, 4–16
Somali Republic, 234, 237
South Africa, 234, 235, 236
South America, *see* Latin America
Spain, 179
Spanish-American War, 75–6
Sprigge, C. J. S., 158n
Stalin, J. V., 66, 117, 120–1, 133, 134
    alters tone of Russian society, 160
steam engine, 54, 60, 200, 204
steam power, in France, 211
steel industry, x, xi, 59, 175
    in Britain, 61
    in Japan, 65
    markets for, 78–9
    in Russia, 67, 95, 102, 103
    in Sweden, 63
    in U.S.A., 219
suburbanization, in U.S.A., 77, 79, 85, 90,
    199
Sudan, 234, 236
Suez crisis, Russia in, 125n
Sukarno, A., 114
Surinam, 234, 236
Svennilson, I., 83, 198
Sweden, 10, 18, 130, 153